A **NAOMI SCHNEIDER** BOOK

Highlighting the lives and experiences of marginalized communities, the select titles of this imprint draw from sociology, anthropology, law, and history, as well as from the traditions of journalism and advocacy, to reassess mainstream history and promote unconventional thinking about contemporary social and political issues. Their authors share the passion, commitment, and creativity of Executive Editor Naomi Schneider.

AT HOME IN THE CITY

AT HOME IN THE CITY

Growing Old in Urban America

||||||||||||||||||||||||||||||||||||||||||||||||||||||||||||||||||||||||||||||||||||||||||||||||||||||||||

STACY TORRES

UNIVERSITY OF CALIFORNIA PRESS

University of California Press
Oakland, California

© 2025 by Stacy Torres

Library of Congress Cataloging-in-Publication Data

Names: Torres, Stacy, author.
Title: At home in the city : growing old in urban America / Stacy Torres.
Description: Oakland, California : University of California Press, [2025] |
    Includes bibliographical references and index.
Identifiers: LCCN 2024014083 (print) | LCCN 2024014084 (ebook) |
    ISBN 9780520288621 (cloth) | ISBN 9780520288690 (paperback) |
    ISBN 9780520963528 (ebook)
Subjects: LCSH: Older people—Social networks—New York (State)—
    New York—21st century.
Classification: LCC HQ1064.U6 N4745 2025 (print) | LCC HQ1064.U6 (ebook) |
    DDC 305.260974709/05—dc23/eng/20240430
LC record available at https://lccn.loc.gov/2024014083
LC ebook record available at https://lccn.loc.gov/2024014084

33   32   31   30   29   28   27   26   25   24
10   9   8   7   6   5   4   3   2   1

For the living and the dead, who have taught me to believe in life after death because you live on in me

For my mother, my father, and my sisters

For Jeanne and Manfred

The good things of prosperity are to be wished; but the good things that belong to adversity are to be admired.

SENECA, *Letters to Lucilius* (28 CE)

Contents

Acknowledgments

ONCE YOU START THANKING PEOPLE, it's hard to stop. And it's near impossible for me to figure out where to begin and where to end, since so many have given me so much to make this book possible. Some people and places that supported me are gone. Others remain. I'm incredibly grateful to have so many to thank and many more whose names may not appear in this space but to whom I am grateful. My cup runneth over.

First and foremost, I thank the people in these pages who made this research possible by sharing their lives with me for several years. I'm forever grateful for your generosity, warmth, and concern for me. Though many have died, you continue to live on in me.

This book is the outcome of a long and uncertain journey. But thankfully I have never been alone. At each stage of my life and education, since my earliest school years, I've found good people to light the way. As the first person in my family to go to college, I've always relied on my teachers for encouragement. They showed me a path I didn't know existed, that led to me first to college, then graduate school, and now to whatever future lies ahead.

I would not be where I am today without my relationships with the college professors who conveyed their respect and confidence in me. At Fordham University I thank Jeanne Flavin, Arnaldo Cruz-Malavé, Orlando Rodriguez, Hugo Benavides, and Father Damian O'Connell, S.J., for their early mentorship and investment in my personal and intellectual growth. Their love and support sustained me through many personal challenges, and they believed in me when I did not always believe in myself.

At Columbia University's MFA Writing program I benefited from Michael Scammell's honest, tough, and constructive criticism. Jaime Manrique, Patricia O' Toole, Lis Harris, Darcy Frey, and Margo Jefferson also provided generous feedback and equipped me with the tools and perspective to keep pursuing my writing.

At New York University I had the fortune of cultivating pivotal relationships that carried me through my arduous but rewarding doctoral studies. I thank my dissertation advisor Kathleen Gerson and my committee members, or "dream team" as I think of them, Colin Jerolmack, Lynne Haney, Dalton Conley, and Steven Lukes, for their warmth, generosity, and scholarly insights. I also thank Ruth Horowitz, Lawrence Wu, Jeff Manza, David Greenberg, Iddo Tavory, Paula England, Florencia Torche, Ann Morning, Jennifer Jennings, Eric Klinenberg, Patrick Sharkey, Guillermina Jasso, Deirdre Royster, Michael Hout, Mildred Schwartz, Kimberly Williams, Judy Harinarain, and Jamie Lloyd, for their kindness, professional advice, and practical assistance. Thanks to Mitchell Duneier for your investment in my research and allowing me to take your ethnographic methods course at CUNY Graduate Center.

I am also grateful to friends and colleagues who cheered me throughout the dissertation slog and beyond, provided feedback on early drafts and ideas, and carved space for fun amid the grind. My deepest thanks to Chloe Anderson, Regina Baker, Julia Behrman, Leslie-Ann Bolden, Madhavi Cherian, Offer Egozy, Esther Elbaz, Damla Gonullu, Adrian Juarez, Emi Lesure, Zalman Newfield, Amaka Okechukwu, Emily Rauscher, Judith Schneider, and Francisco Vieyra. Additional thanks to office mates Jacob Faber and Peter Rich for maintaining a peaceful and collegial work space and to John Halushka, Kaisa Ketokivi, Tey Meadow, Adam Murphee, Alexis Pang, Harel Shapira, and Michael Gould-Wartofsky for feedback in writing groups and workshops.

The University of California President's Postdoctoral Fellowship Program provided crucial support as I transitioned from my doctoral studies to my first tenure-track position. At UC Berkeley, my faculty mentor Claude Fischer provided invaluable feedback on my elastic ties article and further intellectual and professional support. His invitation to engage with the UCNets team introduced me to many wonderful people, including Leora Lawton, Shira Offer, Tara McKay, Keun Bok Lee, and Mao-Mei Liu. The Institute for the Study of Societal Issues provided me with office space, a thriving intellectual community, and an affiliation that continues to give me an important connection to colleagues across the Bay. I thank Deborah Freedman Lustig, Christine Trost, Martín Sánchez-Jankowski, Aaron Cicourel, Melanie Z. Plasencia, Jeremy Schulz, Dani Carrillo, Zawadi Rucks-Ahidiana, Elena Portacolone, and Corey Abramson for their intellectual camaraderie and warmth. In the UC Berkeley sociology department, many faculty generously supported my professional growth, providing career advice, the opportunity to share my work, and feedback on early article drafts. Thanks to Cristina Mora, Irene Bloemraad, Michael Burawoy, Marion Fourcade, Cybelle Fox, Armando Lara-Millán, Mara Loveman, Daniel Schneider, and Andrew Scharlach in Social Welfare.

I could not imagine a more welcoming, collegial, or supportive environment to begin my career than the Sociology Department at The University at Albany. Numerous people across the university and larger community made me feel cared for. I cannot list everyone, but I'd be remiss if I didn't mention Samantha Friedman, Joanne Kaufman, Joanna Dreby, Angie Chung, Kate Averett, David Hureau, Karen Loscocco, Zai Liang, Glenn Deane, Kate Strully, Nancy Denton, David Wagner, James Zetka, Peter Brandon, Richard Lachmann, Zoya Gubernskaya, Jamie Galusha, Chris Bose, John Fritz Schwaller, Ying Huang, Xuemei Cao, Griffin Lacy, Rebeca Herrero Saenz, P.J. Kuno, Cassandra Sever, and Numa Khan.

At UC San Francisco, I've enjoyed interacting with colleagues across the School of Nursing. Thank you to my Social and Behavior Science Department members for our working relationships over the years: Howard Pinderhughes, Janet Shim, Kristen Harknett, Erin McCauley, Jarmin Yeh, Stella Bialous, Susan Chapman, Jennifer James, Ulrike Muench, Sara Ackerman, Leslie Dubbin, Natalie Purcell, and Brandee Woleslagle. Special thanks to Heather Leutwyler, Carroll Estes, and Carole Joffe for their enthusiastic mentorship of me and support for my approach to research. Gratitude to Katherine Tam, Lisa Klope, and Suzanne Leigh in UCSF and SON communications for helping share my writing with the campus community. I also thank my students and advisees for rich insights and candid talks that challenge and uplift me. You teach me far more than I have taught you. Special thanks to Stephanie Arteaga, Tami Boroughf, Renisha Campbell, Thais Forneret, Selam Kidane, Tessa Nápoles, Giselle Pérez-Aguilar, Diana Ponce, Brittney Pond, Amy Rosenwohl-Mack, Kylie Sloan, and Melissa Victor.

The Academic Dead Parents Club (ADPC) has provided crucial space for grief. I don't know what I would have done without your support. Thank you Krista Harrison, Emily Adrion, Meredith Greene, Pei Chen, Sandra Moody, and Anne E. Kelly, along with my bereavement counselor, Stephen Caputo of MJHS Hospice & Palliative Care.

The American Sociological Association's Section on Aging and Life Course has provided an intellectual home and wealth of connection. It's impossible mention everyone who has encouraged my growth in this special organization but I would like to recognize Jacqueline Angel, Duygu Basaran Sahin, Tirth Bhatta, Mark Hayward, Pamela Herd, Jennifer Karas Montez, Jeffrey Lentz, and Ken Sun. I have had the fortune to meet many supporters through numerous channels who contributed to my development, including Sarah Ashwin, Ronald Breiger, Kjerstin Gruys, Anna Haskins, Annie Hikkido, David Meyer, Alex Murphy, Scott Patrick Murphy, Anthony Paik, Brea Perry, Mario Small, David Takeuchi, Chris Wellin, and Rafia Zafar. Thank you all.

My research was funded by fellowships from New York University, the American Sociological Association Minority Fellowship Program (co-sponsored by Sociologists for Women in Society), and the Ford Foundation. I am deeply appreciative for the funding that allowed me to finish the dissertation and for the mentorship and professional development opportunities that have helped me build a strong foundation for my career. A special thanks to Jean Shin and the amazing people I have met through the American Sociological Association's Minority Fellowship Program, which gave me a much needed confidence boost at a critical juncture. Training programs at RAND, the Michigan Center for Urban African American Aging Research, and Summer Institute on Tenure and Professional Advancement have further enriched my growth.

Big thanks to Naomi Schneider at the University of California Press for discovering me, seeing the potential in this project, and patiently shepherding this dissertation into a book. I cherish our friendship. I would also like to thank the rest of the UC Press team, including Artemis Brod, Aline Dolinh, Jessica Follini, LeKeisha Hughes, Katryce Lassle, Teresa Iafolla, Neal Swain, Stephanie Summerhays and generous reviews from Deborah Carr and two anonymous reviewers along with David Trouille's early blurb.

I am also grateful to editors and peer reviewers of journals and edited collections that published early versions of some chapters, including *The Journal of Gerontology Social Sciences*, *Critical Gerontology*

Comes of Age, Qualitative Sociology, Innovation in Aging, and *Sociological Science.*

Writing for broader audiences has nurtured my spirits. I thank the editors who've worked with me over the years, including: Valerie Nelson and Maret Orliss at *The Los Angeles Times;* Michael Larabee and Jen Balderama at *The Washington Post;* Jill Lawrence at *USA Today;* Trish Hall, Matt Seaton, John Glassie, and Honor Jones at *The New York Times;* Lois Kazakoff, John Diaz, Caille Millner, and Matt Fleischer at *The San Francisco Chronicle;* Gary Reed and Yousef Baig at *CalMatters;* Sari Botton at *Longreads;* Eileen Connell and Karen Sternheimer at W. W. Norton & Company's Everyday Sociology Blog. Katha Pollitt and *The Nation Magazine*'s internship program provided me with an invaluable launching pad for public sociology.

Serendipitous friendships and acquaintanceships in the Bay Area have boosted me during uncertain times and challenged me to grow and learn about myself. Deepest thanks to Greg Gutowski, Sebastián Díaz, Fergus Price, Marilyn Ryan Hall, David Kamholz, Marty Schwartz, Martin Allen, Jeremy Krupp, Justin Scovil, and countless others.

Writing is lonely work and I owe tremendous gratitude to the places that gave me a table, booth, bench, or bar stool to think and jot. Workers there looked out for me. For many, I have only a first name or none at all. But I remember you all and what you did for me.

In the San Francisco Bay Area: Capital One Café, Mechanics' Institute Library, Peet's Coffee, Philz Coffee, Royal Ground Coffee, The Beanery, Caffe Trieste, Caffe Greco, Bazaar Cafe, Starbucks, El Paraiso Cafe, Cafe La Boheme, Church Street Cafe, The Blue Danube Coffee House, All Star Donuts, The Grind Cafe, Caffe Bianco, Café Cordoba, Borderlands Cafe, The Romo Cafe, Café Santana, Red Bay Coffee, Berkeley Espresso, Caffe Strada, the Med, Joe & the Juice, Tommy's Joynt, Specs', Vesuvio Cafe, Ha-Ra Club, Geary Club, High Tide, 500 Club, Mission Bar, The Bitter End, Shovels Bar and Grill, Mario's Bohemian Cigar Store Cafe, San Francisco Public Library, UCSF Library, UC Berkeley Library, Oakland Public Library, Berkeley Public Library, Alameda Public Library, The Ferry Building, and Washington Square.

In New York City: Fordham University Library, New York Public Library, Stroko's Gourmet Deli, Starbucks, Maison Keyser, Caffe Reggio, Johnny's Bar, Cafe Panino Mucho Giusto, Joe & the Juice, Romeo & Juliet Colombian Coffee, Essen Fast Slow Food, Cafe 28, Variety Coffee, Think Coffee NYC, Benvenuto Cafe, and McDonald's.

In Albany, New York: The Daily Grind, UAlbany's Downtown Campus library and cafe, Hudson River Coffee House, Panera, Starbucks, Stacks Espresso Bar, and Uncommon Grounds.

Finally, I thank my mother, my father, and my sisters Erica, Shauna, and Joelle. You may not have always understood my steadfast pursuit of education, but I know that you have always wanted the best for me. We all lead very different lives, but we are all survivors. I love you all. Mary Anne Hamel has been an indispensable family friend. And my deepest thanks to Chris Tkaczyk and Manfred Geier. Chris, you began this journey with me and though we were apart for the final dissertation stretch, I am forever grateful for your love, your brilliant insights, and your steady presence alongside me throughout my fieldwork and early attempts to write it up. Manfred, you took a chance on me, joined me on this unpredictable journey, never gave up on me or let me give up on myself. This book would not have been possible without you and your unwavering support and patience. Your unconditional love and humble wisdom have powered me through my worst moments. Whenever I fear my snail-like progress will never amount to much, I hear your comforting voice telling me, "Every drop hollows the stone," giving me the hope to keep pushing. This book is yours.

1

ANOTHER NEW YORK STORY

A place belongs forever to whoever claims it hardest, remembers it most obsessively, wrenches it from itself, shapes it, renders it, loves it so radically that he remakes it in his own image.
—JOAN DIDION, *The White Album*

It was evident that we had come without knowing it to our inevitable place.
—ROBINSON JEFFERS, Poet of California, on seeing Carmel for the first time

WE HUDDLED AT A CORNER TABLE on the final day at La Marjolaine Patisserie, a mom-and-pop bakery on Manhattan's West Side.[1] As snow curtained the windows and icy February air tore through each time the door opened, heavy flakes fell and a little more of the place disappeared. A depleted stock of cakes and baked goods greeted customers. Sooty edges demarcated the ghostly outlines of pastry display cases that had sat for years on otherwise bright white floor tile. The butter-colored walls stood bare but for a leftover Valentine's Day wreath cradling two fuzzy teddy bears beneath a banner that read, "I Love You." With a mischievous glint in his eyes, the owner said that he would leave it for the landlord. He had lost his lease after the landlord had sought a much higher monthly rent and renewal negotiations had broken down that autumn. But despite everything, he hadn't lost his sense of humor about the bitter fight to keep his store open. Buyers for the equipment stripped the kitchen clean, and burly men soon arrived to remove commercial mixers and industrial ovens; weighing over a thousand pounds, they had been planted in the same spot for decades. I felt a twinge of disbelief as movers dismantled a place almost frozen in time, which until a few days before, had seemed as enduring as the hulking trunk of a giant Redwood tree or the base of the Empire State Building.

Under ordinary circumstances most people probably would have stayed home. Snowy sludge slicked the sidewalks, and many elder customers couldn't risk a fall.[2] But neither snow nor rain nor gloom of night kept most regulars away on the bakery's last day of business. I saw many familiar faces—people I had met since becoming a customer six years before. Eugene sat in the corner. Though he'd proven stalwart on numerous occasions and had recently recovered from a second major hip surgery, his appearance still surprised me. Another longtime customer, Carmen, turned up despite a bad cold. "I had to come for the last day," she said, brushing snow from her shoulders and shaking off her black hat encrusted with ice. Red-nosed and sniffling, she clutched a balled-up tissue. Rather than trudge two and half blocks home, she took a cab back. Sylvia appeared at her usual time, around 10 a.m., and Lucy followed in the early afternoon.

More people crowded the store as the day grew long, and a few spontaneously erupted into song, as they often had over the years. The sweet strains of "Bye Bye Blackbird" filled the space:

> Pack up all my care and woe,
> Here I go, singing low,
> Bye, bye, blackbird,
> Where somebody waits for me,
> Sugar's sweet, so is she,
> Bye, bye, blackbird,

No one here can love and understand me,
Oh, what hard luck stories they all hand me,
Make my bed and light the light, I'll arrive late tonight,
Blackbird, bye, bye.[3]

As their voices harmonized, people seemed to forget the reality of their vanishing surroundings. A little more of the place faded with each passing moment. Where would they go tomorrow? An hour before closing, the store nearly emptied of people and fixtures, Eddie filed in at his usual time around 7 p.m., wearing his favorite FDNY baseball cap.[4] His son had urged him to show up for the last day. "I told him he'd better join the witness protection program if I bust my ass on the way over here," he said, grinning as he parked his trusty cane by the wall. At his request I snapped a picture of him at his preferred spot by the window. We were the last two to leave.

As a lifelong New Yorker, I couldn't help but feel surprised to discover La Marjolaine Patisserie still in existence when I stumbled upon the business in 2004. According to the owner and regular customers, a string of mom-and-pop bakeries had occupied the storefront since 1962, ancient by New York City standards. The bakery storefront hadn't undergone much renovation in the intervening years, giving the space a preserved-in-amber quality. Eight tables arranged in a rectangle allowed people to dip into any number of simultaneous conversations around them. Handwritten signs and worn plastic-coated tablecloths lent the place a cozy, if slightly shabby, ambiance. Though a few regulars joked about the distressed furniture, creaky chairs, and holes in the tablecloths, the faded decor hadn't deterred their patronage. In fact, customers' fierce attachments paralleled the writer Joan Didion's assertion that place belongs to whoever "loves it so radically that he remakes it in his own image."[5]

The bakery sat nestled among three residential swathes: public housing projects, low-equity co-ops, and market-rate apartment buildings that still contained rent-controlled and rent-stabilized tenants.[6] Affordable housing protections had allowed many lower- to middle-income residents to remain in a neighborhood now home to upscale businesses and luxury condominiums. A number of them frequented the bakery, which sat in a one-story block-long commercial retail strip leased by the co-op. Brick high-rises that surrounded the strip housed a large concentration of people, whose numbers compared to a small town's population. Green lawns and park space with benches epitomized the tower-in-the-park model of housing that predominated during the era of "urban renewal," when the city tore down tenements to make way for the co-ops and housing projects. These waves of demolition and building construction began in the mid-1940s and concluded in the early 1960s.[7] Ten buildings, each twenty-one-floors high, comprised the co-ops, while the housing projects contained a mix of seven eleven-, twelve-, and twenty-one-story buildings.

Co-op and project residents lived in buildings classified as naturally occurring retirement communities (NORCs), defined in federal law as "a community with a concentrated population of older individuals, which may include a residential building, a housing complex, or an area (including a rural area) of single family residences."[8] These housing complexes and neighborhoods had not been built purposely to qualify as NORCs; they were not made for older adults, nor was residence restricted to older age groups.[9] Rather, in gerontology lingo, NORC dwellers "aged in place," meaning that many longtime residents of these buildings and communities never moved out and have grown old there over time.[10]

I began observing social life at La Marjolaine Patisserie first as a customer and years later as a researcher. Over time I noticed that this slice of the neighborhood not only evoked an earlier era in New York City history but also attracted its share of old New Yorkers, men and women predominately in their 70s and 80s, who comprised the bakery's most loyal customers.[11] They faced traditional challenges associated with old age, such as declining physical mobility; difficulties performing activities of daily living related to personal care, such as dressing;[12] and the loss of friends, relatives, and other social connections. Most had lived in the neighborhood for multiple decades and several for their entire lives. These lifers often attended elementary school together, knew each other's extended families, and carried mental maps of the neighborhood and the long-demolished tenements they grew up in.

For retirees on fixed incomes with plenty of time but who often could not walk more than a few city blocks, the bakery served as a convenient gathering spot with reasonable prices and few restrictions on how long customers could linger. Unlike the fictional bar in the television show *Cheers*, everyone may not have known your name, but they usually offered a friendly hello. People checked on each other, asked about a neighbor's whereabouts, and waved to passersby. The place served as a clearinghouse of neighborhood information, and older customers caught up on news both good and somber, sharing pictures of grandchildren, updates on neighbors in nursing homes, and notices of wakes and funerals. People dropped in several times a week, sometimes multiple times a day. A few didn't buy anything. They preferred this type of place to a senior center, and the bakery grew into an alternative hub of neighborhood life where they could develop the kinds of social ties and support that helped them remain in their homes.

We know belonging matters for elders but less about how, why, and what facilitates a sense of connection and a sturdy network of social ties. How do older people maintain their independence when faced with multiple vulnerabilities? What forms of social relationships exist? How do older people create or resist belonging? In what ways does belonging to a place or a group help people manage crises and everyday challenges? In the chapters that follow, I investigate these questions by examining belonging among elders in New York City, and I uncover how people aged 60 and older struggle, survive, and thrive in twenty-first-century urban America. To understand their experiences of aging in place, I conducted a five-year ethnographic study following longtime residents as they coped with the accumulated losses of neighbors, friends, and family; health setbacks; depression; gentrification; financial struggles; and other everyday challenges. Data collection spanned from 2009 to 2014, beginning in the wake of the Great Recession and concluding seven years before New York City would experience so much devastation as the early epicenter of the United States' Covid-19 outbreak—a devastation that was unimaginable at the time.

These pages chronicle how a nondescript bakery in Manhattan transformed into a public living room, providing company to ease loneliness and to lend a sympathetic ear for the monumental and mundane struggles of late life. What may have appeared to the average passerby as an unremarkable cafe with rickety tables and a well-trodden linoleum floor doubled as the bubbling center of an elder social world hiding in plain sight. From years of careful observation, I peel away the layers of this oft-neglected world and explore the relationships and experiences that Western culture often renders invisible, or when it pays attention, frames as a problem.

The ethnographic portrait I offer also moves us beyond stereotypes of older people as either rich and pampered or downtrodden and frail to capture the complexity of late life.[13] While many struggled and a few had wealth, most people I met fell between these extremes. In these neighborhood places, I met people like Sylvia, an 86-year-old Jewish woman originally from Brighton Beach, Brooklyn. Though she had lived in the neighborhood for forty years, she joked, "I needed a passport when I came." Barely five-feet tall and with a mane of long, dyed-blonde hair, which had turned solid grey in later years, piled atop her head, Sylvia's modest stature belied her strength. She often reflected on the loss of her parents, her husband, her three siblings, her niece, and countless friends. "I'm a veteran without a gun," she said. More recently Sylvia faced challenges spurred by gentrification and the losses of neighborhood places she had frequented for decades, such as the bakery. "I don't want to get evicted again," she said one day at Pete's Delicatessen, where she and the other former La Marjorlaine regulars had begun to gather after the bakery closed. She managed the rent increases on her one-bedroom, rent-controlled apartment, while a revolving cast of younger, more affluent neighbors paid double and triple her then $1,650 monthly rent. The urban landscape beyond her door changed with startling speed as gentrification continued its inexorable march. New bars and restaurants sprouted every few months and displaced neighborhood mainstays such as Mr. Wonton Chinese takeout and Niko's Café. Unlike many of her similarly aged peers, Sylvia could afford to try them but concluded they hadn't opened for her or for "neighborhood people." "They're for a younger crowd," she said with a resigned hand wave.

"In spite of all the bullshit, I try to remain optimistic," said Eugene, a 90-year-old white man of Scottish descent, who lived alone in a rent-stabilized apartment and frequented the bakery daily. His dignified air obscured mounting challenges in late life. Though he had retired from his position as a trade nutrition-magazine editor, he still dressed as if he were headed to the office every day, wearing a sport or trench coat, suspenders, and button-down shirt. The worn leather briefcase at his side betrayed his work history in publishing. With his gleaming white hair and mustache and ruddy cheeks, he once joked when observing how strangers frequently waved to him that he looked like "everybody's grandfather or Santa Claus." During a later stint as a film and television extra, filmmakers tended to cast him as esteemed characters, including as a judge, doctor, boxing referee, and ambassador. He'd appeared in over twenty films as a nonspeaking extra, playing a physician alongside Robin Williams in *Awakenings* and the ambassador to Hungary in the Benicio Del Toro film *Che*, his last role. One bakery regular, Eddie, quipped, "They never pick you to be the criminal or the bum, always a judge or a doctor or something. Guess they don't know the real you. Ha-ha."

Eugene had retained a gallows humor through nine decades of ups and downs, which included housing insecurity and, in recent years, health problems. While he could still afford the $1,080 monthly rent on his studio apartment, paying this well-below-market rent and his other living expenses depleted his dwindling savings and swallowed his monthly Social Security check. Fighting to remain in his home of forty years emerged as one of the most emotionally and physically grueling experiences of his life. Eugene's building had tried to evict him for an allegedly filthy apartment, but they later dropped the case without apologizing for having subjected him to the stress and humiliation of housing court. "It was obviously a ploy to steal my rent-stabilized apartment," he said. Eugene was one of a handful of renters who had remained since the building had turned into a co-op in the 1980s. The following year, a studio on his floor the same size as his apartment listed for $425,000. Larger apartments sold for more than a million dollars. When faced with the prospect of losing his apartment and his independence, which would have forced him to move to Dallas to live with his youngest sister, he preferred to stay and fight. Despite their close relationship, he'd rebuffed her offers throughout the years, explaining, "I don't drive, and they would have to take me everywhere."

Eugene's world grew smaller upon retirement. He continued working as a writer, but once he stopped traveling to his office in the Empire State Building, he spent more time in the neighborhood. The bakery a half block from his building's entrance had provided a new daily destination. When I first spoke with Eugene, he was coming in late mornings for quiche and coffee and often sat with Sylvia. They made an interesting pair; he was a politically conservative and never-married white man originally from a small town in central Texas, and she was an 86-year-old liberal Jewish New Yorker widowed nearly twenty years. She still got a kick out of Eugene's adoption of Yiddish words like *schlep* and *schmuck* years after I first heard them spill from his mouth—a habit that revealed how much New York had rubbed off on this Texan. They avoided discussing politics beyond good-natured ribbing. But movies, I learned with more time in their company, were another matter.

When I started coming to the bakery I observed them cover a range of frothy small-talk topics, including weather, current events, politics, neighborhood happenings, and recent movies. I didn't yet know their names. They laughed together and exchanged friendly banter with other customers whose faces grew familiar to me as I also became a regular and something of a familiar stranger myself.[14]

One early afternoon, snatches of their discussion drifted to my table. I eavesdropped beside them while gazing at a laundromat, small grocery store, and Chinese take-out restaurant on the ground floor of five- and six-story tenement buildings across the street.

"Oh, that movie is very good . . . What was the name?" Sylvia began, tilting her head in rapt concentration. "The one with all the music, where they're dancing in the kitchen . . ." she said, faintly humming the Temptations song "Ain't Too Proud to Beg" from the movie's soundtrack.

"With Jeff Goldblum," Eugene said and joined the humming. "I remember it, they have a reunion after the friend kills himself, but I can't remember the name either."

"With Glenn Close and Kevin Kline," Sylvia continued. "So many good ones in that picture—and the music. But what's the name?"

"It's on the tip of my tongue. This is going to drive me crazy," Eugene chuckled.

I knew the title but hesitated to speak up. Though I'd noticed the pair a few weeks before, since first stopping into the bakery, which had become my makeshift office as I wrote my master's thesis in creative writing, I'd never spoken to them. They appeared to be in their late 70s, making them a good five decades my senior. I was 24 years old then and felt like an outsider among the bakery's older clientele. But I found the entree too tempting and finally slipped into the discussion.

"I think the movie you're thinking of is *The Big Chill*," I said.

"Yes," Sylvia said with excited recognition. "Thank you."

"That's it," Eugene said. "How did you know that?"

"I like old movies." And, with this simple conversation starter, I began the long process of getting to know Eugene, Sylvia, and the other bakery regulars whom I'd spend years observing and interviewing at different neighborhood places.[15]

In my mid-20s, I was not planning to study older people. Initially, old establishments that had survived gentrification interested me—not older adults. But I soon became curious about La Marjolaine's elder clientele, about the neighborhood relationships they formed there and why they preferred this setting to a senior center.

Though three of my four grandparents died before I was born and I had few opportunities to interact with older relatives, I shared much in common with the elders I came to know in the bakery. I'd always considered myself an "old soul." My father and mother, born in 1942 and 1943, respectively, were older than my classmates' baby boomer parents. My sister likened our childhood to growing up with a "time machine." That age gap made a big difference in shaping my sensibilities, and the music, movies, and experiences my parents introduced me to helped me connect with bakery regulars.

As lifelong New Yorkers, we—the bakery regulars—engaged in rollicking, no-holds-barred conversations, using a direct communication style that the linguist Deborah Tannen has described as "high-involvement."[16] Several of us had working-class backgrounds and were the children of immigrants. Many of us had experienced significant loss and illness. My mother died when I was 16. As her cancer progressed, her world shrank to the one-block radius around our apartment. I helped care for her at home while she was dying. During my time as a bakery customer, I also began what would become years of caregiving, first for my father after his kidney and advanced lung cancer diagnoses and later for my sister after her schizophrenia diagnosis and hospitalization. The bakery provided me with a place of respite as I balanced schoolwork with family care. Despite perpetual concerns among the general public about older adults' potential for social isolation, in some ways I was more isolated than them. Since my own diagnosis at age 26 with an autoimmune disease, Sjogren's syndrome, I'd also adapted to living with chronic fatigue, pain, and symptom "flares."[17] Like the older adults I came to know, I needed to pace myself and interact extensively with healthcare providers. Elders checked on my health as much as I inquired about theirs.

I began formal data collection at La Marjolaine for an ethnographic research methods course project during my doctoral studies. Prior acquaintanceship with key figures such as Sylvia and Eugene helped me build rapport and meet other bakery regulars whom I then invited to take part in the study.[18] This fluid group consisted of forty-seven women and men aged 60 years and older, the majority of them women; Puerto Rican, Jewish, and ethnic white (of predominantly Italian, Greek, or Irish descent); and low to middle income. Most people fell into the upper age range of the Silent Generation, who, born from roughly 1925 to 1945, came of age during war and economic depression.[19]

Although I took field notes at this site for six months from September 2009 through February 2010, my observations date to 2004 when I first came into La Marjolaine as a customer.[20] During this intensive six-month period, I observed the bakery on average four to five times a week for a minimum of two hours during mornings, afternoons, and evenings. I recorded my observations until the bakery permanently closed in 2010 after eleven years in business, at which time my study branched out as former customers scattered across the neighborhood and decamped elsewhere. I identified five sites where I hypothesized they might go based on their plans to cope with the closing, housing proximity to the original site, and my knowledge of the neighborhood. I ended up primarily in two sites for four and a half years—McDonald's and Pete's Delicatessen—where different groups of former bakery patrons convened. I came to consider the bakery closing as a kind of "natural experiment" that allowed me to chart how relationships changed after the external shock and how these ties endured, fragmented, or transformed in other fundamental ways.

The number of people I observed regularly whose names I did not always know or who fell into a younger age group is greater than the core group of regulars with whom I spent the most time, totaling approximately 135. My fieldwork also took me out of public gathering spots when I visited people in their homes, hospitals, nursing homes, attended wakes and funerals, and accompanied them to other neighborhood places such as park benches. To gain additional insight into elders' life histories and experiences aging in place, I interviewed twenty-five people recruited from the bakery. These interviews began three weeks after the bakery closed. I asked about biographical information, residential history, social relationships, daily routines, customer experiences, and adaptation after the store closing.

A NOTE ON LANGUAGE

I wrestled with decisions around what language to use to describe those who appear in these pages. I use *older adults, old* or *older people*, and *elder.* Though people often used *elderly* and *senior* to describe themselves, I avoid these words as we lack comparable terms for younger adults, and they may reinforce negative stereotypes that see old people as a different and separate social group. Inspired by geriatrician Louise Aronson's reclaiming of *elder* to connote respect for people over age 65 and to evoke late life's affirmative aspects, I also employ this term. Of the socially devalued category *old,* Aronson writes: "Since the definition of 'old' is having lived a certain number of years, usually sixty or seventy, it seems we have created a society in which carrying that label is so awful that octogenarians leaning on walkers adamantly assert they are not old. Clearly, the human life cycle isn't the problem. Societal prejudice is so strong, and the category old so stripped of respect and social worth, that old people feel compelled to argue against the obvious."[21]

But there's nothing wrong with *old*. Despite its negative cultural associations, I don't treat it like a dirty word to be avoided. As someone whose mother died from cancer at the early age of 53, I hope to live long enough to grow old. My usage reflects a modest effort towards destigmatizing a word that we should not treat as an insult or epithet. In her reflection on language and her choice to use old to describe people over 65, sociologist Arlie Hochschild writes, "It is a commentary on our culture that I should have felt (but mostly resisted) the impulse to soften the term to something like 'older people,' or 'elderly' people, or even 'senior citizens,' an unfortunate phrase suggesting a large boy scout with a gold watch. . . . There is no word to denote people over 65 that has the exact connotations I would like. I prefer the term 'old' because it is straightforward and it sets the tone of this book apart from others that ride over an urgent social problem by saying, in effect, 'old age can be rewarding *after all*.'"[22]

HOW DOES IT FEEL TO BE A PROBLEM?

What is aging like in America today? With a swelling population of older adults, understanding the social, economic, and political challenges and consequences of this unprecedented demographic change warrants our collective commitment to building a society that supports all ages and accommodates shifting needs in late life.[23] International news reports offer dispatches about the "crisis of aging" and warn of a "global population bomb" as countries around the world face declining fertility rates and increased longevity.[24] The media bombards us with advice to ward off the health and cosmetic consequences of aging and offers peppy mantras like "60 is the new 40" to soften the cultural devaluation associated with old age.[25] Companies pitch products aimed at reducing physical signs of aging, such as wrinkles, and sell the promise of life extension. Self-help books direct us to "defy aging" as a process we can and should fight, stop, or reverse; they don't encourage us to embrace or accept the process.[26] And tech billionaires have invested huge sums in anti-aging research.[27] As medical sociologist Irving Kenneth Zola astutely observed about accepting "bodily differentness" that occurs from aging, chronic illness, and disabilities, "Acceptance is acceptance of an inevitable part of oneself."[28] More recently, disregard for older adults has grown amid rising generational tensions.[29] In recent years, "Ok, Boomer" has become the latest cultural put-down for elders, reflecting the struggles of young and old people to take care of themselves and increasingly each other at a time when blame and resentment flows both ways. Amid surging ageism during the pandemic, the disparaging nickname "Boomer Remover" for the SARS-CoV-2 virus trended in early waves on social media.[30]

While we will all grow old if privileged to live long enough, age remains a slippery and fluid social identity, an etcetera category that sociologists have not examined nearly as much as other social constructs such as race, class, and gender.[31] But age is a powerful social organizing principle, and old age is a devalued cultural status. From birth to death age structures our social experiences—on one end as soon as we enter school and, on the other, as those of us who are eligible collect Social Security benefits and enroll in Medicare.[32] Our devaluation of elderhood is evident in the fact that we make fine-grained divisions to distinguish earlier parts of the life course—infant, toddler, child, tween, adolescent, teenager, and young adult—but lump several decades together in late life. Although chronology matters in these larger contexts, age transcends the number of candles on a birthday cake. We construct age in our social interactions and often choose the moments when we consider age relevant to our identities and experiences, though at times people foist labels and expectations on us whether we agree with them or not.[33] Birth cohorts, or groups of people born in a given year or time period,[34] may share some historical and cultural touchstones, but their experiences also diverge based on race, class, gender, sexuality, immigration or migration history, disability, and a host of other social locations. Growing diversity among older adults reveals great heterogeneity in trajectories, life chances, and health and economic outcomes. While status may diminish with age, power can also increase with seniority, especially for those already privileged in terms of race, gender, and socioeconomic class. For example, political analysts have described the concentration of power among elected leaders in their 70s and 80s, such as former president Joe Biden, former president Donald Trump, former House Speaker and Congresswoman Nancy Pelosi, and Senator Bernie Sanders as a "gerontocracy."[35]

This study also reveals how elders internalize larger cultural messages about growing old—namely, that aging is acceptable as long as you don't get sick and look, act, or feel old. In retirement, people once again find themselves among peers of a similar age.[36] Even seemingly innocuous interactions, such as apologizing for a forgetful "senior moment," reinforce negative messages about old age. How do older adults embrace or resist belonging to an identity category or social grouping? What challenges do contemporary elders experience and how do they cope? And what does their situation tell us about the organization of community and family in modern society?

Rather than offer a prescription for how to age "well" or "successfully"[37] or frame aging in America as a "crisis," this book takes up the above questions by providing an in-depth ethnographic account of how people attempted to age meaningfully and with dignity in their communities. They often faced this challenge in the absence of strong or nearby familial support, and they did so in an urban environment that both offered many advantages for older people who wished to stay independent and posed special challenges for lower income residents remaining in some of the most expensive real estate in the country. Unlike previous generations, these elders hadn't moved into the family homestead or to a distant retirement community as they entered their later years. Many found social support in "third places" such as coffee shops, restaurants, and parks yet still struggled to balance connection with autonomy.[38] And growing discrepancies between people's constricted mobility and the neighborhood's changing retail landscape due to gentrification threatened their social ties and larger possibilities for belonging to a community. Even those with stable, affordable housing who had escaped residential eviction suffered what I've come to see as a metaphorical "social eviction," or exile in the form of growing alienation, as they became displaced from the public spaces that had once catered to them and allowed them to claim symbolic control.

"I'd rather die than go to a nursing home" became a popular refrain among the older adults I came to know. They strived to avoid burdening anyone, especially their families, often by cultivating interdependence with others. Most died before moving to an institutional setting, though some suffered a longer period of acute illness and spent a few weeks or months in a nursing facility before dying.

Their aversion to institutional care reflects a broader desire among older Americans to age in place. A recent poll from the American Association of Retired Persons (AARP) found that more than three-quarters of people aged 50 and older want to remain in their community and residence for as long as possible.[39] A growing number of elders live by themselves, with some fifteen million, or 27 percent, of adults aged 65 years and older living alone in the United States.[40] This rise in solo living over the past fifty years represents a "gray revolution in living arrangements," with people older than 75 more likely to live alone today.[41] As sociologist Eric Klinenberg's research has shown, the number of people living alone has risen significantly over the past half century. If people can afford solo living, they choose this arrangement whenever possible, especially when the alternative requires moving in with family at an older age.[42] Yet, the design and infrastructure of most regions remain ill equipped to serve an aging population. For example, insufficient public transportation forces people of all ages to depend on cars.[43] Despite the vast need and desire for home-based care, we also lack adequate funding for medical and nonmedical services, such as attendants to help with laundry, chores, shopping, and personal care.[44] Medicaid and Medicare provide limited home-health coverage, and proposed cuts, which are perpetually on the horizon, often threaten services that help elders remain at home.[45]

As generational tensions flare amid rapid population aging, a care crisis looms. Our social policies incorrectly assume family will step in when elders' needs for long-term care exceed available resources. Given the United States' threadbare social safety net, family often becomes the default source of emotional, practical, and financial support for all ages. Partial measures only duct tape over flaws in a sagging care infrastructure, which works for few and squeezes multiple generations. Growing numbers of younger adults provide paid and unpaid assistance to elders, leaving themselves vulnerable to worsening physical and mental health while also trying to achieve benchmarks associated with the transition to adulthood, such as completing education, securing financial independence, and forming long-term relationships.[46] Often these young women caregivers come from low-income, racial- and ethnic-minority backgrounds. Their relatives experience greater disability and earlier health declines, and research has shown higher rates of caregiving among Latinos at younger ages.[47]

Given the high cost of institutional care, the heavy toll of family-provided care, and the desire to age in place, scholars, policymakers, practitioners, and ordinary people have an interest in understanding the conditions that help elders thrive and remain at home independently. Elders living alone may feel precarious due to rising economic vulnerability, difficulty accessing necessary resources, and bewilderment and frustration in navigating a tangled web of social services.[48] Increasing numbers may become "stuck in place," lacking choice about where to grow old and the social and economic resources to comfortably age in place.[49] Fewer studies have focused on elders' lived experiences; this book adds to a modest but growing body of ethnographic research by furthering our understanding of how places and neighborhood relationships support contemporary urban aging.[50] The old New Yorkers in this book confronted late-life hurdles amid the fallout of commercial gentrification and the loss of the retail spaces that they had relied upon for daily socializing. Many scrambled with their scarce resources to manage steep rises in living costs, and some found themselves unable to cover expenses after outliving their savings.

With the greying of the United States and countries around the world, including high-income countries and regions such as Japan and Western Europe and now low- and middle-income countries, the findings of recent qualitative work are more timely and relevant than ever.[51] Elders in this book exemplify the key demographic trends that will shape old age for generations to come. Most lived alone by choice and remained single, whether because they had been widowed, divorced, or never married. Many never had children.[52] The majority of them were women, who continue to face significant economic disadvantages in old age and higher poverty rates than older men.[53] Given New York City's unique status as the most populous city in the United States and as a global media, culture, and finance center,[54] elders in this study may have a different intensity of experience than older people elsewhere, but they herald rising trends such as having fewer children and multiple committed relationships over a lifetime and facing heightened economic pressures and higher retirement ages. They offer a glimpse into navigating the blessings and burdens of increased longevity and suggest that Generation X and millennial cohorts may experience such challenges even more acutely as they age, though these subsequent generations may also have different opportunities. Thus far, these two cohorts are much less likely to own a home, due to, for example, rising educational debt and escalating real estate prices. Concerns about urban belonging documented in this book may also extend to smaller cities, as younger cohorts find themselves priced out of the costliest cities in the United States. Yet they may also feel more comfortable meeting their social needs with virtual relationships. Lastly, recent drops in U.S. life expectancy signal worrisome trends for younger people that foreshadow poorer health, insufficient preventative care, and an ongoing failure to address increasing drug overdose deaths.[55]

Scholars have long considered older adults vulnerable to isolation and associated negative health outcomes, thus raising the stakes for understanding the size of their social networks and also the quality and character of their myriad social ties. More recently, United States surgeon general Dr. Vivek Murthy sounded alarms about increasing mental distress and loneliness across all ages, but especially among younger people. In a report, he warned that social disconnection posed health risks as deadly as smoking fifteen cigarettes a day and urged strengthening social infrastructure and investments in social programming, the built environment, and neighborhood places such as libraries and parks.[56] Sociologist Eric Klinenberg defines social infrastructure as "the physical places and organizations that shape the way people interact." He argues, "Social infrastructure is crucially important, because local, face-to-face interactions—at the school, the playground, and the corner diner—are the building blocks of all public life."[57]

While older adults face challenges to maintaining social connections, those in urban areas may have distinct opportunities to assuage loneliness. This book helps us understand how elders developed supports beyond close friends and family by marshaling resources near home. They acted as unwitting trailblazers, forging alternate communities as they made their way along an uncertain path that tested their strength, resilience, and creativity. Their cultivation of such informal yet consequential relationships offers an important contrast to the demands of contemporary marriage, which potentially reduces involvement with extended family and community ties. Due to cultural expectations of intense emotional involvement, commitment, time, and energy, sociologists Lewis A. Coser and Rose Laub Coser have described marriage as a "greedy institution."[58] In line with the fluid nature of time and daily routine after retirement, elders often eschewed institutionalized spaces. Thus, their choices provide a possible blueprint for reimagining old age. Despite the critical services senior centers provide, especially for low-income older adults, research has revealed that baby boomers dislike most centers in their current incarnation; they suffer an image problem as "unsexy" and as spaces for the downtrodden.[59] Accordingly, more elders will connect with neighbors and acquaintances in less formal settings. These associations may grow into relationships that are difficult to define and that might therefore challenge traditional notions of friendship and strong social ties; if not "strong," they nevertheless remain important.

Given this flurry of opportunities and constraints, I argue that we should devote greater attention to the neighborhood contexts where informal social bonds blossom. They matter more than ever in cities and are of growing importance in suburban and rural areas, where people may know their neighbors and live closer to family but still crave intergenerational, nonkin ties that allow greater privacy and less obligation. With technological forms of connectivity that no longer require face-to-face interaction, sociologists have debated the extent to which neighborhoods and place matter for creating the connections and networks that provide companionship, a sense of belonging, and robust emergency resources.[60] However, privileging digital connectivity neglects place's heightened significance for older people whose social worlds "tend to be spatially circumscribed."[61] Relationships in public places may allow elders greater standing and recognition as something other than dependent, invisible, or a problem to solve. Alternative social ties stand alongside and, in some cases, rival other structures critical to well-being in old age, such as family and home.

Neighborhood places offered the old people I spent time with a diverse mix of companions and alternate caretaking opportunities, which differed from family contact. Family members often positioned them as recipients of care and subjects of crisis management for serious health problems. Even when elders provide significant financial and childcare assistance as grandparents,[62] obligation and responsibility complicate the kin relationship. People supplemented their living spaces by using a private business's openness and accessibility to fit their needs, and these public places proved as important as home. Ties cultivated in nearby gathering spots enabled elders to receive help with smaller, sometimes overwhelming tasks such as fixing a computer or television remote control. Social connections saved lives—for example, when someone had fallen at home and a friend or acquaintance checked on them after noticing their absence. Outside help, usually unpaid and informal, freed people from overreliance on relatives, healthcare institutions, and elder-serving organizations. But the lack of pay or family obligation also limited this form of assistance.[63]

ORGANIZATION OF THE BOOK

Each chapter examines different consequences of the bakery closure, which reverberated months and years later. At the heart of this book lies the tension between elders' desire for connection and their concerns that too much intimacy with others might result in dependence and threaten their autonomy. This is a story about the multiple meanings of place—place as a temporal location; place as a physical space; and place as a cognitive, emotional, and feeling realm. If we live long enough, we will reach our "inevitable place" in the life course, as poet Robinson Jeffers described in his unexpected discovery of what would become a lifelong home on California's coast.[64] Under favorable conditions, we may discover several inevitable places to belong, whether a park bench, a community center, or a fast-food joint. The older adults I came to know sought their place among these options, and their convergence in time, space, and mind offered most a path towards belonging beyond formal institutions. Our inevitable place in late life doesn't have to be dark, trapped, or despairing but a shifting and flexible site of negotiation, recognition, and reimagining. We may not realize at first that we've found our place but over time may settle in, embrace its tensions and contradictions, and weave webs of sustaining ties. While late life may contain difficulties, detours, and uncertainties, opportunities abound for surprise, innovation, and connection.

Chapter 2 considers how the bakery provided essential ingredients, such as time and proximity, to facilitate practical and emotional support among regular customers. Elders' residences formed the bedrock of their experiences aging in place, but they *aged in places*. Neighborhood places ringed their homes in a radius of walkability and served as communal extensions of their living rooms.

Chapter 3 advances our knowledge of how elders age alone together by gossiping about others around them. Despite gossip's bad reputation and potential for excluding others, talking about others served as a counterintuitive form of connection for older adults. While people's criticisms sometimes delineated a social hierarchy based on differences in physical or cognitive functioning, gossip also provided access to support and fostered cohesion among loosely connected people.

The impending loss of the bakery stirred a special grief for customers. Chapter 4 charts growing recognition of its significance to them as older people with shared challenges, including living alone, limited finances, and declining physical mobility. Elder clientele recognized a common plight, if not necessarily pride in or a lasting embrace of an old-age identity. The crisis spurred a more ephemeral coming together as "the bakery club," as regulars called themselves while they mobilized to save the place they had made their own, mourned its coming extinction, and planned together for the day after.

Cities are gentrifying, yet we know little about older adults' experiences and how commercial gentrification threatens their possibilities to connect in noninstitutional, intergenerational spaces.[65] While important research has focused on the harm of residential eviction,[66] we still have much to learn about the toll of business closings on the emotional and social well-being of their patrons. Chapter 5 examines how indirect displacement due to commercial gentrification estranged even those customers with more secure, affordable housing. I find that different features of establishments, such as cost, surveillance, proximity (distance from people's residences), and physical design and layout shaped placemaking, face-to-face interaction, and a sense of ownership that nurtured elders' independence.

Chapter 6 explores closeness and distance in elders' neighborhood relationships. I present empirical data that complement survey approaches to social isolation and push our understanding of social ties beyond weak and strong by analyzing relationships that defy this binary classification. Usual survey items would describe these elders as isolated and without social support. But ethnographic observations of their interactions with neighbors revealed the presence of "elastic ties": non-strong, non-weak relations between people who spent hours together and shared intimate personal details with those they did not consider "confidants." Nonetheless, they provided the support and practical assistance typically seen in strong-tie relationships. Many social ties fall outside weak and strong; they are elastic in allowing elders and other marginal groups to connect and secure informal support while maintaining their distance and preserving their autonomy.

Examining the physical experience of late life is paramount to understanding how bodily challenges pattern and often constrain older people's social worlds. Chapter 7 considers how people managed the physical and social self amid cultural pressure to eschew dependence. When the body's functional abilities deteriorated they adapted and developed strategies to assuage the threat to their sense of self and their relationships with neighbors, which suffered when mobility declined.

Despite the challenges of recreating their bakery arrangement, displaced elders persisted in finding places to give and receive emotional and practical support. Chapter 8 delves into how they managed their constraints and encountered new tensions and rivalries. They continued relationships and forged new ties while also negotiating spaces that no longer catered to them as older people to the degree the bakery had. Despite reluctance at times to be in each other's company, they made a home in the city that allowed interdependent connections and also sociable moments of pleasure, fun, and laughter.

The book's final chapter considers the study's implications for practice and policy. Given the ageism and stigma attached to organized spaces for elders, I propose modifying senior centers to align with older adults' spontaneous and voluntary uses of public spaces, without rebranding them in ways that diverge too much from their essential purposes, such as providing free or low-cost, nutritious meals.[67] Additionally, reducing bias and improving interactions between medical providers and elder patients remains a critical concern. Besides designing age-integrated and intergenerational programs, we can also create more age-friendly public spaces for elders who seek care and connection in informal settings such as parks, diners, and shopping malls. Finally, along with a substantial investment in affordable housing that integrates supportive services, I recommend strengthening eviction prevention and legal assistance for those at risk of losing their housing.

Sweeping demographic change will shape society and institutions for decades to come, bringing forth new challenges and ways of living. Because of our lack of preparedness and growing precariousness in many realms of social life, societal aging brings new vulnerabilities for older adults. As sociologist Kenneth F. Ferraro writes, "By analogy, a life course can be viewed as a book. The fate of the characters can be gleaned by reading the last chapters, but it is a shallow reading. To understand the life journey of the characters, we read the whole book."[68] Elders of color, LGBTQ+ elders, and those lacking legal status, for example, have experienced greater hardship and different life-course transitions that contribute to cumulative inequality by the later chapters of their life stories[69]—a fact that demonstrates the wisdom contained in the Yoruba proverb, "Where you will sit when you are old shows where you stood in youth."[70]

We no longer live in a society where we can expect one lifelong employer, intimate partner, or place of residence to sustain our needs. But the erosion of these traditional arrangements need not cause alarm if we create policies grounded in lessons learned from prior scholarship and provide significant but necessary investments in long-term care and communities designed for people of all abilities and ages. Previous qualitative studies provide a core foundation for understanding the array of changing needs in late life; but they also leave room for expansion and updating.[71]

Earlier qualitative works have grappled with essential themes of belonging and potential isolation among elders, who are on the fringes of central organizing institutions such as work and family. Some older adults fare better than others, but even those with more privilege still encounter challenges. Classic studies such as Barbara Myerhoff's *Number Our Days* and Arlie Hochschild's *The Unexpected Community* emerged from an era when older people more commonly lived with or closer to family, compared with today's greater geographic mobility, which spreads more family members across the country and the globe.[72] Even older adults with close family ties resist moving in with relatives or prefer to live alone. These studies provide a guide to understanding how different cohorts of older adults reworked anchoring structures such as work, family, and neighborhood at a time when researchers, policymakers, and the wider public can no longer assume a family caretaking model to absorb older relatives.

Qualitative research counterbalances large-scale survey research into older adults' social lives, including the National Social Life, Health, and Aging Project; the Survey of Health, Ageing, and Retirement in Europe; and the Longitudinal Aging Study Amsterdam.[73] While these surveys offer an important portrait of elders in the United States and abroad by collecting data on health and sources of social support, sustained ethnographic observation offers rich insights into the texture of people's daily interactions and how they build supportive networks over the life course.[74] Subsequent generations will refashion old age, and as my research suggests, they will embrace newfound freedoms and possibilities for forging social bonds less entrenched in family and formal institutions.

One day I passed a telling scene heralding the future of aging in urban America. On a quiet, tree-lined block, recycled Whole Foods bags brimmed with empty amber beer bottles. A rolling walker stood alongside, chained to the iron gate of a three-story brownstone. Presumably, the building housed the walker's owner and the party-giver who had disposed of a previous night's revelries (although they could have been from the same person). The juxtaposition reminded me of a similar scene I glimpsed weeks before: someone had secured a folded wheelchair to new bike racks outside a fast-food restaurant. These found objects encapsulated the growing reality of older and younger adults, affluent and not-so-affluent, living side by side. In expensive cities such as New York and San Francisco, which has the lowest share of children among the 100 largest cities in the United States,[75] such scenes have already become more common.[76] The trend in America's high-density cities towards declining birth rates and fewer families with school-age children, coupled with a growing population of wealthy, college-educated whites, has only accelerated in the last decade.[77]

As more people discover cities' benefits, elders in areas undergoing "revitalization" may have to fight to remain in their homes and communities. The poorest face the threat of eviction and end up on the street.[78] Metropolitan areas are ideal places for growing old due to their greater walkability, public transportation, and denser social services. With constraints on finances and mobility coupled with an increase in surplus time spent closer to home, the rising importance of neighborhoods for elders complicates a simpler narrative of aging at home. The advantages that make cities attractive for older adults often draw younger, more affluent professionals who can afford higher rents and desire upscale amenities and businesses. Despite recent increases in crime and growing safety concerns,[79] demand for urban living and rents have remained high amid a chronic shortage of affordable housing.

The buildings that housed the older adults I met during my research represent some of the last large-tract affordable housing left in New York City, a great urban center that once had sufficient protections to allow old people to age in place but that no longer provides a solid base in which to grow old comfortably. At this crossroads, we can choose collective action to ensure tomorrow's older adults—and people of every age—have a chance to find solace, support, and togetherness in their inevitable places. Without intervention, many will experience housing insecurity and dwindling access to the neighborhood spaces that transform a collection of buildings, sidewalks, and storefronts into home. Though unique challenges exist for growing old in twenty-first-century urban America, opportunities abound for improving elders' day-to-day lives. If we can landmark buildings and create historic districts, bemoan follies such as the destruction of architectural treasures like the old Penn Station, we can find tangible ways to support living, breathing examples of old New York like Eugene, Sylvia, Lucy, and Eddie so that they can remain here with dignity and contribute to city life. While this book chronicles older people's journeys after losing their central gathering place, it is ultimately a story about coping with vulnerability and finding ways to negotiate our need for care and connection with autonomy and independence, whatever our age.

2

THE PUBLIC LIVING ROOM

WHEN LA MARJOLAINE PATISSERIE HUMMED with chatter, the bakery felt more like a social club than a business, with the modest price of admission a cup of coffee or tea. "This place reminds me of my grandmother's kitchen table," mused occasional customer Luis, 26. Seasonal tablecloths and custard-colored walls made the place feel warm despite the harsh florescent lighting. Handwritten signs for different baked goods completed the unfussy look. The dated decor seemed an afterthought, but more importantly, the space accommodated older customers' bodies and sensibilities. Cushioned chairs with generous seats and few restrictions on how long patrons could linger imbued the place with homey familiarity, giving people permission to dawdle and form neighborhood relationships. No one minded the shopping carts, walkers, and canes parked alongside tables. Many stopped in after errands, setting down heavy bags and resting weary joints before heading home. Without music playing, people heard each other easily and slid into conversations with neighboring tables. The layout encouraged mingling. Eight tables with two chairs apiece, sixteen seats total, were arranged in a rectangle, allowing people to join discussions or observe from the sidelines and interact as much or as little as they wished in this public living room.

No one ever called the bakery by its given name. Everyone knew what "the bakery" referred to, given its centrality in people's lives. It remained a place with no name, not only satisfying patrons' craving for sweets but their desire for company, for community, and for connection. Sociologist Ray Oldenburg advocates for "third places" such as bookstores and coffee shops as necessary yet endangered sites that help build community, often between people from diverse backgrounds.[1] With colleague Dennis Brissett, Oldenburg coined the term "third place" to describe the inclusive places outside of home (the first place) and work (the second place) where people gather, such as post offices, drug stores, coffee houses, and taverns.[2] This chapter considers how the bakery's setting provided essential ingredients, like time and proximity, to facilitate closeness and the development of practical and emotional support among regular customers.

How did people establish closeness with each other? And what did this form of intimacy look like? In his classic work on the spread of information in social networks, sociologist Mark Granovetter defines strong ties. He claims that we can assess the strength of relationships based on a combination of the following properties: time spent together, intimacy (mutual confiding), reciprocal services, and emotional intensity.[3] Stronger ties contain more of these characteristics. The relations I observed among bakery customers often possessed many, if not all, hallmarks of strong ties. Vignettes in this chapter illustrate how the elders in my study formed relationships that exhibited many of these relationship strands, whether a single hallmark was present or all simultaneously.

The majority of bakery regulars resisted heavy participation in formal organizations, such as churches or senior centers, and thus their interactions in semipublic places like neighborhood eateries served as an important source of social involvement that corresponded to their flexible routines in old age. Even patrons who participated in a religious community or senior center relied on the bakery as a key gathering spot. For those with growing physical limitations, nearby shops helped secure a comfortable quality of life. The bakery's central location and its draw as a safe, affordable, and accessible place, attracted a diverse crowd in terms of race, class, and physical capability. Some spent more waking hours there than at home. Many stopped in more than once a day, creating opportunities for repeated interactions that strengthened ties to each other.

Dottie, 83, a retired telephone company worker, suffered worsening mobility in her last five years. But her warm humor and sharp tongue, coupled with her consistent presence in neighborhood places, helped her to perennially add new acquaintances to a reserve of long-term ties. Less than a block from her apartment building, the bakery's proximity encouraged her devoted patronage despite accumulating physical hurdles. As a lifelong neighborhood resident, Dottie seemed to have friends everywhere. Eugene joked that she knew everyone within a ten-block radius. Though she had an Irish surname by marriage to a neighborhood boy, Dottie liked to remind us of her "full-blooded" Italian-American lineage and quizzed me on how to pronounce her maiden name. She had an older version of a working-class New York accent, which can now be heard mostly in old film reels—for example, in the actor James Cagney's voice and on the crackling recordings of historical figures like New York governor Alfred E. Smith—but rarely on the streets.[4] Dottie's linguistic roots surfaced in her rising inflection and dropped R's whenever she said, for example, beautiful ("bee-yooou-teeful") or girls ("goyles"). Like other customers, she had grown up in the tenements, which the city tore down during "slum clearance" projects completed in the early 1960s and eventually replaced by the co-op buildings. The demolitions displaced her and her family to New Jersey, but she found her way back to the neighborhood, unlike many who never returned. She lived in the housing projects across the street, two blocks from where she was born, and described how the bakery fit into her daily routine: "I come in the morning for my breakfast. I do my errands and come back for lunch. Then, I stop in for coffee in the evening and see my friends."

From the sidewalk I glimpsed Dottie's crown of white hair and glinting glasses through the bakery's large windows as she sat among regulars with her iced coffee and buttered roll. In the mornings, Lucy, a retired secretary in her late 70s known for her bright-red glasses and love of celebrity gossip, held Dottie's table until she arrived. They had a standing arrangement that one would save a table for the other as the store crowded with customers. One brisk autumn day Dottie showed up exhausted and panting. "I'll sit down soon, if I don't drop dead first," she said, gripping the table's edge. Once she caught her breath, Dottie parked her blue metal shopping cart—ubiquitous in walking cities like New York City where people accomplish errands on foot—and filled us in on the story of her lost wallet. "I probably left it in the lotto store [next door] when I was paying," she wondered aloud as she leaned back, stretching her squat legs outfitted in loose-fitting pants and thick-soled sneakers. Before launching into the details, she smoothed her white T-shirt, silk screened with a flirtatious Minnie Mouse cartoon in a flouncy polka-dot dress. A maintenance worker named Henry whom Dottie knew from the projects turned the wallet into her podiatrist's office across the street. "The receptionist called me and said, 'I have something for you.' Thank God," she said, glancing upward as if to the heavens and clasping the gold crucifix pendant she wore every day. "I never carry my birth certificate, but I had it today. I'm gonna give Henry a gift card and a thank-you card to her."

Dottie's friends, Maureen and Tom, were also lifelong neighborhood residents, married for sixty-four years. They often reminisced about growing up together. "I remember the two of us dancing in West Side Park as teenagers," Maureen said. "They held dance contests on the handball court and showed free movies. All you had to do was bring a newspaper to sit on." Dottie chimed in, "We went to P.S. 14," referring to the elementary school a block away. "Did she tell you how I used to play hooky?" she asked with a throaty laugh as she tucked her shopping cart between two tables.

In their old age, they giggled, joked, and gossiped at the bakery. Dottie acted as a second grandmother to Maureen's grandson Joey, who had also grown up in the neighborhood and attended college in Massachusetts. "How's my Joey?" she asked Maureen without fail. "He's good. He sure misses you," Maureen said in her warm, gravelly voice. For years, she and Tom came to the bakery most afternoons. Maureen pushed a rolling walker for support, but the three-block walk from their co-op apartment to the bakery tested her stamina. Like Dottie, she wore comfortable clothes, and her once-dark hair was now equal parts salt and pepper and short-cropped. Tom dressed in crisp plaid button-down shirts and tan khakis. While Tom had no visible mobility issues, his advanced dementia may have accounted for his halting speech and gait. Maureen served as his primary caretaker. Their four adult children lived in the Tri-State Area, including a daughter in the neighborhood. All helped with shopping and took turns checking on their parents. The couple arrived at the bakery's busiest hour, two o'clock in the afternoon, when the late morning crowd was enjoying their last sips of coffee, and many of the old men who lived in the surrounding blocks arrived en masse to talk sports and scratch piles of lottery tickets. Maureen seated Tom and ordered for them at the counter. As Tom's dementia worsened, he could no longer manage much conversation beyond hello, goodbye, and "How are you?" but smiled often and appeared to enjoy sitting among the crowd.

Over the years Maureen's physical issues and caretaking responsibilities had nicked away at her health. She had more trouble walking and fewer opportunities to leave Tom's side. When Tom's dementia progressed and hampered his ability to meet physical needs such as using the bathroom independently, he moved to a nursing home. Maureen shared details about his decline with friends and bakery acquaintances but also confided in the congenial counterwoman, Angelica, an undocumented immigrant from Spain in her late 40s. For two and a half years, she worked the afternoon and evening closing shift, from 2 p.m. to 8 p.m., and many customers trusted her as a confidant. Angelica had the soothing presence of a children's daycare provider, having previously worked as a live-in nanny, and dressed for comfort in baggy jeans, sneakers for long hours on her feet, and roomy T-shirts underneath her white apron. A soft headband held back her wiry black hair, thinning slightly and streaked with grey. In addition to offering an attentive ear and taking in people's stories, Angelica assisted with tasks such as carrying food to customers' tables and writing down information for someone with increasing memory lapses.

Two weeks after Tom's admission to a nursing home across town, Angelica's dark eyes grew red-rimmed as she recounted recent developments. While cleaning up after the store closed for the day, she often debriefed me on events that I missed and shared her interpretation of interactions we had both observed. "She [Maureen] goes every day to see him. He got too confused. He messed himself," she said, pointing to her crotch. "It's so sad. This man, he so nice," she continued, lifting her glasses to wipe tears with the cuff of her cotton-candy pink sweatshirt. "Sometimes, he no recognize her. And he want to go with her. He completely lost. He in his own world." This development didn't surprise me since Tom had recently grown more disoriented. Weeks before I gently had to pry away his fingers when he grabbed my forearm in confusion. Angelica noted that other bakery regulars, such as Eddie, offered extra support to Maureen. Eddie passed by earlier and talked with Maureen for a long time, which was out of the ordinary. "I think on this occasion, he see her alone." Maureen later confirmed these events and shared the pain of Tom's absence after a lifetime together. "It's strange being alone in the house now." But she also expressed relief at no longer bearing the weight of his care alone as she had for years without skilled help from a visiting nurse or home health aide.

The bakery also offered respite to other caregivers, such as Patricia and Dolores. Patricia, in her late 50s, worked nights as a word processor for a corporate law firm and dropped into the bakery in the early afternoons. Originally from the Bronx and the daughter of an Italian-American mother and a Puerto Rican father, she had moved to the co-ops within the last decade. Her parents now lived an hour and a half's drive north of New York City, and I often found Patricia in the bakery with her mother, Anna, and occasionally her father, Louie. Patricia's brother worked in the city and semiregularly drove their mother to spend time with Patricia. Into her 80s, Anna had seemingly boundless energy and spoke of her pride and joy in cleaning her house and cooking big Italian dinners for extended family. She felt most at home in the kitchen. "Yeah, Ma pulls down all the pots and pans from the cabinets, doesn't want any help," Patricia said, at her mother's side. They shared a strong resemblance, with the same deep-set, chocolatey brown eyes, prominent jaw, and thick hair. "That's right, no one comes in my kitchen," Anna laughed as she socialized with other women in bakery.

But as she approached her ninth decade, Anna needed extra family support. "She suffers a lot of back pain, arthritis," Patricia said.

"I remember your mother loves to cook. Can she still do that?" I asked.

"Most of the time."

We saw Anna in the bakery more frequently as Patricia helped coordinate medical care and accompanied her to appointments in the city. I remember my startled dismay, seeing her for the first time wearing a plastic child's bib covered with bright yellow ducks as Patricia assisted with eating.

"Ma, when is your heart doctor appointment?" Patricia asked.

"November twelfth," Anna responded promptly.

Despite growing physical limitations, Anna enjoyed the bakery crowd's company. No one indicated anything had changed, welcoming her into their light conversation and offering their usual greetings and pleasantries. During this time, Patricia informed us of her father's serious illness. "Well, my father is still in the nursing home, but we're hanging in. It seems there's always one thing or another," she said.

Dolores, in her late 70s, also used the bakery for brief breaks from caring for her two adult children in their 40s. Both had never married and lived with her since developing a form of multiple sclerosis that left them unable to walk. She had lived in the neighborhood most of her life, widowed several years before. Many bakery patrons spoke fondly of her late husband, Victor. Dolores's family had immigrated from Spain, and Victor's had migrated from Puerto Rico. She spoke openly about different challenges in her life, as we discussed my own relationship stresses and growing uncertainty about having children amid my family caregiving responsibilities and lack of money. She never gave advice but shared her earlier struggles, including intense family pressure to have a baby. "I thought I was going to have a nervous breakdown," she said and described how she and her husband had given up and visited the country to decompress. Shortly afterwards, she became pregnant with her daughter.

By the time the study began, Dolores's daughter Jennifer, who had once worked as a registered nurse, died at age 46. Dolores continued caring for her son, Hector, at home with help from a devoted team of home health aides and her sister-in-law, who lived in the neighborhood. She stopped into the bakery often to pick up snacks for her son's aides and a small coffee for herself, keeping an eye on the wall clock and another on her wristwatch. In quiet moments, she tucked her bobbed, dyed brown hair behind her ears, dusted her pale cheeks with a bit of rouge, and touched up her blood-red lipstick. Dolores spoke fluent

Spanish with the bakery counter women and, on the phone, with home health-care workers. Her American accent betrayed her New York-born roots. Upon arriving at the bakery, she always noted the time she had to return home, which depended on when her son's aides left for the day." As her own health problems worsened, Dolores stood rather than sat since she had difficulty rising from her chair. "Oh, honey, thank you, but that's okay. If I sit now, I'll never get up," she would say with a gentle laugh whenever I offered her a seat. Late-stage rheumatoid arthritis had caused extreme knuckle swelling and bent her fingers so that they drifted in the opposite direction of her thumbs.[5] She often rested them on the tabletop in front of me. Slight to begin with, Dolores had grown thinner over the years. With fewer pounds on her petite frame, her cheek bones jutted and the sleeves of her long wool peacoat slipped off her shoulders. I worried about her fragile health, especially given my understanding of damage from autoimmune diseases, as I lived with my own chronic illness. But Dolores carried on without complaint.

People folded the bakery into their daily "rounds" in retirement.[6] As older adults become less entrenched in the institutions of work and family, they must develop new routines and relationships. Place has important consequences for understanding their social ties, and considering their neighborhood resources can help researchers form a more accurate picture of risk factors amid different constraints and opportunities. Because elders have fewer institutional attachments, they reveal the circumstances under which place becomes important and how people use places to build social support and a sense of belonging.[7]

Eugene had lived in New York City for 55 years—forty of them in the same rent-stabilized apartment a half block from the bakery. Despite losing a work routine that had whisked him out of the neighborhood each day, when I first met Eugene at age 79, he maintained a full schedule. He went to the movies often, occasionally attended opera performances at Lincoln Center, and dined at "nice" restaurants. He visited friends, even traveling as far as Washington Heights in northern Manhattan to see his friend Maggie. Eugene juggled multiple projects as a working writer, ferrying typewritten manuscripts of his nutrition books to an Upper East Side typing service, which transcribed his documents into a word processing file. He boarded a Metro-North train to Connecticut to meet with his literary agent, as he had years before when he worked at a magazine with an office in Stamford. A few times a year he traveled the country and sometimes abroad, such as to the Philippines, for invited speaking engagements to promote his books. In the midst of these activities, I often saw him at the bakery for breakfast and in the late afternoons for hot honeyed tea to coat his throat before his weekly voice lesson.

Though Eugene peppered his conversations with stories of overseas travel, in his 80s, he stayed closer to home, and his access to those far-flung places dwindled to email and a trove of memories. At age 88, he decided not to renew his passport for the first time. On his final long-distance trip, to Fargo, North Dakota, for a book event, he fell in the airport and required major hip surgery. When Eugene's hip pain grew so severe that he could barely limp to the bakery, he drew on a reserve of goodwill among regulars, who provided practical assistance during his grueling recovery, which included a string of setbacks. In the hospital he received at least twenty visitors, who brought him food, newspapers, cards, balloons, and their well wishes. His first night back home, though thinner and paler, he returned to the bakery for food and company. He lamented that his landlord hadn't repaired his bathroom shower and sink, forcing him to lug pots of water from the kitchen for sponge baths. The situation lasted forty-five days, and as one of a handful of rent-stabilized tenants in his building, he concluded, "They want to kill me. They want me out." Eugene's affable disposition and nimble intellect helped him amass support, and bakery regulars offered advice, lawyer referrals, calls to the building department, and perhaps most importantly, a willingness to listen.

Since then, additional health issues limited Eugene's walking ability. Even with his sturdy wooden cane, he sometimes fell. "People rushed over to help me," he assured us. Lingering exhaustion from a heart attack three years after his hip surgery necessitated a taxi ride to the barber about three blocks away. Eugene told us that drivers often refused payment for shorter trips, as when he hailed a cab to a theater showing the new *Spider-Man* movie a few blocks away: "I had such a nice young gentleman driver, and he didn't want to take my money. Can you believe that? I tried several times, but he didn't want to take it. Happens a lot."

While Eugene's case may seem like an outlier, many dealt with multiple chronic illnesses that compromised mobility. Though Sylvia, 87, had walked sixteen blocks with me slowly but steadily to her doctor's office nine years before, she had more trouble in later years. Arthritis caused severe leg and knee pain, and an untreated left eye cataract reduced her peripheral vision. "I'm not a kid," Sylvia said, updating a growing list of health problems she took in stride. "I don't know why I'm laughing," she said, recounting her setbacks. "I guess humor is all we have." She limited excursions beyond a two-block radius around her home to medical appointments, bank trips, and family visits. The bakery served as a key rest stop in between neighborhood errands and doctor's visits.

During superstorm Sandy and the ensuing blackout, she and Eugene remained stranded alone in their darkened apartments for days without elevator service and unable to climb the stairs. Sylvia's neighbors had left town, taking refuge in their second homes or staying with friends elsewhere. Eugene also rode out the storm alone without a cell phone or even a flashlight. "I was having panic attacks," he said of his hours in darkness. When subway service resumed, I checked on them, bringing extra flashlights and nonperishable snacks such as granola bars, in case they had run out of food.

Another bakery regular, Eddie, 82, also became a frequent customer after his retirement from construction work. His apartment building stood a block and a half away from the bakery. He had lived in the neighborhood since he was a teenager; before that he lived on the East side of Manhattan and before that in his birthplace of Puerto Rico. With his bright blue eyes, fair skin, and accent inflected with more New York edge than Spanish lilt, the revelation of this birthplace surprised me when it came two years after first meeting him.

"Were you born in Puerto Rico?" I asked.

"Yeah," he said, lifting his index finger to his lips and peering around, as if revealing a secret I should keep. "I came on the banana boat," he chuckled when recounting his family's migration history. He didn't advertise his ethnic origins and only spoke Spanish with Angelica when the store emptied. He had a reputation as a curmudgeon, and, with his all-knowing sneer, he struck an air of a tough, street-smart New Yorker, which stood in contrast to Eugene's Southern-gentleman, college-educated gentility. More than once Eddie half-jokingly threatened to hit someone with his cane. When brushing past a customer he disliked, he grunted at sharing space with someone who annoyed him even for a moment.

When I first met Eddie, he was frequenting the bakery almost every day. He cut a comfortable but neat appearance in his usual jeans, white sneakers, and freshly pressed sweatshirt. He had divorced decades before and lived alone. His two adult sons in their 40s lived in California and the United Kingdom. Though he had knee pain and hunched while standing and walking, Eddie worked around his creeping physical problems and maintained his daily routines by pacing himself and resting between errands. Though these outings required increasing effort, they hadn't yet inflicted undue pain. He could walk further then.

In our earliest conversations Eddie spoke of wanting to work due to boredom and financial need. He had retired as a construction foreman in his late 60s, largely due to leg and back pain. He mentioned his physical problems and lack of computer skills as barriers to his return. When Eddie hit his eightieth birthday, pain and swelling in his ankles and legs confined him at home for days. His leg brace and compression stockings provided little relief, and flare-ups increased in frequency from every few months to every few weeks. His next-door neighbor of fifteen years, a retired postal worker in her late 60s, brought him necessities such as milk and the newspaper.

Eddie's poor balance stemmed from a neurological issue that he told me his doctors couldn't correctly diagnose. He explained that he was able to walk without his cane if, for example, he sprang out of bed without over thinking it. The moment he became aware of his missing cane, he faltered. In his apartment he also used a walker. Shuffling alongside me, cane in hand, he took careful yet quick steps, as if by speeding up he could outwit any potential imbalance.

For fear of falling, Eddie stayed home during rain, and afterwards if the streets remained shiny and rain slicked. To protect himself from the Hudson River's strong gusts, he crossed the street about forty feet from the corner crosswalk. He positioned his cane on the sidewalk like the third leg of a tripod to strengthen his balance against the blasting wind. This strategy didn't always work. He spoke of one occasion when the wind whisked him from the middle of the crosswalk and slammed him into a fence across the street. He fell to the ground, and two passersby helped him up and retrieved his cane, which had blown several feet away.

Most evenings at the bakery I found Eddie at his favorite corner table by the window. His strategic positioning allowed him to interact selectively and then steal some solitude by retreating to his newspaper and tea and staring out the window. He turned his face and body away, as if hanging an invisible curtain between himself and the main stage for the action. He deftly carved out a semiprivate "zone" by erecting this "social wall," imagery the sociologist Eviatar Zerubavel uses to describe how we draw cognitive boundaries and organize time and space.[8] I also enjoyed sitting by the windows, and my regular presence at the table in front of Eddie's encouraged interaction. "Hey, Stace," he said to initiate conversation. As many bakery relationships began, we started with small talk about current events and articles from *The Daily News*, later progressing to more intimate discussions about health, family, and self-care challenges.

Midday, Eddie passed the bakery en route to shopping at a rotating lineup of supermarkets on senior discount days; scouring shelves at the Rite Aid pharmacy for the latest cereal and ice cream sales; or making his rounds to the bank, the post office, and his building's management office. He usually stopped in for a few minutes to say hello to me and "the guys and gals," referring to the older men and women who lived in the surrounding buildings. He had known many for decades as a near-lifelong neighborhood resident. This pit stop kept Eddie apprised of local gossip but also allowed him to sit and rest his sore knees.

In lighter moments the bakery provided a venue for him to share anecdotes about his family and brag about his grandchildren, thereby lifting the invisible curtain and displaying a garrulous side at odds with his gruff persona. He drew his material from regular telephone conversations with his sons.

"Mike's going Californian. He's taking up golf," Eddie laughed and said that his other son, Gabe, in England, planned to "crack on him for this." He embellished updates about his granddaughter Emily with unstinting detail. One evening Eddie brought in a family photo calendar his son had sent from England, filled with images of a little girl with blonde ringlets who resembled him. As the calendar circulated among tables, to a chorus of approving murmurs he told us that his granddaughter towered over other three-year-olds and had started to lose the baby fat in her face. "She's going to be a real knockout, but her parents have to watch her. She's too smart. The other day they tried to get her on the phone, and she said something like, 'I'm watching *Tom and Jerry*. I can't talk right now,'" Eddie laughed. "I overheard Gabe [his son] call her a 'cheeky little devil.'"

Sociologist Mark Granovetter identifies emotional intensity as a feature of tie strength, though he does not define this quality. Emotions offer an important lens into people's investment in each other. The interactions I observed contained a spectrum of intense emotions, including concern, empathy, frustration, anger, distrust, and camaraderie. This range often reminded me of the complex ups and downs in family relationships. Occasional clashes I witnessed among bakery regulars recalled squabbles I've had with my three younger sisters.[9] The presence of positive and negative emotions also betrayed a deeper involvement between customers who often claimed only a passing connection or a casual "nodding" relationship with each other, a seeming contradiction I explore further in Chapter 6 on the presence of "elastic ties." Even traditionally frowned upon practices such as gossip, discussed in the next chapter, revealed surprising closeness and mutual concern among customers.

Different expressions of care threaded into the fabric of social interactions. For example, George, a Black man in his early 60s, offered frequent thoughtful gestures to several bakery regulars and workers, including Angelica. George lived in Brooklyn and spent time in the bakery with his fiancée, Diane, 60, who had grown up in the neighborhood. Twice widowed, she had returned after two decades living in South Carolina and moved into her sister's project apartment for a fresh start. George and Diane hoped to save for their own place but finding affordable housing on their low-paying jobs had proved impossible thus far. He worked at a soup kitchen, where he served many older adults, and she held an office assistant position at an AIDS non-profit organization.

One evening among many, George warmly greeted me with his usual, soft cadence, "Hello, princess."

"Hi, George. How's Diane?"

"She's fine. I just dropped her off."

"Do you have far to go home?"

"No, just to Brooklyn." He'd stopped by to say goodnight to Angelica.

"Hello, my dear," she said and put aside her sweeping. "Do you want some bread?" He declined.

"Good night, Angelica," he said. That brisk night he wore a Yankees cap to keep his bald head warm, with his usual baggy jeans and sand-colored Timberland boots. Readying himself for the journey home, he zipped his black bomber jacket over a hoodie sweatshirt before heading out.

"Goodnight, my friend. Take care," Angelica said with an airy timbre.

People weighed cost when deciding where to gather, and for many, their limited income led them to the bakery where they could purchase a small coffee or tea for $1 and a buttered roll for 65¢. The owner and head baker, Guillaume, an immigrant in his early 60s from Lyon, France, stocked staples like apple turnovers, baguettes, and quiche, along with bagels, challah bread, and hamantaschen in a nod to his Manhattan location. Most items cost less than $2, and the low entry price assured patrons of the reliable company of others.

Guillaume allowed customers to linger but not due to altruism, as he explained. Most of his profits came from catering and wholesale orders, not the walk-in cafe. He divulged this information when we discussed a story in a small neighborhood newspaper on the bakery's imminent closing. "Patrick O'Connell [the building complex's general manager] says I don't have any customers, but the cafe is only five to eight percent of my business," he scoffed, brushing silver strands of hair from his piercing eyes. "What does he know?" Guillaume said it helped business if people saw a packed store when they walked by. At peak times like two o'clock in the afternoon, the bakery had standing room only but, even when crowded, felt spacious enough for all. A regular named Theresa in her early 70s described the appeal for her, "This place reminds me of the cafes they have in Europe. You can sit all day, and nobody bothers you."

Guillaume worked seven days a week, from five in the morning to about two-thirty in the afternoon. I rarely saw him out of his white baker's jacket. During breaks, he pulled up a chair to chat with customers and stretched his long legs. Regulars sensed that he favored some over others, because he chatted more with bigger spenders. But people expressed comfort in knowing that, if they bought something, no matter how meager their purchase, they could sit as long as they liked.

Loose supervision allowed people to make the place their own. When the owner left, customers could "break" the rules. Some stayed for hours without purchasing anything. Many people treated the bakery as a rest stop on their way home, buying nothing. They usually stayed longer than a few minutes, especially if they ran into someone they knew, and chatted with Angelica. Her laid-back presence allowed patrons to bend rules further. She didn't enforce prohibitions against outside food or using the restroom. One evening a few women had a pizza delivered and passed around extra slices. Others brought Chinese takeout from across the street. The scent of stir-fried beef and broccoli mingled with the perfume of fresh-baked, buttery croissants. On busy days when Angelica had no time to eat the homemade vegetable soup she brought for dinner, she warmed it up for Eugene, cutting into the owner's profits. At day's end she distributed bread and other unauthorized freebies, such as day-old muffins that she didn't think should sell the following day. "She gives the whole place away," Eddie said with a satisfied chuckle. He disliked Guillaume.

Not only had the bakery's proximity and low levels of surveillance provided a comfortable place to linger, but the changing nature of time in late life had also compelled people to spend more time together. In the absence of work and family obligations, many of the retired customers struggled to fill surplus time and created routines that helped structure daily life. They transformed this space into a "home away from home." For others, such as Maureen, Patricia, and Dolores, who continued caretaking for spouses, parents, and adult children, the bakery provided respite. Unhurried moments encouraged relationships between people who may never have crossed paths earlier in life.

Lucy and Sylvia shared their difficulties managing excess time. Lucy mentioned her boredom whenever Eugene listed the writing projects he juggled. She envied that he stayed busy and never seemed to grow lonely even though he lived alone. "Yes, I always have something going," Eugene said. He had learned to enjoy solitude as a boy, often spending time alone after his mother died as he shuttled among different relatives. "He's lucky. Not everyone has that. I sure don't," she said. Sylvia also sought escape from boredom and stress. Playing lotto helped. "I find it very entertaining," she said of her favorite scratch-off ticket "Bingo Boxes." I purchased a ticket and discovered how easily I lost myself in the scratching. The game took a half-hour to play. Even the New York Lottery understood its entertainment value, suggesting on the ticket's back that players scratch one number at a time "for more suspense." Because of their advanced age, bakery regulars confronted another paradox of time: They had less to waste and felt compelled to use it wisely.

People forged intimacy by revealing past and present concerns, including health, loss, and gentrification. Confiding opened the door to developing other features of strong tie relationships, such as providing practical help and emotional support. They reached into the deeper past to share personal information about childhood events and fast-forwarded to incidents from the last few years or days. During a discussion about neighborhood safety, prompted by Lucy's paging through the local crime blotter, an 84-year-old woman named Phyllis announced, "I was raped" and described the attack she endured as a teenager. On another occasion, she graphically detailed her older brother's accidental death in World War II under friendly fire. She visited his grave at the National Memorial Cemetery of the Pacific in Honolulu, Hawaii, whenever traveling to her son, who lived in Japan. Other discussions of personal histories included fond reminiscences and strained memories of family relationships and the loss of relatives and friends. Eugene spoke with great emotion about losing his mother at 9 years old after she had contracted tuberculosis while bringing food to infected neighbors. Likewise, Sylvia often shared stories about her deceased parents, siblings, husband, and most recently, a middle-aged niece. One morning at the bakery, between sips of coffee and bites of poppy seed Danish, Sylvia spoke of another recent loss.

"You know, I lost two close friends recently. My childhood friends," she said.

"One was a bridesmaid at your wedding, right?" I asked, as she had mentioned this friend many times.

"Yes, and the other lived in Arizona. They sent her body back to Brooklyn. I just received something from her daughter. She said she knew how hard it was for me to go to the chapel in Brooklyn," Sylvia said. After a long pause, she continued. "Ironically, the irony of living is that the longer you live, the more you say goodbye to. My biggest fault is that I miss people too much. This reminds me of them. That reminds me of them," she said, pointing to the floor and empty space in front of her.

Given these elders' advanced ages, present concerns often involved managing the practical, emotional, and financial challenges of health problems. No matter the discussion topic, whether the scandalous gossip on Page Six of *The New York Post*, a prior run-in with a neighbor, or a recent telephone call with relatives, health infiltrated most conversations. People divulged great detail about their medical history. They consulted each other about their health-care decisions and navigating frustrations with the medical establishment and received assistance evaluating their options. This third place provided them with somewhere to vent and a pool of reliable listeners.

During a discussion on these topics, Judy, 63, revealed her breast cancer diagnosis at 18 years old and described her follow-up treatment. Phyllis blamed herself for her diabetes, claiming, "It was my fault. I ate too much sugar." Sylvia discussed her heart attack and a brain hemorrhage that still affected her memory and hearing. She offered asides on other medical problems, such as severe seasonal allergies and nasal polyps that hampered breathing. A worsening cataract would cause complete vision loss without a surgery, which she was delaying due to her anxiety about the procedure. More recently she had foot pain that her podiatrist, Dr. Gurvits, told her resulted from fluid build-up. "I asked God to please take it away. 'Let up, let up,' I said. Enough," Sylvia said. "And you know what, it did. So hopefully tomorrow will be a better day." Lucy detailed ongoing treatment for chronic arthritis and her high out-of-pocket costs for prescriptions and medical visits. She often provided a full report of her doctor's appointments and the subsequent stress at the pharmacy whenever she learned that she had to pay more than anticipated for her medications.

Besides health, people also discussed complicated relationships with family and everyday challenges, such as managing finances and errands like shopping. They also revealed feeling increasingly insecure in their current housing and living arrangements, especially those who resided in market-rate buildings. Sylvia worried about retaining her apartment, saying, "I don't play my music loud, I don't turn my TV up. I'm just afraid they're going to take me out one day." She mentioned wealthy new neighbors on her floor, a young couple, and admired the well-paying jobs and long workdays that covered their rent. "They rent the empties. I'm squeezed by these high payers," she said of the newcomers moving into vacant apartments. Residents with more stable housing in the projects and co-ops expressed their own concerns. For those in the projects, such as Dottie, worries about safety, deferred building maintenance, and delayed apartment repairs loomed large. Co-op residents demonstrated greater security with the physical condition of their buildings, but gentrification left some, especially those with lower incomes, feeling moored on an island of affordable housing, surrounded by a sea of high-priced retail establishments.

As the bakery faced its imminent demise, Eugene's plight knitted together his worries about health, physical vulnerability, and housing insecurity. During his recovery from hip surgery, which I discussed briefly above, he chronicled his ordeal in installments over six weeks. His building had neglected to repair his bathroom shower and sink, allowing the situation to continue upon his arrival home from the hospital. Eugene's comfort with confiding in bakery regulars set the stage for them to help.

One early October evening, he arrived around 6:25 p.m. "Hello there," he greeted me, Theresa, Sylvia, and Dottie.

"How are you?" Sylvia asked.

"Well, thank God I'm alive," Eugene said before ordering at the counter. As he circled back to sit with the group, he added, "It's tough for an old guy like me. Give me a break. I'm 84." I'd never heard him call himself old before.

He said a flood in his bathroom from mid-September had prevented him from taking a shower for over three weeks. Water only worked in his kitchen, forcing him to carry pots of water to the bathroom for sponge baths. He also hadn't been able to lock his front door for the past four days.

I observed that this neglect sounded like harassment, remembering an article in *The New York Times* I read some years before about retired longshoremen who suffered harassment via neglect during building renovations. I summarized the article for Eugene. He agreed. "If I owned my apartment they'd be here in a second. I'm rent stabilized, so they don't give a shit. They want me to die. There's a bitch in the office . . ." he said, explaining that she hadn't helped him despite numerous requests.

Eugene had lost noticeable weight; his round belly had disappeared. The color had also drained from his normally ruddy cheeks, giving him a wan pallor. He didn't have much appetite, he explained in between languid forkfuls of Quiche Lorraine. Slumped in his seat, weary sighs segmenting his speech, he told us that he had contracted a bedsore and urinary tract infection in the hospital and needed to use "a urine bag," or catheter, now. He laid bare his physical reality without shame, as a matter of fact rather than complaint.

Sylvia joined in. "I'm over the hill. Going over the hill," she said, referring to her piling medical problems. "If one more thing goes wrong . . ." she trailed off. She asked Eugene if he received her get well card, which she had entrusted with another bakery regular, Lorenzo, to deliver during his visit. "Yes, I got it."

Dottie sat quietly in the corner, looking distracted. Dolores came in for a few minutes and explained her reticence that evening. I hadn't seen Dottie for several days, but Dolores saw her earlier. "Her neck still hurts. She's bad off, not herself. With all the people talking, she didn't talk so much today."

"How are you? I haven't seen you in a long time," I asked her.

"Well, I've got my hands full with Hector," Dolores said. She had to go soon, since her son's aide left at 7 p.m. Unable to leave him alone, she skipped her building's informational meeting about an upcoming HVAC replacement project. "That's fine with me. There's a lot of elderly people, and they yell so much. They don't want to pay more rent. I'm elderly too . . . but there's too much yelling."

Eddie arrived a half hour later and drew on his construction background to advise Eugene about pressuring his building to make repairs.

"You should call the building department and then tell your building that you did. Then, you should say that the Veterans Administration Hospital told you to call, and they'll be calling your building."

Eugene nodded. "That's a good idea," he said.

"You gotta eat," Eddie urged. "How about some pumpkin pie?" he suggested and pointed to the pastry display case.

A few days later, despite Eugene's absence, Eddie continued discussing the plumbing situation and repeated his suggestions. "He needs to call the health department and the building department. They hear 'Vets hospital,' and they'll be there the next day." Eddie also assessed Eugene's physical condition and recovery from surgery. "He thinks it's gonna take a week. It's gonna take a year," he said, shaking his head. "The thing that gets me is he could have gotten a fitted one [a walker]. I told him that one's for the house. Everyone has them. And he needs to get a chair [a power lifting chair] from Vets. The regular recliner, you sink. I wake up at 2 a.m., and I need the cane to get up."

Nearly a week later, Angelica left me a voicemail: "Hi, Stacy. I'm in the store if you want to call back. I'm working. Eddie, he want to ask you something." I called back, and Angelica put Eddie on the phone.

"Yeah, it's kind of important," he said, explaining that, while in the bakery alone two days before, when another counter woman named Dani was working, Eugene had called the store asking for me. "Then he said that he'd talk to anyone there. She hands me the phone. He gets on and says, 'Eddie, I'm desperate. I need underwear.'" Eugene told Eddie that an ambulance took him to Bellevue Hospital four days earlier, and the emergency department held him for thirty-two hours in a room without a phone or television.

Eddie brought underwear to the hospital for Eugene the following day. "He told me that the doctor said the plumbing situation at home was his fault. The visiting nurse called an ambulance. Police said that they wouldn't take him to Vets. Last thing I told him, you gotta ask your [literary] agent if she has a lawyer. And you gotta call the store and tell us where you are. But I asked Angelica today, and she didn't hear anything."

"Well, we found Eugene . . . again," I said as we ended the conversation. Last time we "found" Eugene, he had just returned from the emergency room after a few falls. I could scarcely imagine Eugene's options for support without the bakery.

The next day, I bumped into Diane and George as they left the bakery. "Eugene's in there. You have to talk to him," George said, raising his eyebrow from behind thick-lensed, Coke bottle glasses.

"Yes, he's really upset," Diane said, buttoning the navy blazer she wore over a flowy white blouse and ankle-length skirt. Her wig of chestnut curls complemented her golden skin, several shades lighter than George's deep brown complexion. I found Eugene sitting with a silver-haired man I hadn't seen before. Eugene introduced him as a neighbor in his building. After his neighbor headed home, Eugene said, "He's nice. He visited me twice in the hospital when I had my surgery."

Eugene offered an opening statement to whet our appetite for the story he prepared to unspool. "Well, I've been through hell," he said. Eddie and I sat at nearby tables by the window. Jeannette listened attentively, hovering by the door.

"You look it. Your face shrunk and everything," Jeannette said bluntly before heading out.

Eugene explained that he had fallen the week before, and a visiting nurse called an ambulance, landing him in the hospital. "Didn't this bimbo know the rule?" he said, referring to the ambulance policy of transporting patients to the nearest hospital. They declined to take him to the Veterans Administration (VA) Hospital, as he requested, which had his medical records and provided his health care. "One nurse refused to let me go to the bathroom. But another nurse took pity on me. She let me place two phone calls. I told them I refuse to spend another night here." They discharged him after he signed a liability waiver.

"It's a miracle they released me. They said they didn't think I had a working toilet and couldn't release me. It took all day to let me go home. I got home at 8 o'clock at night," Eugene said, his jaw tightening.

"Is that right," Eddie said. "That's a shame."

"At some point this stupid psychiatrist came in. She asked, 'Did you leave the water running all night? Do you know what year it is? And what month? Is it the middle or the end of the month?'"

"How old do you think the psychiatrist was?" I asked.

"About 30," Eugene said.

"This is Paris. You're a courtesan. Now take your clothes off," Eddie guffawed. "Yeah, there's water running in your head. They probably told the psych you did this [left the water running]. Where the hell did they get that from?"

"At one point, this bozo next to me was crying all night. They asked him why, but I didn't hear the answer," Eugene said.

"Because I'm in this ER," Eddie said.

"When I came home, I asked the building superintendent, 'Why did you tell the doctors at the hospital it was my fault?' The super said, 'We didn't say that.'"

Eugene's hospital admission activated the cancellation of his visiting nurse and physical therapy sessions. "Case closed," he said, resigned to a contorted bureaucratic logic he couldn't understand.

Eddie pressed Eugene not to give up, "You gotta do it. You can't hem and haw. Get after them."

Phyllis and Judy came in together. Not yet retired from her banking job, Judy stopped by less frequently and mostly in the evenings, still dressed in her office clothes. Chunky bracelets adorned her plump arms, and rings sparkled on multiple fingers. Eugene updated them on his ordeal.

"We didn't know where you were. We thought maybe you went to Texas," Judy said, squinting from behind glasses and thick brown bangs. People had trouble keeping track of Eugene's whereabouts, including his sister who would contact me when she couldn't reach him by phone or email. I updated her as I learned more information.

Days later, Eddie came in an hour before closing. Walking past Eugene, he covered his nose with a napkin, smirking. "Hey, I don't have a shower," Eugene said in smiling protest at Eddie's joke. Eddie urged Eugene to stay on top of the situation.

"Did the lawyer get back to you?" Eddie asked about a public interest attorney Eugene had contacted.

Eugene explained he couldn't reach his ringing phone in time, missing the call on account of his cumbersome walker. The law office left a message. She had gone for the day, so he emailed her.

"You gotta tell Vets," Eddie said. "And tell the doorman that you have a leak when the water's supposedly shut off and that you're going to call the fire department. That's what they do here [in the co-op buildings]. Drives them crazy. Now they have one after-hours guy. He fixes everything."

"Yes, that's a good idea," Eugene said, his eyes searching as if tucking away the suggestions in a mental filing cabinet.

We shifted our discussion to the swine flu, which had garnered news attention recently. Eddie filled us in on the latest information about the emerging threat, which he'd gotten from an article in the newspaper left on the table. "I already got my flu shot," he said.

"That won't protect you against the swine flu," Eugene said. "I never get a flu shot. Half the time they don't work. They make one for one strain, like the Hong Kong flu,[10] and another one makes everyone sick anyway."

Eddie groaned. "Listen to this guy who just came out of the hospital. Again. Well, I get mine."

"The guy next to me was coughing. Who knows. Maybe he had it. Or maybe it was a fake cough. He was taking everything else [medications]," Eugene said. He complained that the unhoused, Spanish-speaking man wailed nonstop and that he had to listen to Spanish-language television all week. "This poor guy couldn't tell his caseworker where he was. But he hotwired the TV." His stereotyping revealed resentment at feeling forced to share space with someone he considered lower in social status.

Eddie turned to me after Eugene had left, "If that bloody thing [the pipe] goes, he'll be swimming."

Reciprocity formed the backbone of many bakery relationships and colored exchanges between regulars. This give-and-take included swapping information, favors, and small gifts, which proved critical to people fighting to maintain their independence in old age.[11] Though rarer, one-sided exchanges quickly strained relations. On her birthday, for example, Phyllis shared her disappointment and frustration with lopsided giving. Though she often treated people on their birthdays, no one reciprocated her kindness that day. She bought a birthday cake for herself, telling Angelica while she paid, "I grew up very poor. We didn't have enough food, and I never had a birthday cake. I worked my whole life." As Angelica sliced the cake, Phyllis added instructions not to give everyone a piece. She complained about Theresa, Bill, and "the guys." "They're so cheap," she said.

Later that day while closing up, Angelica offered additional context for this tension. I'd seen Phyllis treat others but never saw anyone buy her anything. Angelica confirmed these patterns as she pulled down the store's metal security gate. "She always buy to others, but they don't buy to her. She bought Theresa a little cake on her birthday—$3.50—and Theresa, it's like she didn't have any reaction. She didn't say nothing." Afterwards, Phyllis expressed her disappointment with Theresa's ingratitude. Angelica knew that omitting anyone from Phyllis's birthday cake would spark controversy. "So I cut it into very tiny pieces, so everyone could have a taste." She also expressed surprise at Phyllis's childhood poverty. "I never would think . . . I would think she had money, she was rich or middle class."

I agreed. "See, you never know."

Eugene's case illustrates how people participated in the giving and receiving of information. He served as the group's resident nutritionist due to his fifty-plus published books on vitamins and health and provided a wealth of information for years. Carmen, a soft-spoken Puerto Rican woman in her late 70s, expressed her gratitude to him for educating her about vitamin D, especially after her sugar levels bordered on diabetic. She credited her knowledge of the vitamin's benefits to helping her successfully avoid more serious disease. Recipients also shared information with others. Lucy followed Eugene's suggestions to treat her arthritis and relayed his recommendations for preventing macular degeneration to a friend. Eugene's knowledge reached others years after the bakery closed. When Angelica received a breast cancer diagnosis, I passed along his suggestions to her when I accompanied her to surgical consult appointments. Upon request, Eugene also conducted web searches for people and fact-checked information.

Eugene also received vital information. Sylvia advised him about Senior Citizen Rent Increase Exemption (SCRIE), a program that helps people age 62 years and older with fixed incomes avoid rent increases.[12] She asked me to pick up an application for him from their district's state assembly member's office six blocks away, too far for them to walk. Lucy said she would bring one the next day. Eugene and Sylvia lived in rent-stabilized and rent-controlled apartments surrounded by neighbors who paid three and four times as much. Both had experienced unfair and confusing rent increases. The harassment Eugene experienced forced him into housing court, at which point the management company abruptly halted eviction proceedings. Information exchange aided their survival in a gentrifying city. Co-op residents encountered less housing-affordability pressures since annual income determined their rent. Eugene also received important information from Eddie, who also accessed health care at the VA Hospital and offered tips to expedite prescriptions and navigate the clinic of rotating doctors and the backlogged physical therapy office.

Beyond information sharing, people also exchanged gifts, small loans, and other practical help, such as picking up something from the store. When Eugene had trouble paying his bills, Sylvia provided a few loans in $20 to $40 increments and confided to me that she didn't expect him to pay her back. When I admired her rich tapestry scarf, Sylvia told me that Phyllis had given her this gift. For several years, a large group of bakery regulars took each other out for a birthday dinner. Many treated each other to coffee and food at neighborhood eateries. Knowledge of a person's limited finances also prompted generosity, for example, towards Jeannette, who lived in the housing projects, wore threadbare clothing, and had no cell or landline phone.

THE TIES THAT BIND: AGING IN PLACES

Sociologists' interest in social integration dates to the discipline's founding in the classic works of sociologists Emile Durkheim and Georg Simmel.[13] The extent to which isolation has waxed and waned has fueled perennial debate about whether we in the United States are "bowling alone" or more connected than we appear.[14] Social media have inspired twenty-first-century handwringing over potential isolation, a departure from earlier optimism about new forms of connection.[15] More recently, United States surgeon general Dr. Vivek Murthy warned of increasing mental distress and loneliness at all ages, especially among younger people, and recommended the public avoid or limit technology usage to minimize digital harm.[16] The Centers for Disease Control also cited record high sadness and suicide risk among adolescent girls.[17] Concern about isolation stems in part from negative outcomes related to a dearth of social ties, such as increased stress and poor mental and physical health. Robust networks provide a sense of belonging, social support, and access to resources, such as cash and other practical assistance.[18] "Social capital" also acts as a public good, and higher levels of trust and cooperation can benefit the larger community.[19]

Scholars, popular media, and professionals in health care and social service fields often portray isolation as a problem of old age.[20] Older adults face multiple risk factors for social isolation, including higher rates of living alone, physical illness, and clinical depression.[21] The number of elders living alone has risen throughout the late twentieth and early twenty-first centuries, often due to partner loss but also because they choose to live alone.[22] Urban areas tend to have higher rates of solo dwellers, challenging cities such as New York City to identify those most vulnerable to isolation.[23] While living alone increases elders' isolation risk,[24] this household arrangement does not predetermine loneliness or a lack of companionship.

A substantial scholarly literature has documented the harm of loneliness on physical and mental health.[25] Loneliness-related health problems include cognitive decline, heart disease, weakened immune systems, and depression.[26] Prior research has found participation in social activities and the perception of feeling supported are associated with better cognitive function in older adults, suggesting that diverse and expansive networks offer greater exposure to complex social stimuli, which may boost brain health.[27] The loss of social network members through death or other transitions, such as retirement or moving to an assisted living facility, complicates remaining connected.[28] Networks may also contract through selective paring down. Socioemotional selectivity theory, developed by the psychologist Laura Carstensen, argues that older people prune networks to increase positive emotions and exchanges, whereas younger people more likely seek information and professional opportunities from a larger number of contacts.[29] Despite these challenges, the prevalence of late life isolation remains unclear. Health declines may limit activity, but research has also shown that older adults experience less loneliness and isolation than previously thought and that social interaction and volunteering increase with age.[30]

Place rises in significance as health, finances, and retirement increase time spent in residential neighborhoods.[31] In his study of personal networks, sociologist Claude Fischer finds that older people's social worlds "tended to be spatially circumscribed," leaving few options other than those people living within their communities with whom to form supportive ties outside family.[32] Reliance on neighborhood-based social ties may grow for those with physical limitations and those who no longer drive.[33] Older adults may struggle to leave home and the immediate area due to health problems that impede long- and short-distance trips.[34] National Health Interview Survey data show that 28.4 percent of adults aged 65–74 and 44.3 percent of adults more than 75 years experienced some physical limitation, with 12.3 percent of adults aged 65–74 and 24.6 percent of those aged more than 75 reporting difficulty or an inability to walk a quarter-mile.[35] The geography of streets and sidewalks may matter more in urban areas, where people rely on public transportation and walk to local shops and parks.[36] Limited finances may also hamper travel.[37] Sociologist Arlie Hochschild observes the significance of economic and social class for developing neighborhood relationships, with working-class older people drawing heavily on community ties, perhaps blunting the loss of work-based ties in retirement.[38]

Urban scholars have argued for place's importance in understanding community and social network formation.[39] Thomas F. Gieryn's discussion of "a space for place" in sociology emphasizes that place is "doubly constructed" in the minds of people who imbue its physicality with meaning.[40] Investment often leads to emotional attachments as people associate special places with different strands of their biographies. Over time attachment may deepen, creating an "interactional past" and a trove of memories,[41] encouraging ownership of physical spaces and people to become "public characters."[42] Caretaking of places can also extend to caring for others who inhabit them.[43]

Third places offer "a home away from home" and a sense of control and ownership through their physical accessibility, casual decor, and unassuming design.[44] These venues encourage relationships of proximity (neighbors), service (sales clerks and waitstaff), and chance (strangers).[45] Third places also foster warmth due to their lively, playful, and welcoming atmospheres and a freedom in casual conversations, which often include gentle joking and teasing.[46] Voluntary, informal, and often anonymous, such gatherings stand apart from more serious and obligatory interactions at home and work.[47] Elders' interactions in fast-food restaurants, shopping malls, and parks may offer one of few avenues for social contact outside formal settings where they receive services, such as a doctor's office or a senior center.[48]

Many older adults eschew age-separated, institutional spaces such as senior centers. While organized centers represent a significant policy intervention to reduce isolation, the number of senior center attendees has declined nationwide.[49] Stigma and internalized ageism explain some of this decline. Many elders dislike socializing only with other old people and prefer intergenerational activities in non-age-specific community centers and informal settings.[50] Declining participation also reflects baby boomers' changing preferences, a generation famous for declaring, "Don't trust anyone over 30"[51] and characterized by post–World War II material surpluses and individualized lifestyle choice. Given many boomers' identification with younger generations, negative stereotypes of senior centers filled with frail and lonely older adults discourage their attendance.[52]

Instead, many elders enjoy multigenerational public spaces bustling with children, families, workers, and other passersby.[53] In retirement, the second place often fades while the third place rises in prominence, helping elders socialize and structure their days. For those with limited physical mobility, the proximity of neighborhood third places makes them important physical spaces outside of home that still harbor a homey feeling. Aside from emerging studies on the "digital third place,"[54] most studies on older adults' use of public space examine how elders socialize in "commercial third places," such as malls, fast-food restaurants, and cafes.

Many approach shopping centers not as consumer hubs but as places to "do nothing" or to enjoy "people watching."[55] Due to their safety and comfort, inclusive physical amenities (such as benches), and low or no cost, some elders visit shopping malls solely for social contact and physical exercise, such as walking.[56] Fast-food restaurants serve as another popular third place for elders. For example, public health researcher Michael Cheang observed a group of older adults in Hawaii who frequented a Honolulu fast-food restaurant. He found that this spontaneously occurring group not only provided structure, meaning, and social interaction but also leisure, fun, and laughter to support long-term well-being.[57] Likewise, journalist Michael Tsai profiled 76-year-old Barbie Kihara, a fixture for eighteen years at McDonald's in Honolulu's Manoa Shopping Center. She came several days a week, staying up to fourteen hours per day, to knit, crochet, and teach others the craft. When she stayed home to recover from a broken hip, concerned customers inquired with management about her whereabouts.[58] Public parks also afford elders open space to cultivate social ties. Using still photography in Israel, geographer Rinat Ben Noon and social work scholar Liat Ayalon captured the presence of older adults in parks. They found that, although most arrived alone, almost half formed a group there, revealing the importance of these spaces in facilitating social interactions.[59]

At Home in the City adds to this growing literature on late life and enlarges our understanding of why and how older adults use third places, why some prefer them to more formal and institutionalized spaces, and how service providers can reach their patrons. For the elders in this book, their apartment residences formed the bedrock of their experiences aging in place, but they *aged in places*. The neighborhood venues that ringed their dwellings in a radius of walkability provided crucial opportunities to connect with others and avoid isolation, serving as communal extensions of their living rooms and the homes they longed to return to after any absence, whether a stressful hospitalization or a pleasant visit with relatives.

3

AGING ALONE, GOSSIPING TOGETHER

ONE EVENING AT THE NEARBY GALAXY DINER, in between dishes that our attentive waiter brought, Sylvia and I discussed the people she liked and those she dreaded seeing at the bakery. She had known him since the diner opened.

"My waiter of thirty years," she chuckled as he set down her steaming tea mug and slice of Challah slathered with butter. Without needing to ask, he had her usual order ready.

"Thank you, Alan."

"Of course, Sylvia," he said with a familiar smile. "I had more hair then," he said, pointing to the remaining wisps of black hair on his smooth shiny head. "Me too," Sylvia joked.

Turning to those she favored, Sylvia said, "I like Eugene. He's intelligent, on top of things. He has a good sense of humor. Oh, yes. How we laugh sometimes when he comes in the mornings." Though out of earshot of anyone else, she lowered her voice and continued, "You know, he doesn't like everyone."

She told a story to illustrate. "There's this photographer. He can't stand him. One day he comes in, and Eugene saw him coming and said to me, 'Oh, no. Save me!' I was going to go, but I sat a little longer to protect him." "The photographer" referred to a retired newspaper photographer who lived across the street from the bakery. Almost no one called him by name. That day she lingered long enough to prevent him from cornering Eugene. Despite being generally well liked, Eugene had clashed with others over the years. Sylvia shared more examples. "And Susan. They [Eugene and Susan] had some words, he said." She mentioned some heated political discussions between the two. Susan leaned leftward in her politics, while Eugene identified as conservative. "You know, Rob didn't like Susan. And she thinks he adored her." Even in death, former bakery customer Rob also had not escaped gossip's web. A neighborhood fixture, Rob died three years prior in his early 60s. When he went missing, bakery regulars called the police and then searched for him until they discovered he'd had a heart attack during his nightly bicycle ride along the Hudson River. A regular named Arthur helped identify his body. Rob's ghost hovered over the bakery, and people invoked his memory often.

When she exhausted her list of people that Eugene disliked, Sylvia laughed, "I don't like everybody either."

"You shouldn't have to," I said.

She launched into complaining about those she disfavored, "The woman with the problem with her neck [Theresa]. The other night I saw her kicking the crumbs on the floor to the garbage. She's losing it."

"Theresa?" I asked, though others had referred to her with the same language: the woman with the problem with her neck.

"Yeah. Theresa," she said, shaking her head. "And Lucy. She talks very loud."

As I spent more time in the places that elders frequented, I discovered widespread gossip among regulars. Much like previous studies, I define gossip as talk in the absence of a third party who is the subject of the discussion.[1] They talked often about other older people they encountered in neighborhood establishments, semipublic venues such as the bakery and other nearby eateries, along with other shared spaces such as building lobbies and park benches. I argue that despite gossip's bad reputation and exclusion potential, talking about others also served as a counterintuitive form of connection for older adults living alone, especially those without a spouse or close kin. While in some instances people's criticism delineated a social hierarchy based on differences in physical or cognitive functioning, gossip also provided access to support and fostered cohesion among this loose collection of people. Despite its negative reputation, gossip allowed them to access less conventional forms of social support close to home and proved an important source of social involvement.

My work expands gossip research by turning attention to the connections that older adults formed in daily conversations with each other and about each other.[2] In revealing the ways that gossip's motivations and processes may differ among older adults, especially those more vulnerable to social isolation compared with other previously studied populations, this chapter advances our knowledge of how elders age alone, together, by gossiping about others around them. I identify three main ways that gossip helped people avoid isolation: gossip as a means of setting group limits and establishing the boundaries of acceptable behavior, as entertainment and activity, and as information sharing. A fourth aspect underlies these features: gossip as a relief valve that allowed people to blow off steam so that they could diffuse tension, minimize confrontation, and continue sharing space with those that irked them. The vignettes in this chapter represent countless interactions I observed over five years, and many illustrate overlapping themes.

THE OUTER LIMITS

Gossip allowed people to set personal limits and establish community standards of acceptable behavior and discussion. Talking about others in their absence provided an outlet to express disapproval without the need for confrontation; but it also reinforced potential conformity pressures to restrict expression that others would not approve of or calibrate their presentation of self.[3] For people with the greatest need for neighborhood spaces due to a lack of strong family support, few material resources, and cognitive and physical declines, the bakery served as a central location to alleviate the isolation they experienced in other parts of their lives. A handful stood on the fringes of bakery social life and of the other neighborhood spots where regulars socialized. While this group of elders struggled to fit in and gain acceptance and were often the subjects of gossip, they had a sustained presence and often interacted with others.

The most loathed person at the bakery was a woman in her middle to late 70s named Jeannette. She lived alone in her public housing project apartment, in the same building as Dottie, and stood out as one of the few people who had no landline or mobile telephone. Jeannette had never married, though one holiday season she produced a Christmas card with a picture of distant relatives who lived in her home state of Oklahoma. She had little money to spend at the bakery. Every winter she unearthed a long, black 1980s puffer coat, which grew more threadbare each season. Her poverty in itself had not placed her on the fringes, although some commentary focused on her lack of money. Customers complained about a number of things; in her absence, they remarked on what they perceived as her crass manners and provincial ways and her habit of looking for people to buy her coffee and food.

About the latter tendency, Eugene said, "She's a scam artist. That's why she hangs out with Salvatore [another bakery customer], so she can get a handout." Salvatore, in his early 90s, often bought Jeannette coffee. He didn't speak much, but his pronounced accent revealed his Italian origins. He came in the late mornings with his home health aide, a Jamaican woman in her mid-50s dressed in cheerful pastel nursing scrubs. She projected a patient and warm but firm demeanor when she sensed Salvatore getting fatigued and that the time had come to take him home.

Unlike other objects of public attention, Jeannette showed no obvious signs of dementia, such as repeating herself, which had pushed others toward the edges of the group conversation. As Angelica observed in a discussion about why customers disliked Jeannette, "She has a good memory," ruling out cognitive shortcomings as an explanation for her unpopularity.

In addition to lacking polite conversation filters and social grace, people most often cited Jeannette's negativity and racism as reasons they preferred not to associate with her. The 2008 presidential election brought out her most offensive, racist language. She freely admitted that she disliked President Obama due to his race. Weeks before the election she said, "What's going to happen if he gets elected? We'll have a chimp for president." Each time I saw Jeannette she had armed herself with inflammatory stories about President Obama from *The New York Post* and steamrolled over others with her objections to the latest Obama-era policy. People began to ignore her during these tirades. Although Jeannette appeared to think she was still speaking with them, she ended up talking to herself. Instead of confrontation, they tried changing topics. On one heated occasion, Lucy said sharply, "Okay, that's enough. Let's talk about something else," and flipped through her copy of *The Daily News* for inspiration. "Would you look at that?" she said, holding up a picture of star Jennifer Lopez in a string bikini. "Mamma mia, hot stuff."

One late afternoon, through the bakery's large windows, I saw Jeannette walking with Helen. Jeannette had stopped coming in the last few weeks. Angelica said that she'd reduced her bakery time due to cost, not ostracism. "She can't afford it," she said and reviewed how she had given Jeannette discounts until she started taking advantage. "I think she go more to McDonald's now," Angelica said, which I confirmed with sightings of Jeannette there some mornings. I found it interesting to observe these two fringe characters together. For different reasons, bakery cliques tended to ignore or shun them. Helen was a petite, snow-white-haired woman who trailed off at times. Some portions of her speech made perfect sense, and others suffered from chunks of missing information, like a verbal ellipsis. Most regulars gave up on stringing together these disconnected thoughts and stopped engaging until she grew silent. But having reached some consensus that Jeannette had brought the treatment upon herself, people shunned Jeannette in more pronounced ways.

One day, after a two-week absence, instead of passing by, Jeannette came into the bakery. Helen was waiting outside, dressed in her typical outfit of a pale blue sweater overlaid with a black fleece vest despite the muggy weather. Jeannette wore oversized dark shades, a pale pink trench coat slightly yellowed around the cuffs and collar and toted a red plaid handbag. She usually dyed her stick-straight, chin-length hair medium brown, but without touch-ups, more grey showed at the temples.

"Hi. I just came from McDonald's," she said to Angelica, clutching a wrinkled paper bag from her visit. "I'm going home," she continued.

"Do you want something?" Angelica asked her.

"No, I'm just looking around," she said, moving among display cases filled with glistening sugar cookies and ornate cakes topped with halved strawberries, chocolate shavings, and frosted flowers. She turned to the women seated and said hello. They reciprocated in polite but disinterested unison. After surveying the store once more, she said, "Well, bye now," and walked out. Helen headed downtown, and Jeannette turned in the opposite direction towards her building. Afterwards, the group discussed Jeannette.

Theresa started. "She's not stupid, but there's something wrong with her," she said. "Always talking about Black people. A couple months ago, she said something to Lucy [another customer]. 'That's not right,' I said. I didn't mean to embarrass her, but it's not."

"It's terrible," Carmen agreed. "Terrible."

This type of discussion often occurred in Jeannette's absence. But despite people's objections and frustrations with her behavior, they never cast her out of group interactions. She remained in the fold of social life, albeit on the periphery when people tired of her. Amid grumbles that she "mooched off" people, a few treated her to food or a beverage out of pity. Dottie sometimes bought her a buttered roll or coffee. "I feel sorry for her," she said.

One evening after 8 p.m. when the store closed, while Angelica finished cleaning, I asked why she thought people tolerated Jeannette when no one seemed to like her, especially the women. "I think they feel pity. And they know what it is to feel lonely. They don't want to be in the same situation. They understand this. She's [Jeannette] just a pain in the ass but the bottom of the line . . . she alone. Dottie is the one who brought her. Because she helps her," Angelica said. Our discussion revealed that Dottie not only pitied Jeannette but increasingly depended upon her. Angelica had observed Jeannette coming into the bakery more in the past week. She volunteered to run small errands for Dottie, such as fetching something from the store, and walked home with her. Dottie relied on a number of women who frequented the bakery to help her. One afternoon she had asked Theresa to get her bananas; I also pitched in and picked up a package of Depends underwear, which she had promised her neighbor, from the pharmacy and milk from Johnny's bodega. "Dottie can't walk so good," Angelica explained why Jeannette was helping her. But some criticized this arrangement, such as Eugene, who called Jeannette "Dottie's lackey."

Afternoons brought many older men to the bakery. One November day, most of the guys that comprised the midday crowd showed. Carl, who was in his late 70s and had thinning brown and white hair arranged in a neat comb over, a friendly spray of freckles, and a ready smile, sat with a taciturn man around his age. Harry had frizzy black hair and a generous belly that hung over his belt. Arthur sat furthest from the door. He had a rangy figure, with a slight forward bend in his shoulders, and wore a navy wool jacket and royal-blue New York Giants cap atop his full head of wavy, steel-colored hair.

Jeannette and Helen occupied a back table beside Bill, who sat alone. His grey hair verged on white, and his perpetually ruddy complexion matched the red satin Giants jacket he always wore with the team name embroidered in blue and white.

"How are you ladies?" he said, offering to buy Jeannette and Helen coffee. His generosity surprised me for two reasons: their lack of popularity and his irascible demeanor, especially when sparring with the guys about different topics ranging from sports to current events.

"I like mine very light," Helen said in a barely audible voice. Jeannette issued no instructions for her coffee.

While he paid at the counter, Jeannette told Helen, "He's a nice man, even if some of the women don't think he is."

When he returned, setting the cups down on their table, she repeated this sentiment to Bill, "*You're* a nice man even if some of the women don't think you are."

"Only one woman doesn't like me," he grimaced and launched into a diatribe, without mentioning the woman's name. Jeannette agreed with him. "Yeah. She talks bad about you with Dottie and all the rest of them."

Arthur stepped outside for his afternoon smoke. He earned the nickname "professor" because he had once worked at Columbia University, though not as a professor. He had some prior teaching experience and liked to expound on different topics for bakery regulars, drawing on history, philosophy, and politics. He slipped a cigarette from the red and white pack of Marlboro Reds nestled in his shirt breast pocket. While Arthur smoked, Flora's husband Walter stopped by and talked to him. They peered out onto the avenue, squinting in the sun's direction, which blazed from downtown.

While he smoked, Bill and Jeannette criticized smoking generally and Arthur's smoking in particular. "I don't understand why he does that," Bill said.

"He has a bad cough," Jeannette observed.

"Oh yes, always hacking. I'm afraid he's gonna cough up a lung one day."

"And his breath stinks," Jeannette said.

"Yeah, yeah. Smells awful."

Overhearing their gossip, I had to admit inwardly that his clothes gave off a strong tobacco odor.

"The best thing they ever did was ban smoking in restaurants," Jeannette said.

Behind-the-back comments about Arthur's smoking occurred often. The moment he stepped outside for a cigarette, discussion ensued. Regulars bad-mouthed his habit even when he didn't come to the bakery and during his prolonged absence several months before. I wondered if their gossip reflected some people's jealousy that they couldn't smoke anymore. I couldn't foresee Arthur quitting at his age, in his early 80s, since he had so far escaped serious smoking-related illnesses such as emphysema or lung cancer. Thus, gossip in this instance served to reinforce community norms of health and conduct rather than halt Arthur's behavior. Talking about him also offered an opportunity to recurrent targets of critique, such as Jeannette, to disrupt established patterns and gossip about others.

An occasional comment about someone's physical or cognitive deficits is different than sustained commentary. The line between acceptance and rejection from the bakery's social groups remained fine. But when a person became a frequent subject of behind-the-back discussion, this indicated that they had fallen to the bottom of the hierarchy. Open talk about these unpopular figures also served a purpose beyond idle chatter. A polarizing figure like Jeannette helped build group solidarity. Those who joined in gained access to this connection. Reaching some consensus about the limits of acceptable behavior provided cohesiveness to a gathering of people with no official membership requirements or procedures. Gossip in this situation also served as a release valve that allowed people to share space when "stuck in place" with others and maintain interdependent relationships despite the inevitable strains.

As Eddie supported Eugene through his health and housing woes, his comments about Eugene betrayed not only concern but also frustration—and a need to demarcate boundaries around what he considered appropriate behavior. One evening in the bakery, as Angelica announced closing time, Eddie returned to Eugene's plumbing problems and slipped in a last reminder to consult his neighbors about the building's responsiveness. By Eddie's logic, if the people living above him had their plumbing problems fixed in a timely manner, the neglect of Eugene's problem would provide evidence of harassment, which, they assumed, was motivated by the fact that he was a longtime rent-stabilized tenant who paid nowhere near market rent for his spacious studio apartment. "You check with the guy upstairs and see if the guys did the work. Then you smile and you walk away," he said.

"Thank you, sir," Eugene chuckled. Eddie held the door for him before pausing at the counter to pick up some day-old bread from Angelica.

"I'm gonna stick up the joint. I only have a few more months," he joked. She handed him a large plastic bag filled with bread that hadn't sold, mostly palm-sized rolls browned with an egg-wash crust. He stuffed $1 in her tip mug. As usual, she told him he didn't have to give her anything. He laughed again about his "plan" to rob the bakery. "I'm going to make the big heist at Christmas."

When Eugene had left, Eddie turned to me and said, "I said that to him four weeks ago. I get mad . . . for that volume [of water] . . ." As on numerous occasions, he expressed anger at Eugene's building management for their negligence but also annoyance that Eugene hadn't followed his advice.

"It's his own fault, you know. I told him to go to the Hospital for Special Surgery or Joint Diseases. He would have been a year younger," Eddie said, lamenting Eugene's physical deterioration from delaying surgery.

Furthermore, he disapproved of Eugene's involved discussions with Lucy and Theresa about his situation.

"That one who puts her glasses on top of her head . . . with the loud voice," Eddie started.

"Lucy," Angelica interjected while she swept.

"Yeah," Eddie said. "I sat over there," he pointed to a table farthest from his usual spot in the corner by the window. "I make like I'm reading the paper. I don't want them near me."

"He avoid," Angelica said to me, with a knowing snicker while Eddie continued.

"You should have heard them. That one [Lucy] she must have said eight times, in eight different ways. 'This is inhuman,'" referring to Eugene's ordeal. Eddie continued, "I told him, 'You can't talk about this.'"

"It's done," I said, summarizing his assessment.

"Exactly," Eddie said.

"They ask him [Eugene] constantly," Angelica confirmed.

"He sounds like an old woman." Eddie reenacted Eugene's chronicling of his misfortunes for the bakery crowd, fixing a mock weepy expression on his face, the corners of his mouth turned down in an exaggerated frown like a sad clown. "You don't know what I've been through . . . forty-five days . . . those bozos," he imitated in a shrill voice, borrowing one of Eugene's favorite put-downs: bozo.

"I wrote him a note. You gotta do two things. One: You gotta clean up that apartment. 'You gotta cleaning woman?' I ask him. He said, 'Yeah.' You gotta clean up that apartment so they don't think you're one of the Collyer Brothers." Turning to me, Eddie raised his eyebrow and said, "Remember the Collyer brothers. Fifth Avenue?" emphasizing his point about Eugene's interest in avoiding comparisons to the infamous hoarding brothers. Then, as if speaking to Eugene, Eddie said, "Two. You gotta paint that apartment. You can't have them thinking you're a senile old man. And he said, 'Yeah, you're right.'" Eddie exhaled a deep, weary breath with a slight groan. "I like Eugene. But he's gotta learn. Vivian . . . She got into him. She said, 'You gotta help yourself.' She called me the other day about another matter and then it turned to Eugene . . . for a half hour," he said, exasperated.

After Eddie left, Angelica analyzed his negative response to Eugene's behavior. "This is my opinion. He has a very different personality. Eugene is open. He needs to talk with the people. He [Eddie] is closed. He don't talk to too many people. He talk to Maureen. Dottie. Imagine, she's friends for twenty-eight, thirty years, and he don't talk to her much. He talk with four or five guys . . . Eugene talks with people. He walks in and he tell them right away what's going on. And they ask him because they know he's expecting. Eddie thinks this is too much, that it's embarrassing." Angelica echoed my own observations of Eddie's gossip serving as an outlet for his indignation when others violated his personal standards of conduct and restraint.

Another controversial figure who tested the limits of tolerance was the old man whom everyone called "the photographer." He had worked for many years as a professional photographer for *The Daily News* and other media outlets. I almost never heard anyone call him anything else. People hadn't prioritized learning or using his name. For years he tried to befriend different men at the bakery. I often witnessed his fruitless attempts to engage Eddie and Eugene. Their interactions were strained, and talk about him in his absence revealed a need to vent their frustration, allowing them to share space with a person they found difficult and needy.

During Eugene's hospitalization, the photographer turned to his next best option and attempted to speak with Eddie. That evening Eddie had stopped in at about 7:10 p.m., his usual time, dressed in his "uniform" of a brown sweatshirt, blue wool jacket, jeans, and sneakers. He took his favorite corner seat by the window. A half hour later the photographer arrived in a wrinkled beige shirt and faded jeans. His stringy grey hair peeked out from under his worn baseball cap and his longish beard hung wild and straggly. A bulky professional camera hung from a Nikon neck strap, contrasting with his typical disheveled appearance. He beelined to Eddie's corner.

"This is the guy I need to talk to," he shouted, plopping down in a seat at the table beside him. Eddie looked straight ahead as if wearing blinders. He said nothing, growling in acknowledgment. The photographer leaned in and talked about trying to get in touch with Eugene, still in the hospital, with no success. He then fired off seemingly random discussion points. "Ever want to go to New Mexico?" he asked and offered to host Eddie at the desert house he owned.

"No."

"I've got a couple of books if you want them. Gratis," he said with a crooked Cheshire cat smile.

"No thanks," Eddie grunted.

The photographer asked Eddie how long he had lived in the neighborhood. "Seventy years," Eddie said tersely. "I've been here sixty plus years," the photographer volunteered after Eddie declined to ask about the length of his residency.

I felt like the photographer stayed forever. Time passed uncomfortably slowly. I knew that Eddie disliked this man—not that his feelings were in question, given his scowl and exasperation in his eyes. He looked ready to explode and thwack him on the head with his cane if he didn't leave soon. The men talked for fifteen minutes at most, perhaps as few as ten. Sensing that Eddie had not warmed to him, he said, "I can't get out of the chair, that's the problem," accounting for his prolonged presence. He lifted his stiff body out of the seat. Part of what he said was true. I'd noticed that he had more trouble moving lately. Still, he'd lingered due not only to his physical limitations but also to his desire to talk to Eddie.

"He's in bad shape," Eddie said under his breath as we watched him leave. The photographer dragged his feet, leaning on his cane as he shuffled out the door. "No, no, no. I can't take this. He does the same thing to Eugene," Eddie said afterward. I turned back to face him. I had stopped chatting when the photographer came in. His doggedness had edged me out of the conversation, making me feel invisible. Afterwards, I felt a little guilty for not bailing Eddie out, which he may have expected, but the photographer's persistence left little room for intervention. I also felt a bit heartbroken observing Eddie rebuff his desperate efforts to win him over.

"I didn't want to be rude, so I just said, 'No, no, nope.' He's just lonely, I guess," Eddie said. But his awareness of the photographer's loneliness hadn't translated into a willingness to engage further. His avoidance reflected a prominent difference in how men and women interacted with people they disliked. While both expressed their distaste, men had few qualms about demonstrating their lack of interest. Women more often shared space, meals, and conversation with peripheral and even reviled characters.

"You and Angelica owe me." Eddie was referring to the fact that he didn't tell the photographer that we had visited Eugene in the hospital. "If I did, he would have got into you." But I doubted this. The photographer would have likely welcomed a Eugene update, but he indicated that he wanted to talk to Eddie, not to me or Angelica, and I was pretty sure he would have felt the same even if we possessed desirable information.

"You know, he [the photographer] crosses in the middle of the street," Eddie said with disapproval as he looked out the window.

"Goes right to his door." His annoyance echoed his previous concerns about the photographer's dangerous jaywalking with his poor balance.

"He alienates himself," Eddie continued, which struck me as ironic because he often kept to himself and talked extensively with only a few customers, including myself and Eugene. But unlike the photographer, who grasped for company, Eddie separated himself by choice.

"There's a woman who used to come in here," Eddie said, referring to Jeannette. "She did the same. When they [photographer and Jeannette] got together, whoa, it was doom and gloom." I'd forgotten the flavor of their interactions until he reminded me of this pair. The two talked, usually negatively, about politics or other local stories in *The Daily News* or *The New York Post*, complaining about politicians and other ire-provoking news items.

About a month after the painful encounter with Eddie, I found the photographer seated diagonally across from Eugene at a neighboring table. Eugene wore his brown leather jacket, paisley button-down shirt, jeans, and Derby dress shoes. Before leaving, he tried one last time to break through, inviting Eugene to a bar with a first-beer-free special.

"I haven't had a drink in a month. Hey, could you use a drink?" he proposed.

"No," Eugene responded.

"Do you like sweets?"

"No."

"I've got half a Toblerone," the photographer offered.

"No thanks," Eugene said. As he left, Eugene relented a bit. "Well, take care . . ."

Afterwards, Eugene said, "He's going to kill himself," repeating criticisms he and Eddie had leveled against the photographer for eating sugar-laden snacks, despite his diabetes. "He's always giving me candy," Eugene continued, shaking his head in disapproval. But he also added information about a recent kindness. "He brought me fruit while in the hospital. I was thinking, I should have said, 'Take me home' when I was at Bellevue."

Eugene's hard line surprised me, since, unlike Eddie, who was more cautious, he interacted with most everyone. But avoidance of figures perceived as "downtrodden" or otherwise unattractive companions accomplished an end. Their distancing illuminates prior findings about older adults' pruning of social networks, reducing social contacts to include only those who maximize positive emotions.[4] Eddie's selectivity in his social interactions hints at late life's freedoms. As a retired person, he had no job that obligated him to get along with others or act as a team player. His separation not only facilitated trimming his network to suit his needs but also helped him fashion an identity as an old person who excluded less desirable associates. Nonetheless, constraints compelled him to find strategies to coexist with others in this shared space.

THAT'S ENTERTAINMENT

Gossip allowed older people to stay socially involved as other work and family structures receded. Hanging out in neighborhood establishments formed an important part of their routines and talking about local characters provided entertainment. This activity not only helped fill their days but also gave elders purpose and a reason to leave house. In an interview after the bakery closed, one former customer mentioned missing "the drama of the place."

More tolerated than well liked, Theresa, who started coming in after her retirement as a secretary for four decades in a neurologist's office, managed to join other women by simply always being around. Angelica imitated Theresa's excuses for her lateness, "'I'm sorry I came late. I had to do things this morning; that's why I didn't come this morning.'" I smiled at her apology because Theresa could never arrive late—she had no appointed arrival time. As if speaking to Theresa, Angelica said,

"If you don't want to come for a week, I don't care. You don't have to have a note from your parents. It's not your job." She continued, "I feel like saying, 'That's okay. No one cares.' She doesn't have to come here every day. But for Theresa, it's as if she's missing a spectacular part."

Increasing discussions about Theresa occurred in her absence. As the study progressed she could not recount the plot or name of a movie she had seen the same day. Angelica helped her with tasks such as writing information down that she requested and setting the correct time on her vintage wind-up watch. Many bakery regulars expressed losing patience with Theresa as she exhibited signs of early to middle stage dementia, including repeating herself, memory loss, and misplacing things.[5]

Phyllis, a longtime resident of the co-op buildings, who projected the persona of a youthful, active senior, merely tolerated Theresa. With her startling blue eyes, high cheekbones, and careful attention to wardrobe and accessories, Phyllis always looked polished, betraying her modeling history before working full time as a secretary while rearing her children. Others at the bakery often remarked on her vitality.

One day Sylvia voiced appreciation for Phyllis accompanying her to the podiatrist when she had undergone treatment for a painful heel spur. Phyllis had also given Sylvia information for an Atlantic City trip organized by the co-op senior center. I caught up with them as they sat side-by-side over breakfast and coordinated dinner plans at a nearby diner. Phyllis wore a royal-blue sweater, matching blue headband atop her fluffy, white-blonde hair, and a shiny, black, puffy jacket fashionable among young women.

"I can't get rid of you," Phyllis joked with Sylvia as she dashed off for fruit shopping.

"She has a lot of vim and vigor," Sylvia remarked after Phyllis had left. With a throaty laugh she added, "I don't."

Though Phyllis frequented the bakery several times a week, she put down the women "who sat there all day and drank coffee." She distinguished herself as someone with wider interests and delighted in discussing her activities, which included trying new restaurants, taking multi-mile walks around Manhattan, going to museums, and visiting her son and his family in Queens. She identified excursions beyond the neighborhood as giving important reprieve from the older people she lived among in the co-ops.

She disparaged the vast majority of older people with whom she had crossed paths and expressed aggravation about Theresa's cognitive deficits. She told a group that included me, Dottie, and Lucy about Theresa's repeated questions earlier that morning about Phyllis's two sons, including their names, jobs, and where they lived.

"How many times do I have to tell her?" Phyllis asked, so infuriated that her voice shook. When I probed further she clarified her distress. She mentioned that she had gotten so rattled having to repeat everything for Theresa several times that she had forgotten two important things during a later phone call. Her agitation betrayed the contagion threat she felt, almost as if Theresa's cognitive deficits had rubbed off through proximity or excessive interaction.

Others also exercised caution around people they perceived as downtrodden, whether due to their cognitive decline or a depressive nature. They expressed needing to protect themselves from excessive contact with people whom they found draining with the same gravity as they would protect themselves from infectious illnesses like flu or pneumonia. I often observed people lose patience with others, especially with those who "talked too much" or repeated themselves. Sylvia noted the exhaustion of dealing with needy, difficult, and confused people. "I just can't do it anymore," she said with palpable anxiety and fatigue in her voice. She spoke of the tough time she had looking after herself, managing bills, chronic illnesses, and unexpected nuisances such as plumbing problems. Lucy echoed a similar need for escape. "There's too many seniors everywhere. And they want to talk to you about their problems. All day long. I got my own problems," she said and griped about the old people she avoided in the small seating area of the super-market where she ate breakfast each morning.

Meanwhile, Lucy and Dottie shared their own Theresa stories. They recounted how she had called them multiple times that morning to check the scheduled arrival time for a cable station news crew to cover the bakery's imminent demise. Theresa had called Lucy first, saying she wouldn't call Dottie, but later called Dottie twice. On other occasions, Sylvia had offered her own assessment: "She's losing it." Eugene agreed, "Theresa is in trouble. She doesn't know what day it is."

The most glaring incident to indicate Theresa's low standing occurred one busy evening when customers packed seven of the bakery's eight tables. Lucy told me that Theresa had gone to play lotto and promised to come back but had left a long time ago and not yet returned.

"She must have gone to Italy," she quipped. Lucy also mentioned that Theresa left her umbrella, pointing to the familiar umbrella with a white handle and clear plastic canopy segments leaning against the wall. Theresa had a special attachment to this item as I and most every-one else that evening knew. She brought it everywhere, often on clear-blue-sky days with no rain forecasted.

Flora, another lifelong neighborhood resident, said with characteris-tic sarcasm, "You know she loves that umbrella. 'It's very expensive,' she told me. Ha!" She curled her lips with condemnation. Her dark eyes narrowed as she recalled how Theresa had refused to loan it briefly to one of the afternoon regulars because of its supposed worth. Everyone commented on Theresa's preoccupation. Usually unflappable, Carmen, who often ate with Theresa and other women at a nearby diner, could not suppress a giggle.

Lucy, who also dined with her several evenings a week, laughed and said, "Maybe she thinks she's Mary Poppins."

"Always with that umbrella," another murmured.

Carmen gave a knowing look and pointed out, "And it's not even raining today."

People passed around stories about times that Theresa had misplaced her umbrella and panicked. Once, she had nearly come unraveled when she couldn't find it at the bakery and searched for it at the diner she frequented a block away and later her apartment. On that evening she had returned well after the bakery closed to report that she had located it at home, after having insisted to Angelica that someone had stolen it. Hearing this tale, Flora inspected the prized umbrella, holding it up for the store's audience and showing off its dark blue logo from a chic hotel that betrayed its history as a promotional giveaway.

"This isn't expensive," Flora scoffed. "She got it for free," she said, twirling the umbrella like a baton before setting it down. About ten minutes after closing, the crowd gone for the night, Theresa returned to retrieve her umbrella.

"Where is everybody?" she asked. "Do you know where they went?"

"I guess they went home," Angelica replied.

"Oh," Theresa said, her lean face heavy with disappointment.

After Theresa had left, Angelica mused, "I wonder what they're going to do when this place closes." I asked if she thought people would try to dodge Theresa after the bakery shuttered. Angelica pointed out the difficulty of avoiding her. "If Theresa doesn't see people, she asks me, 'Where is everybody? Where is Dottie? Where is Lucy?'" When Theresa fired off her litany of inquiries, Angelica said she told her, "I don't know, I just got here." She broke into giggles. "Sometimes I want to say, 'I don't give a damn.'" Angelica's frustration made me smile because she had incredible patience. Even when faced with Theresa's onslaught of questions, she retained her equanimity, only telling me here what she'd like to say, not what she had.

Gossip did more than allow people to release tension, making direct confrontation less likely, as we will see in the next vignette; it also did more than help the group to shun the company of more burdensome figures, like Jeannette. Talking about Theresa in her absence allowed her peers to joke at her expense and thus entertain themselves and create humor in storytelling. They forged closeness by sharing in-jokes. For example, the mere mention of Theresa's umbrella provoked eye rolls and commiserating laughter. Communal comic relief also helped some manage their own health anxieties and fears of dementia.

Gossip delineated a hierarchy that assured those who participated that, even if not at the top, they had not fallen to the bottom, where Theresa, by virtue of the amount of negative attention she received, dwelled. But the story is more complicated than a group simply disparaging an outlier. As they discussed her, they tracked Theresa's worsening dementia. Even when expressing frustration with Theresa for reasons that went beyond her cognitive problems, many continued to interact with her. When she could no longer live on her own and moved closer to family in New Jersey, they continued trying to contact her despite problems reaching her brother. Her involvement with neighborhood people over several years of decline may have prevented her from losing her independence earlier.

I HEARD IT THROUGH THE GRAPEVINE

Engaging in gossip requires sufficient intimate knowledge to be able to competently talk about others in their absence.[6] Neighborhood places such as the bakery allowed people to linger and drop in multiple times a day so they could people watch and accumulate information about others. Amassing and sharing information not only provided fodder for gossip but also promoted the development of social support and set the stage for helping those in need. Overhearing others' troubles motivated some to assist.

People openly discussed others' physical and cognitive problems. Talking about health declines and speculating about future trajectories remained a popular pastime. For example, I often observed assessments of Dottie's problems walking in her absence. Sylvia, a year younger than Dottie, told me that she and another bakery regular, Lorenzo, had planned to play slots that weekend at a Yonkers casino, a short train ride away. But she asked me not to let anyone else know, especially Dottie, because of her problems walking. Dottie had expressed interest in joining them on a future outing, but Lorenzo and Sylvia decided that she could not keep up and withheld an invitation. About a year and a half later when I visited Eugene in the hospital after his surgery, he told me how "the ladies" had visited him and how Lucy complained about bringing Dottie given her mobility problems, which made getting her in and out of the taxi difficult.

"She's enormous," Eugene exclaimed. "No wonder she can't move." Those alongside him nodded.

"And if she keeps going this way . . ." Phyllis warned.

In situations when people discussed someone behind their back due to wanting to spare someone's feelings or to avoid awkward scenes, as in Dottie's case, exclusion still created distance and distinctions, even if unintended.

While Dottie's physical problems left her out of some group activities, talk about her ailments didn't shut her out. Due to her sociability, accumulation of friends and acquaintances, and lifelong residence in the neighborhood, Dottie remained at the center of the bakery's social world. In addition to negative assessments about her size and growing health problems, people's discussion also revealed genuine concern. After the bakery closed, she remained on people's radars even though she had difficulty walking to McDonald's, where many former customers gathered. People called to check on her and helped her in and out of taxis to her apartment three blocks away. When a heart attack resulted in Dottie's hospitalization, nursing home admission, and eventual death, visitors' daily updates spurred others to visit and call, sparing her greater isolation. Gossip served as an important conduit for information to reach others and thereby kept her hooked into neighborhood social life even as her mobility declined.

Eugene's openness in sharing his physical problems and worsening housing situation worked in tandem with the circulation of information among bakery regulars. He confided in them, and they kept the updates and opinions flowing through gossip, thereby bolstering support among those who received the daily digest of Eugene news.

As Angelica locked the door and readied the bakery for nightly closing, Eddie and I lingered. We remarked on the quality of time, with all of Eugene's recent ups and downs; we both felt drained.

"It's only Tuesday. It feels like Friday," I said.

"Yeah, I know," Eddie said. He told me he had attended a wake the week before for a neighbor and had another upcoming in Bayside, Queens. "It works on you after a while. It's been nonstop since Ma died," he said soberly. "It works on you after a while," he repeated, trailing off into silence. The store grew quiet, making the neon sign humming in the window and swishing of Angelica's sweeping broom sound deafening. All of a sudden, Eddie grew animated, disturbing the solemn energy. As if an extension of his arm, he pointed his cane to the empty spot where Eugene sat earlier that evening. "I told him two weeks ago. The pipe's broken. That's it. It's not your fault," he said with a blend of care and frustration. "It gets to me. He wants you to do it," he said, referring to Eugene wanting me to help him. "When I was here on Saturday, he said, 'Is Stacy there?' I said, 'No! I'm here. What do you need?'" Eddie said, almost shouting, addressing an absent Eugene. "What gets to me about him," he said, lifting his cane towards Eugene's vacated seat, "is those people are trying to kill him. They want him out."

At 8:05 p.m., a few minutes after the bakery closed, Dottie and Lucy passed by. Dottie waved to us, her fair complexion and powder white hair bathed in the cherry glow of the store's crackling neon sign. I stepped outside. They knew all about Eugene and his hospital ordeal.

"It's a nightmare. I saw Eugene today and I was like, 'Wwhhhaaa???'" Lucy said loudly, noting her shock at his weariness and how much weight he had dropped. Dottie also mimicked a spooked reaction, stepping back with stiffened shoulders as though she'd seen a ghost.

"He has to sue," Lucy said. She had won three successful lawsuits, for workplace age discrimination and for personal injuries from a cracked sidewalk and a piece of wood that flew off a flatbed truck and landed on her foot. I recapped details in the newspaper article I'd read about harassment of old longshoremen via neglect and renovation of the buildings where they had lived for decades. "You're right," she said, lowering her voice and concurring with the idea that he had possibly suffered harassment. She said Eugene would have fared better if he lived in the co-ops, her residential complex.

GOSSIPING: WHAT WE KNOW

Gossip remains especially understudied within sociology and the social sciences. The few social science studies have clustered mostly in anthropology and psychology. One reason for scant gossip research, despite its ubiquity as a social phenomenon, lies in the challenges researchers face in studying this form of talk. Most gossip research tends to use observational and ethnographic methods, which helps explain the healthy representation of anthropology in gossip studies, though social scientists have also surveyed undergraduate college students.[7] To become privy to research participants' gossip, scholars must first establish access and then rapport, often a time-intensive and delicate process in the field. Gossip researchers have called for more sophisticated methods to encourage additional research, such as developing experiments and leveraging social network data.[8]

As mentioned earlier in this chapter, I define gossip as talk in the absence of a third party who is the subject of the discussion.[9] Gossip retains a negative connotation, though it can range from mundane information with little evaluative content to disparaging remarks and insults. Despite the scarcity of gossip studies, scholarly literature recognizes this talk as an important form of communication—one that provides information, influence, entertainment, closeness, friendship, group cohesion, social control, social comparison, and self-evaluation.[10]

Anthropologist Max Gluckman argues that an important requirement of group membership is the ability to gossip and learn about a group's scandals. He claims that the more "exclusive" a club is, whether that exclusivity derives from its members' elite status or marginalization, the more gossip one finds.[11] In my study, exclusivity stems from people's advanced ages and modest resources in a culture and a city that prizes youth and wealth. Previous empirical studies that have examined the function and import of gossip for older adults find similar dynamics. Gerontologist John Percival's ethnographic study in three senior housing complexes finds rampant gossip in these age-segregated settings, promoting closeness in the information exchange but also spurring residents to withdraw and avoid interaction.[12] Anthropologist Cathrine Degnen's qualitative study of elders in a small English village finds that neighbors gossiped and created similar hierarchies by categorizing each other as "old" based on floating social constructions of age and monitored peers for signs of "oldness" related to appearance and ability.[13]

THE AGE OF GOSSIP

In line with Gluckman's argument about gossip and group membership,[14] people's talk about each other betrayed emotional intimacy, monitoring, and caretaking that provided connective tissue for people who could have otherwise fallen off the social radar. Talking about neighbors elevated conversation to an "event" to look forward to.[15]

Any study of gossip necessitates consideration of the social context in which the gossip occurs.[16] While a deeper discussion of setting occurs in subsequent chapters, place remains an important consideration in the larger study and for understanding the gossip I observed.[17] But I will highlight some ways that place and neighborhood context threatened and facilitated possibilities for social interaction and gossip. People's gathering spots dwindled due to growing physical limitations and a changing retail environment that closed longstanding establishments and posed new economic barriers to accessing their replacements. Many became "stuck in place," lacking the social and physical resources to age comfortably in place.[18] As physical issues arose and retirement ended old routines and imposed new ones, people creatively exercised agency and formed ties with people they never considered before, such as neighbors. Even with gentrification, which closed more affordable gathering spots, surviving low-cost establishments offered opportunities to interact and provided easy entry; these were not organizations with membership barriers and responsibilities but intergenerational spaces with a disproportionate number of older customers.

People adapted to their changing circumstances and drew ties from the places they could access in late life. This work expands previous scholarship on the import of casual relationships and "consequential strangers" to people of all ages who interact with these non-intimates in settings such as the workplace, school, gym, and neighborhood bar.[19] Despite their less defined roles, these non-intimates have meaning in people's lives. My findings suggest such ties have increased in significance for elders living alone. As other social network studies have found, people often confided in those they didn't feel close to but who were available and willing to listen.[20] Gossip served as a special social glue that embedded them in these webs of convenience and allowed them to maintain ties and share space despite any frustrations. Relieving tension by venting about others in their absence prevented more direct confrontations that could have led to exclusion and made them feel unwelcome. Gossip suggests one way that people preserve ties with network members they consider "difficult," ties that scholars have found more prevalent in constrained contexts like families where the respondent has little room to banish someone.[21]

Sustained observation allowed me to understand processes and observe changes in people's patterns of talk and social relationships over longer periods of time. Researchers have often cited the need for longitudinal studies on loneliness, social support, and isolation in order to develop effective interventions.[22] This field study contributes to emerging knowledge about alternate sources of connection and enlarges our understanding of the important role humor and laughter play in older adults' social interactions with each other.[23]

Most people stood on the giving and receiving ends of gossip. They discussed others and served as the subjects of gossip. Often their talk recalled the murmured conversations in a family, small town, or high school cafeteria. While at times comments turned disparaging or reinforced hierarchy, which comports with Cathrine Degnen's findings on how elders demarcate boundaries of old age, this study highlights the counterintuitive benefits of gossip for older adults living alone and aging in place.[24] Even seemingly negative gossip often kept vulnerable people socially involved, opening the door to receive help and an entree to pleasurable conversation that bolstered their motivation to socialize despite multiple hurdles.

4

THE BAKERY CLUB

YEARS BEFORE THE BAKERY CLOSED, older people who lived in the surrounding buildings had plenty of nearby businesses where they could socialize over a cheap cup of coffee. On the same block, they had also once frequented other inexpensive establishments leased by the co-op, including a Subway sandwich shop and corner delicatessen, and a no-frills pizza shop housed in a row of tenement buildings across the street. A convenience store next door to the bakery that sold lottery tickets, newspapers, candy, and other sundries served as another informal hangout. Older men congregated over a small card table in the back and carried on boisterous conversations in rapid Spanish while a radio blared. Taxi drivers dashed in on their breaks, sprinting between their cabs and the store to avoid parking tickets. Men huddled outside with their eyes fixed on fistfuls of scratch-off tickets.

The low cost and proximity of these establishments attracted elders with shared challenges. Many subsisted on lower incomes and contended with mobility problems that limited trips outside the neighborhood. For some, walking a few blocks had become a painful endurance test. Store closures forced people to travel further for essential errands, not only causing inconvenience but real struggle, as Maureen shared one day while hunched over her rolling walker with her husband, Tom, at her side. "I'm mad about Emigrant [a shuttered bank three storefronts away from the bakery]. I've been banking there for forty-five years. Now I'm going to have to walk all the way to Fifth Avenue." One by one, these businesses had closed in the two years preceding the bakery's closure. The sandwich shop converted to a tax preparation office; an upscale pizzeria replaced the corner deli; the no-frills pizza joint was reborn as a Sushi restaurant; and a tapas bar doubled in size and displaced the lottery store with its expansion.

As more affordable alternatives shuttered, the bakery emerged as a central gathering spot. Some bakery regulars had rarely gone there when they'd had more options. Others had divided their time and dining dollars between the bakery and neighboring businesses. But after the lower-cost establishments on the block folded, the bakery remained the only place left for many, like the last surviving restaurant on a deserted, small-town main street. In a twist, narrowing options had brought people together by squeezing them into fewer spaces, increasing opportunities for more frequent interactions that promoted closer relationships and deepened a sense of belonging.

In the bakery, elders had eked out a haven in a city, in a country, and in a culture that largely devalued them. Most other spaces didn't prioritize their needs; the exception was institutional sites set aside for older people, such as senior centers. Advertisers had long abandoned them as a target demographic, other than for prescription drugs and assistive devices aimed at the over-60 crowd. Scammers rang their phones all day. Disembodied voices harassed them with lies about the fabulous cruise they won or the imminent cancellation of their Medicare and

Social Security benefits unless they divulged protected personal information. Much like anthropologist Barbara Myerhoff describes in her classic study of older adults who congregated at a Jewish senior center in the 1970s, they found support and freedom in togetherness with their age peers.[1] In a space where old outnumbered young, they created a flourishing place where they could laugh, sing, tell dirty jokes, and reminisce about cultural touchstones such as the popular movies and music that had soothed them through many hardships, such as coming of age during "the war," as they often referred to World War II.[2] They appeared content with the bakery, rarely expressing deprivation with their options for places to gather until this center of their social world cratered, leaving a void and people searching for place.

The impending bakery closure stirred a special grief for its elder customers and revealed attachments to place and to each other not always apparent on the surface. This chapter sifts through this loss and charts their growing recognition that the bakery was significant to them as old people with shared challenges, including living alone, being limited financially, having declining mobility and physical health problems, and enduring the accumulated losses of close friends and family. I view the closing as an example of those unusual conditions under which older adults, many of them women who resisted identification with each other based on their advanced ages, realized some similarities in their social locations. They often drew hierarchical distinctions among themselves based on cognitive and physical functioning,[3] but the closing served as a rare opportunity to band together in recognition of their common plight and embrace fleeting social solidarity based on age, if not necessarily pride or an old-age identity.

This chapter explores the processes through which bakery regulars began to form a coherent and cohesive group as they assembled a "group in fusion," or a "series," borrowing language that feminist philosopher Iris Marion Young uses to describe a fluid form of social organization around shared projects and goals. The crisis sparked a more ephemeral coming together as "the bakery club," as regulars called themselves when they mobilized to save the place they had made their own, mourned its coming extinction, and planned together for the day after.

A PLACE FOR OLDER PEOPLE

Murmurs had swirled for years of a possible change in the bakery's tenancy. The owner, Guillaume, spoke openly of his discussions with the landlord's management office about their interest in securing a higher-paying occupant for his space. In 2009, those rumblings materialized into a concrete threat.

One late September morning around 10:30 a.m., the weather still warm and waiting for summer to release its grip, I arrived at the bakery to meet Sylvia. Dottie and Phyllis sat beside her, stone-faced. A lease termination notice hung on the door—a rude reminder of the looming extinction many had forgotten about—and a photocopy rested beneath each glass tabletop. A petition to save the bakery sat at the register.

The morning's buzzing conversation hovered over the bakery's fate. As more customers shuffled in, the chorus of lamentations swelled.

A woman with thinning red hair in her late 60s complimented Guillaume on the meringues. Her younger friend, who appeared in her late 30s, agreed, "They're delicious. The flavor jumps out at you." The older woman added, "Other meringues are mass produced, like rocks. They're not pretty in the mouth. But these are . . . pretty in the mouth." She came for the sugar-free turnovers but sometimes left with sugared products, she said, despite her efforts to resist.

Her friend left early. The red-haired woman and I chatted about the bakery closing.

"We'll have to load up on the meringues before the end of February," I said.

"You know, New Yorkers need a place like this," she said. "Joe's is nice, but it's jangly," she continued, jerking her arms like a marionette to illustrate another neighborhood coffee shop's nervous energy. "The people are nice, people hang out with their newspapers, but it's . . . jangly." She said she had found the bakery "later in life."

"Some people have been coming here for twenty years," I said. She nodded, fiddling with the cuff button on her faded denim shirt. "Myself, a regular customer for the last five," I said.

"I can't believe it. Why?" she bemoaned the closing once more before leaving.

Dottie's eyes darkened as she declared that she wouldn't come into the new place. "Oh yes you will," Phyllis countered in a skeptical, don't-be-silly tone. Dottie either hadn't heard or disagreed but didn't respond.

"It won't be the same at other places, like McDonald's. Sure, people will go there . . . but it won't be the same," George said, rubbing the back of his head with subdued resignation.

Diane nodded. "That's right."

"We've been coming here for the last eighteen years. When all the crowds were here," Sylvia said. "And Dottie," she whispered, casting a concerned glance her way while turning to me. Dottie sipped her iced coffee and stared silently ahead with uncharacteristic stoicism.

"They're saying this is a place for the elderly," Sylvia said, insulted.

"Well, you've got to use what you've got," I said, hoping to assuage any self-consciousness she may have felt. Later that morning, I overheard two old women at the register discussing the situation. "This is sort of a gathering place for older people. They have their breakfast, go back," said one to the other. Her observation of customer demographics carried no hint of negativity, though Sylvia had taken umbrage.

A few days later when a photographer arrived ahead of her reporter colleague covering the closing for the neighborhood newspaper, she said with a whiff of condescension, "This looks like a senior center." A collective groan from offended regulars followed. She surveyed the room a few seconds longer, peering down from behind her dark shades at customers as if viewing a museum exhibit. The reporter soon arrived and spoke with Diane, George, Dottie, Josephine, Spiro, Arthur, and Theresa.

A quick glance at bakery patrons on any given day confirmed the establishment's greying clientele. Despite the air of ridicule, the photographer had offered an accurate assessment. Customers that day mirrored a senior-center crowd. But people's aversion to others emphasizing their ages hit a sensitive nerve. The pronouncement had punctured the bakery's veil of openness and intergenerational gathering, shrouding the space in old-age stigma.[4] People's reactions also suggested eagerness to avoid the perception that they deserved pity. A few mentioned other hangouts and activities, ensuring that others knew they had options. For example, though Sylvia came into the bakery many evenings, she insisted, "I just come in the mornings. I'm not usually here in the evenings." Eugene stressed his lack of dependency on the bakery's social groupings. "I love people, but I'm perfectly content to spend all day alone. I have so much to work on, and I never get lonely." Spiro, a regular customer in his late 70s, cited his busy calendar curated around dancing at different Latin nightclubs. Many women, most notably Phyllis, pointed to other outings and errands that filled their days. Others, including Lucy, Gladys, Theresa, Carmen, and Dottie, mentioned patronizing nearby diners where they sometimes ate dinner together.

When people caught wind of impending closure, they mobilized a last-ditch effort to save the bakery. Customers signed a petition and spoke with local media. Guillaume told me separately, "Raúl [his assistant baker] went to the park benches with the petition. Some people didn't want to sign. Some didn't know."

A few days later, customers packed every table. The place hardly appeared on the brink of closure. Amid the usual chatting, everyone seemed energized by their efforts to save the bakery. On this bright afternoon, Maureen, Tom, Dottie, and Spiro folded bakery news into conversations about their recent outings. Dottie recounted a recent bus trip to Macy's department store. She was satisfied with her completion of the physically demanding journey. "I was proud of myself in a new way," she said. Spiro cut a dapper figure in his navy suit, red diamond-patterned tie, and gleaming black dress shoes. He rotated among Manhattan's Latin night clubs to dance, sample the dinner buffet, listen to live salsa music, and "watch the pretty women." That afternoon he stopped by before heading to "the Copa," shorthand for Copacabana club. "They're all Puerto Rican there now. Except me," he said with a puckish grin, owning his Greek-American heritage. Dottie gushed, "I love Puerto Ricans. They're my best friends." In the midst of their chatter, she mentioned her plan to hang "Save the Bakery" signs and listed stops on her itinerary: her beauty parlor, podiatrist's office, laundry room, and every floor of her building. Spiro nodded. "Yeah, I signed the petition. Too bad," he said, glancing down as he stroked his chin in a gesture of futility.

Intrigue grew as customers circulated bits of information mined from rumors and intelligence people had collected in conversations with co-op board members. With increased attention on the lease dispute, conflicting accounts emerged from the bakery owner and the landlord. According to Guillaume, at first the landlord hadn't offered a renewal lease, and then he had asked for excessive monthly rent. Building management countered that Guillaume had wanted to retire and had rebuffed their renewal offer. Regardless of the details, the outcome was the same: the owner couldn't get a lease renewal on terms he could afford, and the store would close. Loyal patrons felt caught in the crosshairs and slighted by building management for not working harder to reach an agreement with the owner, who ultimately expressed interest in staying. Given the breakdown in negotiations, customers concluded that management wanted a sleek new business and, in disregarding the longstanding establishment, had rejected its older patrons.

Many distinguished their support for the business and its value as a community space from the owner's personal plight. One blustery evening, as strong Hudson River winds whipped my hair and pummeled street signs, I bumped into Lorenzo and Sylvia chatting on the corner opposite the Galaxy Diner. Before Sylvia and I headed there for dinner together, the three of us huddled for several minutes on the sidewalk and discussed the imminent closure. Lorenzo stood over six feet tall, without the stooped posture of many older men at the bakery. His thick mane of luminous silver hair grazed his shirt collar. In his dashing 79-year-old figure, I saw remnants of his younger self, a marine and onetime member of a 1940s-era Puerto Rican youth gang in the Bronx.[5]

"You know, I could care less about Guillaume," Lorenzo said, his dark eyes flashing, nostrils flaring. "But I signed it [the petition] because it's a place for the people, the neighborhood," he said, recalling his days as a community organizer working with street gangs in East Harlem, Brooklyn, and the Bronx in the 1950s. Lorenzo's distinction marked the third or fourth time someone had stressed allegiance to place above the owner, who had a reputation for being unkind, cheap, and exploitative. Lorenzo said that he once saw Guillaume steal workers' tips from the tip jar and stuff them in his pocket.

Sylvia shook her head with a swift tsk-tsk. "That's awful. Awful," she said in a quaking voice. "But you know, I wouldn't care if Dracula ran the place. I just want it to stay open," she said later as we crossed the street, arms linked to steady her balance.

Other regulars shared stories about Guillaume as news of the impending closure spread. Sheila, a recently retired postal worker and Eddie's next-door neighbor, mentioned once telling Guillaume that she had gotten some old bread. He blamed Raúl, the assistant baker, and summoned him from the back kitchen to talk to her. "Of course I knew it wasn't Raúl's fault. I felt so bad," she said in a low voice, gravelly from decades of smoking.

Shifting gears, Eddie said, "This French guy [bakery owner] is the cheapest guy on God's earth." He complained to Eugene, Angelica, and me about how Guillaume wouldn't turn on sufficient heat in the winter. "He's too cheap to get a unit up on the roof." With no air conditioning, the bakery sweltered from the combination of summer heat and radiating warmth from the ovens. Eddie urged him to improve the cooling and heating systems several times. "Guillaume has a million excuses for why he won't do this," he said, shaking his head with annoyance.

Regulars reassured each other about their motivation to save the bakery. Many people's low opinion of the owner remained an open secret, though some newer customers seemed unaware of the owner's different sides, such as Marilyn, a petite woman in late middle age with corkscrew blonde curls and a penchant for joining bakery conversations. She expressed tenderhearted outrage about the closing and empathy for Guillaume. "You can tell he really treats his employees well, because they're so nice and look happy," she said with a sentimental clasp of her hands.

Angelica shed light on Guillaume's treatment of employees. His assistant baker, Raúl, 37, began working at the bakery as a teenager before Guillaume took over and remained after the change in ownership, for a total of twenty years at this location and eleven years as Guillaume's employee. Together they had roughly sixty-four years of combined baking experience. Despite Raúl's long tenure, Guillaume never sponsored his Green Card to obtain legal status, leaving Angelica perplexed. Of Raúl, she said, "He has a real skill—bakes everything. It would have been easy for him to get his papers this way." She shared that an employer had also exploited her by reneging on sponsoring her immigration documents, saddling her with several thousand dollars in legal bills, which she paid off for years. Multiple customers mentioned that Raúl never took a day off. Bakery workers received no benefits, and Guillaume paid his employees—most undocumented—in cash, off the books. Angelica still paid her taxes using an Individual Taxpayer

Identification Number since she lacked a Social Security number and hoped to maintain a "good record" in her quest to obtain legal status.

Customers also expressed concern for workers' job losses. In response to their offers to help her find employment, Angelica divulged some specifics about her current position and what she sought in the future. She worked about thirty hours a week, started her shift in the early afternoon, and earned $225 in weekly wages with an additional $50–$60 in tips. She liked the job's stability and less than full-time schedule, which allowed her to tend to her health and afforded recovery time from severe chronic migraines. She hoped to find a three-to-four-day-a-week schedule, working for eight to ten hours per day. As much as she enjoyed interacting with customers, Angelica preferred a store without seating to spare her additional cleaning and serving. She often worked unpaid overtime, staying past her shift to clean. Dottie and I planned to accompany Angelica to inquire about hiring at Del Ponte's, another neighborhood bakery without customer seating that met many of her desired specifications. Sylvia put in a good word for the bakery's morning cashier, Dani, at Pete's, a nearby deli. She landed a comparable job there for the next few years.

"What I'm concerned about is her . . ." Eddie said, lifting his arm towards Angelica. "She's gonna be out of a job."

"We talked about it," I told Eddie. "She said she never had trouble finding a job in all her years here, and she's keeping her eyes open. I also know a few places. He [Guillaume] also makes all his money at the end of the year, so I think he'll be here till at least January. You know him and money."

"True," Eddie said.

THE LOST WORLD

As negotiations between the landlord and the bakery owner deteriorated, people prepared practically and emotionally for losing a place that had taken root as a central part of their lives. The emotional processing of anticipatory grief included reminiscing as people looked back while also pondering a future without the bakery. They drew on shared history to memorialize the place and its people, excavating memories that revealed deep attachments and recalled the wisdom of novelist Sigrid Nunez's observations on grief: "What we miss—what we lose and what we mourn—isn't it this that makes us who, deep down, we truly are."[6]

Some expressed overwhelming feelings of expectant loss. Sylvia called to let me know why she left early when a local news station arrived to produce a segment on the store closure. "I wanted to pour my heart out. But it was just too much," she said. Others voiced bitter distrust, such as Eddie, who had harsh words for the co-op management and its handling of the lease debacle. "That Patrick O'Connell [the general manager], what a bullshit artist. Those phony bastards," he said after reading a neighborhood newspaper story on the bakery closing. He banished the crudely refolded paper to the table's edge. Dottie channeled her anger through humor. One evening slightly after 8 p.m., with the store closed for the day, I lingered with Angelica as she swept and packed up to go home. Dottie and Lucy passed outside. Dottie waved, and I stepped out. She had spoken with Guillaume earlier. "He says it's over. I said we'll have to have a party and then break all the windows," she said with a hearty laugh. "I look for you every morning," Dottie continued.

"I'll be in tomorrow," I said.

"Good, we'll see you then," Lucy said. They continued home in the same direction. Their kindness also stirred a twinge of anticipated loss for me as their parting words for the evening reminded me of how they had pulled me into their web of care. I also felt unease, on the precipice of a changing world that had in some ways become my own.

The impending bakery loss stirred memories and feelings about other lost places and people. Regulars lamented other casualties of gentrification and invoked the large-scale "urban renewal" or "slum clearance" projects, depending on the perspective, that had displaced them earlier in life. As younger people, many had lost their homes when the city demolished the older tenement housing stock, where they spent their earliest years. This included the building of the co-op towers and commercial strip that housed the bakery, which had displaced them from the surrounding blocks. Dottie, Maureen, Tom, and Eddie vividly rendered the character of the neighborhood that predated the co-ops. They shared stories of old New York traditions, such as stoop sitting, ball playing in the streets, and neighborhood mothers watching children from their low-slung apartment windows. Their memories offered a counternarrative to claims of urban blight that had paved the way for the destruction of their childhood homes and sidewalks. As Eddie told me pointedly, disputing official accounts in that era of decaying tenement housing, "I know you're gonna write about these things one day. Make sure to tell them it was clean." He reminisced about his mother washing the stairs of their tenement building before their displacement and eventual move to the Bronx. "I don't know what they were talking about with cold water flats. We always had heat and hot water. Those were good buildings. I know," he said, bolstered with the authority of his construction background.

Maureen, Tom, Dottie, Eddie found their way back to the area while many others hadn't. Some people who began their lives in other parts of the city had also lost their entire neighborhoods. Phyllis, the daughter of immigrants from the former Czechoslovakia, had grown up on the East Side in Manhattan's Gas House District,[7] eighteen city blocks on an eighty-acre area of land that was subsequently razed to build Stuyvesant Town–Peter Cooper Village, a massive private housing development comprised of 110 buildings and 11,250 apartments, which is home to thirty thousand residents today.[8] Upon its opening in 1947, the complex prioritized housing for returning World War II veterans and barred Black tenants until 1951.[9] After the mass eviction of her family and some eleven thousand neighbors,[10] Phyllis and her family moved to the Bronx before returning to Manhattan later in life. In 1945, *The*

New York Times called the displacement "the greatest and most signifi-cant mass movement of families in New York's history."[11]

Anthropologist Mérida M. Rúa terms such repeated disruption in the lives of older adults "aging in displacement."[12] Her qualitative study of Puerto Rican elders in Chicago finds that gentrification stood as the latest cycle of displacement for many who experienced previous dis-ruptions linked to migration and Federal slum clearance programs that caused widespread housing loss. Elders first endured displacement after migration from their birthplaces, lost homes and neighborhoods in the wake of mid-twentieth century urban renewal projects, and in late life had to say goodbye to treasured places amid neighborhood change. Many older adults in my study had navigated similar trajecto-ries of loss as the children of immigrants and migrants from Ireland, Italy, Greece, Spain, Puerto Rico, Central and Eastern Europe or as immigrants and migrants themselves. Even those who hadn't experi-enced housing loss in New York City connected present-day gentrifica-tion and affordable housing shortages to family histories of persecution, immigration, and earlier housing scarcity. Although Sylvia hadn't endured such housing displacement in New York City, she often referred to her family's flight from the Russians in Latvia. In conversa-tions about gentrification and neighborhood change, she invoked the post–World War II housing shortage and her brother's difficulty find-ing an apartment upon his return from fighting in Europe. Eventually he and his wife—"a bitty thing but tough," as Sylvia often described her sister-in-law, who had survived a Jewish forced labor camp in France—settled in Sheepshead Bay, Brooklyn.

Now elders who had experienced previous waves of displacement faced a new kind of "social eviction."

The bakery served as a public memorial space to grieve the dead long after funeral services had ended and to collectively mark the passage of those who had no service, whether because they lacked family to arrange it or because they had eschewed formal mourning rituals. It was a place where people became more than strangers, where others knew them well enough to remember them, and it was an information clearinghouse to learn about others' passing. For elders facing increased mortality, the bakery also offered a kind of rehearsal space to contemplate other losses and their own eventual deaths.

One late autumn morning, bakery people informed each other about the latest death of a neighborhood resident. The bearer of this sad news used the full name of the deceased, Manny Garcia. Others needed help placing him.

"He had white hair," a voice volunteered.

"He went to the garden every day," another offered.

"Oh shit," Dottie said when she determined the man's identity. That morning, as on many others, they engaged in a group memory project and stitched together a patchwork tapestry of the deceased man's life, helping each other understand why they should mourn his loss. Manny Garcia worked in a local community garden around the corner and walked by the store daily. Dottie gestured to indicate how he always tipped his cap in passing. As she touched her hand to an invisible hat, I pictured him strolling by wearing dirt-caked gloves, carrying his bag of gardening tools. Customers often lamented the frequency of death and funeral talk. But I always reflected that at least bakery people noticed someone's absence, cared to locate the departed, and paused to remember them with others. They acted as custodians of a communal space that served as a repository of memory, a place where they would neither be forgotten nor entirely remembered.

Workers also expressed sorrow and attachment to deceased bakery patrons. Angelica spoke of "the little lady" that came most days with her companion Theresa. "She was a great woman," Angelica said. "She died very suddenly. She went to the hospital and then she was gone."

The woman's daughter brought her a mass card. "'My mom had very nice things to say about you,' the daughter said," explained Angelica. The woman who died had also given Angelica tips despite discouragement from Theresa, who rarely tipped. Angelica lifted her glasses to wipe a tear. "You realize in this place how many people gone . . . since I been here. You see people, then you don't see them anymore." Her depth of emotion surprised me since the woman spoke little, though she always appeared cheerful and kind to Angelica. Death uncovered surprising revelations.

PLANNING FOR THE DAY AFTER

When La Marjolaine's owner confirmed that Loaf, a high-end Manhattan bread bakery, would supplant him as the new tenant, customers planned in earnest for their post-bakery reality. In evaluating their options, elders considered shared challenges such as limited walking ability, modest fixed incomes, and a greater need for a community hub since they lived alone and had free time in retirement. Phyllis investigated on behalf of curious bakery regulars who wondered if Loaf could suffice as a replacement; she walked to an uptown location a mile and a half away. Her dispatch was animated; her voice rose and fell for emphasis as she detailed the store's layout and pricing. With widened eyes and sunspot-flecked hands, she dramatized her journey for an attentive audience trying to parse what her observations meant for them. The folded-up takeout menu she extracted from her tasteful knockoff Gucci handbag circulated like a note passed among high schoolers before smartphones. The din of murmurs grew as people studied the prices. "Look at this: $4," someone said. "Oh," came another disappointed sigh. Phyllis nodded, casting doubt on the likelihood of this new establishment gaining traction as a viable substitute. "There's nowhere to sit, only a few chairs and a counter by the window. And the prices are higher," she said with satisfied authority, smoothing the sleeves of her silken, baby blue blouse. She appeared to enjoy her position as knowledgeable messenger to her age peers, with whom she felt she had little in common beyond chronological age.

Phyllis stood out as the epitome of what gerontologists and the larger medical establishment might term "successful aging," a paradigm that focuses on the achievement of a disease-free old age with minimal loss of physical and cognitive functioning. The successful aging paradigm emphasizes lifestyle choices and healthy habits, such as a nutritious diet and physical exercise—a worthy aspiration, which is often unattainable for those elders who have faced greater financial hardship, discrimination, and cumulative disadvantage during their lifetimes.[13] Aging scholars have critiqued the concept for obscuring the privilege that bolsters physical, emotional, and cognitive health in late life and for instead attributing outcomes in old age to individual choice. Thus the geriatrician Louise Aronson has proposed "comfortable" aging as a more appropriate goal than disease elimination.[14] Despite her hardscrabble beginnings, Phyllis had managed to achieve these aging ideals and took pride in her self-care routines, logging her daily activities and diabetes management efforts. She projected herself as the model of a busy, energetic senior. While others looked to Phyllis as an example of "vim and vigor," she held in high regard her own elder role models, such as Connie, her next-door neighbor and friend of multiple decades. Phyllis lauded Connie's strength, intelligence, and service during World War II in the Women's Army Corps (WAC).[15] A few years older than Phyllis, in her early 90s, Connie led an active life: she shopped at the farmer's market, frequented the library, and read widely. I often saw them dining together at the West Side Diner.

A week later, Phyllis shared highlights from another reconnaissance mission to Loaf's downtown location. "It's very expensive," she said, gesturing to the invisible rows of Focaccia she described as though unveiling game show prizes. "The people here aren't going to pay for that." Her dim assessment foreshadowed elders' challenges finding a comparable space.

While a few people attended one of the neighborhood's four senior centers, including a woman named Joan who protested budget cuts to senior services at the state capital, most expressed dissatisfaction with them. "I hate old people. And I don't want to sit there all day and play mah-jongg, or whatever they do," Eugene offered as an explanation for avoiding them. He chuckled afterwards. Though he claimed to hate older people, he spent most of his free time with similarly aged peers. But his desire to distance himself from other elders, or at least the lack-luster company he expected in age-separated institutional spaces, revealed internalized ageism common to many older people and prevalent among those with whom I spent so much time.[16] His comment reflected not only his appraisal of elders' limited options for socializing but also hierarchical distinctions among different classes of old people. Sylvia also expressed negativity about senior centers. "That's not for me," she said. When prodded, she mentioned attending a hospital-based support group after her husband's death nearly two decades before as a deterrent. "I went once and never again. It was the most depressing thing ever," she said. Sylvia viewed senior centers as similarly "depressing," though she had never visited one because she felt people who "needed help" went there. Some used centers for select services. Eddie took advantage of a monthly MetroCard bus parked outside one center, which spared him climbing stairs down to the subway to add money to his discounted transit pass. Nevertheless, he abstained from the center's other activities.

Lucy also expressed reservations about senior centers, not because of internalized ageism but because of her resistance to identifying with other elders solely based on their advanced ages. A never-married single woman, she spent a lifetime creating relationships and a daily routine that kept her out of the house and always on the go. In her usual booming voice, she spoke of feeling worn out. "Getting old sucks!" she roared after tallying the day's troubles. She punctuated her stories so often with this catchphrase, the punch line served the same function as a period at the end of a sentence. Since retirement, Lucy had shifted her time, attention, and energy from the demands of paid work to caring for herself and her body. Despite laments about boredom, she packed her day with a panoply of activities, including visits to the bakery, grocery shopping, dinner with friends, and the occasional movie or theater performance. Less palatable errands, such as her full calendar of medical appointments, also helped structure her day.

Lucy often shared her financial stresses when she gathered with other regulars. Rising health-care costs and confusion about her medical plan's benefits caused much misery. She whipped out her mail—medical bills and notices from Medicare, her supplemental Medigap health insurance, and her New York State EPIC prescription drug plan—and offloaded her papered woes onto the communal table. The latest headaches in these envelopes guided her contributions to the evening's discussion. She worried about the impending rollout of Obamacare health plans and potential changes to her Medicare benefits. Lucy spoke often about feeling threatened with another older woman named Vivian, who also expressed concern and anger at President Obama.

One evening in Vivian's absence, Lucy recounted how Vivian had urged her to organize around Medicare with the women who attended the senior center in her building. Incensed, she explained, "You know what she wanted me to do. She said, 'You should go down to the senior center in your building and get some of those women to protest with you.' How do you like that? She wants me to protest. She wants me to do the work. Well, I told her she should go over there and protest. Those women are not like me. They were married and had children. They didn't work. They go down there and knit."

Lucy disliked that Vivian was pressuring her to organize, but she also objected to others grouping her with the senior center women simply based on age. Despite sharing membership in a 65+ age group, residence in the same building complex, gender, and race with these older white women, Lucy focused on their divergent life histories. Her resistance shows that age-based solidarity remains complicated, even without any stigma attached to old people. Growing diversity means that age-separated spaces such as senior centers may have difficulty satisfying a range of needs and preferences. Service and health-care providers must carefully consider such heterogeneity when designing spaces and programs. Years later Lucy mentioned how much she enjoyed attending a new senior center focused on serving sexual minority elders, though she didn't openly identify as LGBTQ+. She cited the center's comfortable atmosphere, good company, and delicious, low-cost meals as major draws. Her preferences speak to the appeal of public places, such as the bakery, for a diverse body of older adults, compared with many institutional, elder-serving spaces that sometimes flattened their differences or required that they identify as old.

THE BAKERY CLUB

As the closing drew nearer, many customers started calling themselves "the bakery club." People's identification as club "members" marked a shift in how they related to this place; instead of merely inhabiting a place they enjoyed, they forged a collective defined by the place. People also used "family" and "fellowship" to describe their association with other patrons. Examining this coming together in a life-course context helps us understand the conditions that raised awareness, however brief, of age's significance to them and their status as older people. Their self-designation as members of a "club" provides a useful way of thinking about how age-related circumstances compel people to realize mutual needs based on the commonalities of birth cohort, living alone, retirement, gender, class, health, and physical mobility.

Most people expressed disappointment and feelings of being unmoored from an important anchor with the bakery's demise. Some voiced burning anger that the co-op buildings, home to many of the neighborhood's elders, had betrayed them by pursuing a higher paying retail tenant rather than preserving an establishment that had served older residents for decades. Unsurprisingly, Eddie emerged as a vociferous critic. He bemoaned gentrification's toll and his own difficulties subsisting on a fixed income. Mayor Michael Bloomberg drew Eddie's ire for "making the city for the rich," and he criticized real estate projects the mayor had spearheaded during three terms in office. In the months preceding the closing, Eddie spoke at length about his anger at the co-op's decision not to offer a more favorable lease and about the harm the closure would cause the neighborhood's older residents:

> You know, that was real rotten what the co-op did. Not to renew. I can't believe they would do that, after all these years. I mean, who do you think was going there all that time? The people in your own buildings, that's who. Who's gonna go to that new place? Not me. And a lot of older people, they've been going there for years. Where they gonna be without that place? Nowhere. They can't afford anything else. What else's left around there? Bill and Arthur said they're going to go to the benches behind [co-op] building two. And they will, but what about in the cold weather? Where then? Maybe the lobby. But who knows. People don't like it if you sit there too long either.

Even those who bad-mouthed elders based on their physical and cognitive shortcomings acknowledged this collective loss for old people. A surprising reversal came from Phyllis, who reaped the benefits of gentrification as a long-term resident and seemed enthralled with most neighborhood changes. She had long criticized those that she decided spent "too much" time in the bakery. Though she conveyed muted regret at its loss, careful to point out that she hadn't frequented this place as much as others, two months after the store closed she disclosed unprecedented anger about the co-op's handling of the lease dissolution. "It wasn't right. The bakery was part of the co-op. A lot of older people depended on it. They went every day. I'm going to say something to Mike," she said, mentioning her son's childhood friend, who served on the co-op council. "He told me to get in touch with him if I ever had a problem." Though he had no power to alter the situation, Phyllis felt compelled to object formally. She recognized the bakery's importance as a neighborhood institution for elders and held the buildings that housed them responsible for looking after their needs, which included maintaining welcoming and affordable retail spaces. In this moment she rallied ever so briefly with former patrons, despite asserting her own lack dependence on the space.

TOUCH OF GREY

I arrived at 6 o'clock one evening and joined Eugene and Sylvia at adjacent tables in the back. As dusk yielded to darkness, we discussed a recent robbery spree. Sylvia said she found complete details in the free weekly neighborhood newspaper.

"Yes, someone robbed the bank over there," Eugene said and pointed towards the shiny new branch a block away.

"There's a lot of crime they don't report," Sylvia said. "But you can read all about it here." She tapped the police blotter three times with such force the paper sharply rattled.

The freebie paper had earned a devoted following among neighborhood elders, judging by their fidelity in reporting the crime blotter's latest misdeeds. Eugene and Sylvia's discussion that evening exemplified a tendency that researchers have historically called a "paradox." Elders often fear crime more compared to younger people, even though older adults have a lower risk of criminal victimization. Recent scholarship adds nuance to these findings, showing that elders' greater caution, such as avoiding certain places or walking outside after dark, reflects a reasonable response to growing vulnerability and the potential for more severe physical and emotional consequences of an attack rather than an irrational terror of crime.[17] Such fears ran high among the older adults I observed, which I found interesting given that, with gentrification, crime declined in their neighborhood. Old people had good reasons for increased feelings of vulnerability. Telephone and mail scams targeted them, and some had experienced crimes of opportunity. Most expressed feeling physically vulnerable on the street, whether they feared someone would harm them or worried about falling.

Eugene endured multiple muggings in his later years. Once while walking home on a quiet side street, tipsy from wine, two men knocked him to the ground and stole his wallet. "It was my own fault," he punctuated the story. During the study, a thief who had made the local papers for preying on older men attacked Carmen's boyfriend in the subway station on his way home from her apartment. The mugger ambushed him in the station's stairwell, choked him, pushed him to the ground, and stole his wallet. Many elders wanted to get home before the hour grew "too late" or "before dark," though others worried less or not at all. Those concerned about the lateness of the hour still felt at increased risk of victimization in a gentrified neighborhood that had seen significant reductions in crime. These fears preclude older people from the full benefits of historic crime drops that have occurred in large American cities since the 1990s.[18] Former mayor Michael Bloomberg promoted New York City as the "safest big city in America."[19]

Safety inequities also existed within the same few blocks. Elders like Dottie and Jeannette, who lived in the projects, faced structural conditions that warranted increased concern. Pockets of disorder persisted in and around their seven-building housing complex. They monitored their surroundings with a greater vigilance as they contended with broken elevators, delayed apartment repairs, drug dealing, and street crime. A young cashier, Jasmine, who lived in Dottie's building and had worked briefly at the bakery, described the ordeal of walking down twenty-one flights of stairs one morning due to chronically broken elevators. She noted the smattering of burnt-out light bulbs that left her descending stairs in total darkness and scurrying past "people smoking crack." Elders' fear of crime and their perceived and real susceptibility to injury also compelled age recognition and acknowledgment of shared anxiety around safety.

Our discussion of muggings and robberies led Sylvia to another observation about dismissive treatment due to age. She told us that her young neighbor's dog walker habitually left her key ring lodged in the apartment's front door and that she'd warned against her foolhardiness. "I told her, 'There's a lot of traffic on our floor during the day. People come in and out with deliveries, to fix things in people's apartments.'"

"Don't get me wrong, I completely trust 'our guys,'" Sylvia said, emphasizing her confidence in her building's maintenance staff. After her warning, she said the woman told her in a huff, "'I've done this for six years.' She said that she leaves the keys in the door so she doesn't forget where she puts them." Sylvia bellowed, "So she doesn't forget them. Ha! Even me, with my brain and my scar tissue . . . I don't do that." The "brain" and "scar tissue" referred to her brain hemorrhage and heart attack some twenty years before, which, she often pointed out, sometimes caused forgetfulness, though she didn't seem more forgetful to me than anyone else in their 80s. In their last encounter, Sylvia said the dog walker squeezed past her to the elevator and refused to speak to her while they were inside it. "She wouldn't even look at me, but I told her, 'It only takes one time.'" The woman stormed off when the elevator opened. "Sure, she's been doing this for six years, but what if one day you're not so lucky."

"That's right," Eugene said in a told-you-so singsong. "Is she out of her mind?"

Sylvia shifted to a more reflective tone. "When you're a senior, they get such an attitude if you tell them something"—she paused while searching for the right word—"unacceptable to them." She turned to Eugene, who sat diagonally across from her and said, "You know, they hate us."

"I know," Eugene said with resignation. "Well," he said, dragging his fingertips forward underneath his chin in a favorite Italian gesture, the *Non mi frega*, or the "I don't give a damn." Eugene gave this hand flick a little something extra, seeming to add, "Fuck off."

Sylvia said of her young neighbor, "I don't think she's going to get rid of her [the dog walker]. She said a friend recommended her. I'm concerned for her. She's young. They're all so young."

"You're the house mother," Eugene said with a smile.

"Yeah," Sylvia said, smiling to herself. "Sans pay," she added, tracing the phrase in invisible letters with her index finger across the glass tabletop.

The idea of belonging to an exclusive club due to age emerged as a frequent theme with Sylvia. A few days later, she highlighted her status as the oldest patient at her primary-care doctor's office. She had often mentioned her standing as the eldest resident on her floor, but I'd never heard her single out her age in a health-care context. "I'm the oldest one who goes there," she said of the office where she received care for about four years. Her previous doctor had retired after treating her as a patient for more than twenty years. She still sometimes referred to her current physician as her "new doctor." "Yes, it's true," she continued. "Some offices aren't even taking seniors."

I concurred and shared how I'd encountered this predicament a few months earlier when searching for a new primary-care doctor for my then 68-year-old father. My phone calls met with numerous offices turning away new Medicare patients due to lower insurance reimbursements.

A CLUB NO ONE WANTS TO JOIN:
THE SOCIAL NATURE OF AGE

What incentive do people have to identify as old? In Western society, especially in the United States, old age remains a devalued status, a club no one wants to join, recalling the famous Groucho Marx joke: "I don't want to belong to any club that would accept me as one of its members."[20] Ageist comments online about the bakery closing highlight why elders resisted identifying by their shared chronology and sought to avoid the stigma attached to places associated with old people. The tenor of these comments spanned from jokes about the disposability of older patrons to antagonism. For example, a commenter on a local food and restaurant news blog quipped, "A good pane di comune is worth any number of old ladies." Other gibes went a step further: "They [Loaf] can hire the ones who have Parkinson's to shake the cocktails if they get a full liquor license!"

While growing older may confer benefits such as increased status, wealth, and power, in the United States people often incur steep social, cultural, and financial penalties in old age. Most would have more to lose from embracing their advanced ages than they do from bowing to cultural pressure to pass as younger through concealment measures such as coloring grey hair and avoiding assistive equipment such as canes, hearing aids, or bifocal glasses.[21] Two challenges complicate identifying with one's age later in life. First, old age is a status you "grow into." Thus, many elders don't recognize age as their primary social identity and consider other dimensions, such as race, ethnicity, and gender, to be more important than age. Second, they often avoid identifying with similarly aged peers because of stigma. Internalized ageism discourages many older adults from developing an age-based identity and interacting with other elders, creating distance from those who can offer support and understanding. Resisting age as a primary category of identification allows them to sidestep the stigma of a "spoiled identity," to use a term coined by the sociologist Erving Goffman.[22] Of a person who lacks acceptance, Goffman writes, "He is thus reduced in our minds from a whole and usual person to a tainted, discounted one."[23] Furthermore, he outlines the potential for isolation when the social difference of those who have been discredited surfaces: "This discrepancy, when known about or apparent, spoils his social identity; it has the effect of cutting him off from society and from himself so that he stands as a discredited person facing an unaccepting world."[24]

As sociologists have challenged the biological basis gender and race, understanding the social nature of age requires moving beyond biology or chronology.[25] Separating age from numerical calculation illuminates its varying importance across culture, geography, and history. Historical gerontologists have tracked both shifts and enduring continuities in how we imagine the life course, including the "invention" of childhood and adolescence and the constancy of old age as a recognizable period of life; they have also reached some consensus about when to designate someone as "old" despite gains in life expectancy.[26] Improvements in older adults' health in recent decades have prompted some to subdivide people 65 years and older into multiple groups, such as "young-old" (65–74 years), "middle-old" (74–85 years), and "oldest-old" (85+ years) to better capture diversity.[27] Aging scholars Bernice Neugarten and Dail Neugarten also distinguish between "young-old" and "old-old" based on social circumstances such as finances and community integration, writing, "Thus, a young-old person might be fifty-five or eighty-five. The term represents the social reality that the line between middle age and old age is no longer clear."[28]

Feminists' conceptualization of gender as a social construction and as the site of interlocking oppressions[29] provides a blueprint for understanding age as a social construct.[30] Age is more than the number of candles on a birthday cake and one of many social positions we occupy. Yet, within sociology and gender scholarship, the study of age hasn't garnered as much attention as race, class, and gender. The fluid nature of age and shifting membership in different age categories, along with longstanding bias favoring research on younger people, has often led to age's neglect or inclusion as an "et cetera" category rather than a primary site of analysis.[31]

Sociologist Cheryl Laz makes age visible and unearths assumptions about the relationship between chronology and age, arguing that we view age not as an "objective" or "natural" number but as an interactive process.[32] She draws on symbolic interactionist theory, a sociological tradition that prioritizes the meanings people create in face-to-face interaction,[33] and expands sociologists Candace West and Don Zimmerman's concept of "doing gender"—which involves the way people construct or contest gender in their interactions—to examine how people "perform" age in different social contexts.[34] Highlighting the micro-context of everyday interaction, Laz argues that age is a "managed accomplishment," or an act that requires ongoing work as people reconstitute or resist dominant conceptions of age in their responses to social expectations and assumptions. Although people exercise agency and creativity in how they construct their ages, they remain accountable to others' perceptions and judgments, which are shaped in part by the larger social structure. For example, our interactions occur against a backdrop of expected age norms and ideas about age-appropriate behavior and activities, pressuring us to explain "off time" life-course transitions like having children "early" or completing education "late" and to justify our fashion choices as we grow older, especially if they challenge social expectations.

WHAT'S MY AGE AGAIN?

The questions that feminist scholars have raised about the appropriateness of grouping women together into a single category bear on age given heterogeneity within different age groups. Should we group older adults together? If so, when? Accounting for diversity, I and others argue that age remains a meaningful social organizing principle, especially in age-graded, age-stratified industrialized nations like the United States, which have specific age benchmarks tied to the distribution of government benefits such as Social Security and Medicare.

Many elders hesitate to identify as old because of widespread cultural devaluation, and protesting ageism requires claiming membership in a stigmatized group. While the social justice and advocacy organization the Gray Panthers remains a notable exception for confronting ageism and other forms of systemic discrimination, age stigma motivates many older adults to avoid other elders.[35] Age's malleable boundaries age also complicate belonging, and a person can experience both age privilege and disadvantage over the life course.[36] Shifting membership in different age groups distinguishes age from other power relationships. Fewer people change racial or gender status, but we all grow old or die.[37]

The bakery closing prompted people to consider how age shaped their circumstances and sparked a momentary coming together, evoking the work of feminist philosopher Iris Marion Young. She grappled with preserving a way to group women together while avoiding the pitfalls of ascribing a shared identity to diverse, multidimensional women.[38] Her approach to considering women as a "serial" collective paves the way for imagining a time-limited group organized around the life course that draws on situations and issues rather than identities. Young's work offers a path towards recognizing contexts in which age becomes more salient, allowing elders to group around key issues of growing concern later in late life.

Young adapts philosopher Jean Paul Sartre's concept of "seriality" and proposes that we consider women as a "social series," or as a "less organized and unself-conscious collective unity."[39] Sartre distinguishes a group from a series, defining a "series" as a different type of social collective and not a group in the traditional sense. People in a group identify with one another and recognize solidarity among themselves. Members in a series may or may not. Each person occupies different sets of series and has a distinct vantage point. Belonging to a series doesn't guarantee anything about someone's characteristics or what they make of their multiple social positions. For example, a person can belong to more than one series ("race," "class," "age," etc.) and choose which, if any, are important to their identity. The same person may relate to them differently depending on social context or, as I argue, during disparate parts of the life course.

Young uses Sartre's example of people waiting for a bus to show how an object (in this case, a bus that never arrives) rather than shared identity and characteristics can activate a collection of people to form a series around this activity. United in the goal of riding the bus, they don't necessarily identify with each other or recognize themselves as engaged in a mutual endeavor. However, this collective problem can spark organization. By eliminating the requirement that people share common features or social locations, seriality moves beyond identity as the basis for membership.

Groups can spring from a series and later revert to a series. In Young's example, the people who complain and strategize a plan of action have formed a "group in fusion."[40] Spontaneous groups can either institutionalize (e.g., by setting meetings or electing officers) or disband and return to the series level of social organization.[41] In the preceding pages, the bakery closure is like the bus that never shows. This situation sparked a brief group activation, as customers signed petitions, participated in media efforts to garner attention, and commiserated about threats to their communal space. But once the business closed permanently, customers mostly dispersed and curtailed further action, though for years they expressed collective loss and recognition of the place's importance to older residents. They supported each other in age-related discussions about ageism, self-care, challenges to independence, and perceived vulnerability to crime. Some advocated with an occasional letter of complaint to a newspaper; politician; or institution, such as a facility where they received medical care, and spoke up during interactions when they felt slighted, ignored, or discriminated against.

Viewing old age as a series allows an inclusiveness and expansiveness appropriate to age's fluidity as a social category. Feminist scholar Margaret Cruikshank presents a compelling justification for applying Young's approach, writing: "'Old' can be thought of as an *affinity group* rather than an *identity*. Such groups form, grow, dissolve, and spring to life again depending on circumstances. Within affinity groups, 'old' can seem fluid and indeterminate, relevant to this situation or issue, irrelevant to that ... Much space exists between denying age and claiming it as an identity" (emphasis mine).[42]

Serial memberships also help surmount the identity issues and internalized ageism that impede coalition building and political organizing around age-based identities. They contain the seeds for mobilization and discovery of mutual needs, while also leaving space to recognize social difference and structural inequalities. For example, safe, affordable, and accessible housing remains a crucial and unmet need for many people over age 65, but a series organized around age should acknowledge that many LGBTQ+ elders face additional concerns about disclosing their sexual identity and securing safe living arrangements.[43] In senior housing, they may fear being "forced back into the closet" due to discrimination based on their sexual minority status.[44] Similarly, elders searching for housing upon release from prison encounter discrimination and barriers related to chronic health conditions and limited finances.[45]

I argue that the bakery closing activated a "series" called old age, showing how situations and policy changes that affect older people may motivate them to rally around age despite their usual reluctance and social heterogeneity. During the study unprecedented proposals to close hundreds of New York City senior centers, increasing gentrification, and face-to-face interactions that revealed pervasive ageism, uncovered age's importance as a dimension of structural location and an untapped point of political organization.[46] Broader problems that could activate different series into an ephemeral or longer lasting group include health-care access, independent living, social infrastructure funding, public safety, climate change, emergency preparedness and evacuation planning for natural disasters. Depending on their mix of social identities, people may relate to different angles of a similar problem. For example, the racially motivated rise in violence against Asian and Asian-American elders during the Covid-19 pandemic uncovered age-related vulnerabilities and heightened safety concerns for older adults but most of all exposed longstanding racial and ethnic discrimination and harm in the United States.[47]

The Covid-19 pandemic in the United States made age visible in new and familiar ways, revealing solidarity but also tension between older and younger age groups. Initially, public health experts and government officials concentrated on older adults and urged people over age 60 and those with underlying medical conditions to isolate due to heightened vulnerability to complications, severe illness, and death from Covid-19.[48] People across the country heeded calls to check on older neighbors and family members sheltering at home and volunteered to deliver groceries and other necessities. At the chaotic start of vaccine distribution, media accounts profiled volunteer efforts to help older adults overwhelmed with scheduling scarce appointment slots amid technology and public transportation barriers. A Saturday Night Live skit ("Boomers Got the Vax") parodied the early vaccine rollout and the strains between privileged boomers eligible for earlier shots and younger generations already scraping by financially, awaiting their turn. Drawing inspiration from the hip-hop music video for The Notorious B.I.G.'s (featuring Mase and Puff Daddy) "Mo Money, Mo Problems," SNL cast members reeled off satirical lines such as: "Baby boomers greatest generation / Got all the money / Now we got the vaccination / Crash the economy three whole times / But when it comes to the vax / We the first in line . . . You whine and cry while we dine inside / We run the world since 1945."[49]

Ageism surged in the pandemic,[50] with the disparaging nickname "Boomer Remover" for the SARS-CoV-2 virus trending early on social media.[51] While many Americans supported public-health safety measures, accounts also emerged showing growing doubt and resentment about continuing stay-at-home orders, seen by some as an unfair sacrifice forced on the young and able-bodied to protect the old and immunocompromised.[52] In positive and negative ways, the pandemic increased our consciousness of age, bringing ageism to the foreground, drawing attention to age stratification in American society, and revealing interconnections between different age groups. Intergenerational households safeguarded older family members living in proximity to younger relatives who held frontline jobs in health care and service sector positions that required on-site work. Other families experienced prolonged separations as they delayed visits and social gatherings with elders who lived independently and in nursing homes.

The pandemic also revealed organizing potential around issues affecting older people and shared challenges across age groups that require cooperation, increased funding, and inclusive policy solutions. For example, a lack of high-speed broadband thwarted old and young in meeting their social, educational, and health-care needs. Elders and people with disabilities protested together at a San Francisco AT&T store to demand free, accessible, and reliable internet access for older, disabled, and low-income residents of the nine Bay Area counties. Protester Maria Guadalupe Siordia-Ortiz, age 67, whose unreliable internet connection had prevented her from scheduling telemedicine appointments, said: "These times caught us. For us, it was something so sudden. The children are growing up with all this, but not us, and we feel kind of left out . . . We need to be connected. We need to have the opportunity, the chance to be part of this world." Another protester, Cora McCoy, 80, said "Free Wi-Fi would help our pocketbooks and improve our connection," and she listed her internet-related needs, including talking to family and friends, attending online religious services, and helping her 13-year-old, co-residing grandson access virtual learning and complete homework assignments.[53] Overlapping concerns about equitable access to resources and social connection recall the Gray Panthers' motto "age and youth in action,"[54] providing a template for bringing old and young together around mutual needs, whether bolstering people's ability to secure information and health care through technology or deepening investment in the creation and maintenance of safe, accessible community spaces for all ages.

5

REBUILDING THE WORLD OF YESTERDAY

CITIES ARE GENTRIFYING, yet we know little about older adults' experiences of these neighborhood changes.[1] Most research—for example, Matthew Desmond's acclaimed work on the eviction epidemic in America—has concentrated on affordable housing shortages and risk of residential eviction for low-income residents.[2] But this trend neglects a fuller understanding of how commercial gentrification threatens older people's connections in noninstitutional, intergenerational spaces and ultimately their social and emotional well-being. I find that different features of "third places" such as proximity (distance from residences), cost, physical design and layout, and surveillance facilitated or precluded face-to-face interaction and a sense of ownership that nurtured independence and the development of social support systems. This chapter contributes to limited scholarly knowledge about elders' experiences of gentrification, a growing concern as population aging converges with the increasing cost of living.

Most previous studies investigating urban aging have focused on safety in neighborhoods experiencing physical decline and high crime rather than on the effects of growing affluence.[3] Many scholars and policy makers now view urban environments as ideal for older adults who wish to remain at home independently. But while cities offer concentrated services and shops within walking distance, my study has also found that gentrification can intensify social exclusion based on physical limitations. The shuttering of neighborhood businesses harmed those who depended on these spaces for connection, support, and a reason to leave the house every day. Thus, in this social context, people's bodies imposed an avoidable hurdle as they could no longer find gathering spots steps from their front door. The bakery closing intensified age and class stratification among former patrons, as differences in income, education, health, mobility, and physical functioning shaped possibilities for socializing. Those with money had more options about where to go. Those without had McDonald's.

Many lost a vital anchor when the bakery closed and the epicenter of their social world cratered. Narrowed options weighed on people's routines and psyches, making them feel like nomads in the neighborhood where they had lived several decades or for their entire lives. A cramped doughnut store with scarce seating remained the lone, lower-cost eatery in this stretch and failed to draw the same crowd. The bakery's retail space sat vacant for nearly two and a half years, waiting for its reincarnation as a branch of Loaf, an upscale Manhattan bread shop. When this higher priced establishment finally opened, a younger, more affluent clientele moved in.

GOING THE DISTANCE

Other sites tested people's ability to walk there or to surmount mobility barriers in other ways, such as taking a taxi or bus. McDonald's and Pete's Delicatessen, where several former bakery customers regrouped, stood at opposite ends of the few blocks surrounding the bakery. McDonald's sat on a busy avenue in a space leased by the co-op. Its location four blocks from the bakery made it a convenient gathering place for many elders. But for those who couldn't walk further than the bakery without strain, McDonald's stood beyond reach.

Given that McDonald's required a cab ride back and forth for him, Eugene went to Pete's for breakfast and for dinner or coffee in the evenings. "It's a little too far," he said of McDonald's, a few weeks after joining others who had gathered there in the days after the bakery closed. In bad weather, Eugene avoided slippery sidewalks by taking his building's underground tunnel and exiting from an adjoining building's entrance. One year, construction scaffolding snaked around the block from his building to Pete's, protecting him from the elements and recreating the tunnel's safe passage.

Sylvia split her time between gathering with others at Pete's and dining alone at the Galaxy Diner across the street. Both eateries stood a block and a half from her apartment. She shared some personal history with Pete's, unknown to me. Several years before, she, her late husband, and "the guys" came into Pete's "all the time." "In those days, an Egyptian guy owned the place. The guys and us came here when Irv [Sylvia's husband] was ailing. They [the men working there] were so good to him," she said, explaining that the owner and other men, a mix of friends and workers, looked after her husband as he grew sicker with cancer, shortly before he died. They kept him company at Pete's, allowing her to shop in the evenings and run errands she couldn't accomplish during the day while caring for him at home. "All the guys were there, Martin . . . they're all gone."

Whenever she heard neighborhood gossip about the group at McDonald's, she said, "Oh, I haven't been there in years," as if McDonald's was a far off, distant place. Eddie went to Pete's, pushing himself to walk the extra block and a half. He frequented Pete's far less often than the bakery. When he couldn't make it, he called with a note of apology and proffered an explanation, such as ankle swelling or fatigue from a full day of appointments at the VA Hospital clinic.

People's physical challenges threatened a sense of belonging and reinforced exclusion after the bakery closure. Dottie, 83, managed cascading health problems in the last five years of her life and expressed growing isolation after the closing. The bakery had stood less than a block from her building. Her daughter Linda said, "I knew if I was ever looking for Mom I could find her in the bakery."

Dottie joined the women who regrouped at McDonald's, but her declining mobility complicated socializing. "It's not my favorite place, you know," she said of McDonald's. When she could afford it, she sometimes went to the Galaxy Diner and the West Side Diner, two closer eateries popular among elders, a block and a half away from the old bakery. Later at Pete's, Sylvia mentioned seeing Dottie at the Galaxy recently. "She's having a lot of trouble with her leg," she said, exasperated. Dottie's arthritis and knee pain turned a short walk into an arduous trek. Though she had stopped at the bakery nearly every morning and evening, deteriorating health reduced her McDonald's trips to once per week until soon weeks passed without anyone seeing Dottie. As I walked with her home one day, she spoke of her sorrow about the bakery closing and the effect on her life. "It's not the same," she said, comparing McDonald's with the bakery. "We had it good. But now it's gone. That broke a lot of friendships. Everyone goes their separate ways. This one there, that one here. It's not the same."

At McDonald's, Dottie met with a group that averaged six women. Yet she felt both left out and the center of unwanted attention. Since the closing, she felt she had fallen off the radar of other bakery regulars. "Eddie used to call a lot. He'd ask, 'How's your brother? How you doin', Dottie?' I guess no more, 'How you doing, Dottie?'" I asked when he last called. "Not since the bakery closed," Dottie said. "But that's okay. I'm a loner. I'm by myself. Everybody's got their own life," she said one afternoon while we sat beside each other at McDonald's. The other women chatted among themselves. She also mentioned not speaking with Sylvia since the closing. "I don't hear from Sylvia no more. She don't call. And now she's hooked up with Phyllis and Judy. I don't blame her. They like to go places where they walk a lot." But the attention that Dottie received because of her mobility problems made her uncomfortable. "They know I'm coming, and they all show up because I don't come out a lot. The girls all want to help, but I feel bad. Lucy said she wanted to walk me home, but she just got there. It's not fair," she explained. She also spoke of losing freedom and control of her schedule now that she needed to coordinate plans with others: "They come later. I come about 2:30. What do they do all day? Lay in bed? I can't do that." If she couldn't manage the walk home, Dottie said, "I take a taxi."

Dottie often walked home with Jeannette. But one late October afternoon Jeannette left without her, suggesting that perhaps relations had broken down between them. Dottie had hinted that she wanted to leave with Jeannette. "Oh, you're leavin'? I'm going too," she said to her. But in the protracted moments that Dottie required to slide out from the hard plastic booth, Jeannette seemed not to hear or ignored her. Jeannette peered down as she started to walk out alone. I caught up with a few more women who had showed up, but I soon had to leave and offered to walk Dottie home. "Oh, would you?" she said with relief.

Escorting Dottie home was no small favor, as I discovered. The three-and-a-half-block walk took me about five minutes alone, but with Dottie, required forty.

After a few plodding steps, Dottie breathed hard. She hunched over her metal shopping cart, which doubled as makeshift rolling walker, and leaned her forearms on its handle. Steering over unpredictable sidewalks proved daunting. After crossing the street, she struggled to wheel her cart up the sidewalk ramp and avoid the large puddle of water in the curb cut. I placed the cart on the indented part above the water, but my miscalculation upset Dottie's balance. A smooth-cheeked Asian boy about fifteen years old offered to help. He tried lifting the cart onto the sidewalk, but Dottie gripped the handle tightly like it was a life raft rather than letting go and having nothing to hold onto. She relied so much on her cart for support that it seemed an extension of her arm. I explained that she needed to grasp it for support. We came to a standstill.

Although the entire incident lasted no more than three minutes, time crawled. Our Good Samaritan looked bewildered and furrowed his young brow. I grew stressed too, feeling trapped in the moment, like we were in quicksand. After we secured Dottie and her cart on the sidewalk, he wished her "a safe rest of the day." At the next corner we stood a second for Dottie to rest. In a weary voice she said, "You know that's been happening more often [people wanting to help]. It's nice, but I don't like it." I thought of how her fallback plan, a taxi, also posed difficulties since she needed others' help getting in and out of a cab. She sopped sweat dripping down her blotchy red face with a McDonald's napkin. We continued walking. Mid-block she mentioned needing to lean against a car—another break built into her routine. As she approached one with her outstretched hand, the dashboard lit up, and the vehicle pulled away. We walked past several empty spaces until we found another. "This one's good," she said, panting and resting her forearm on the car's hood. Once she caught her breath, she joked, "I might get sued." As we continued, Dottie said, "I was supposed to buy something, but I can't remember what. Oh, that's right, milk." I suspected she knew I would offer to fetch it for her, as I had in the past, and asked if she wanted me to go to the store. A wide smile stretched across her face. "Oh, would you?" she said and handed me a few singles.

Dottie paused to say hello to three or four people, slowing us further. We finally reached the corner. A hard plastic strip overlaid the concrete crosswalk divider, newly installed as a part of a recent bike lane project. I imagined that the designers had intended this feature to help prevent falls, but as Dottie struggled across, I wondered how other wheelchair and walker users fared and worried about her losing her balance. Her cart's wheels tangled in the maze of raised bumps, requiring fierce effort as she pushed and pulled to free it. Attempting to bypass the troublesome divider would only expose her to speeding traffic.

As Dottie walked ahead to her building a few doors down, I ran to the store and picked up a half gallon of milk and a copy of *The Daily News*, which she'd added to her errand request. The two items totaled $3.50. A rip-off, I thought. The newspaper cost 50¢, the milk 3 bucks. Johnny's, a bodega several storefronts up on the same block, charged a dollar less for milk, but Dottie couldn't always walk there. When I reached her building, she was limping up the stairs. I thought she would have taken the wheelchair ramp. "I made a mistake," she said. "I saw some cops and thought they were going to help," she explained, pointing to her cart left on the sidewalk when the police didn't assist. I lifted it up the three steps.

Dottie asked me to keep her company in the lobby, a departure from other times when I helped her to the entrance and we would say our goodbyes outside. Light grey enamel covered the lobby's cinderblock walls. Three red signs with white letters hung above each elevator, one dead center between the two: "Riding Outside Cars is Dangerous and Deadly." Dottie always complained about how the sluggish elevators never arrived, passed her floor, and remained broken for weeks.

Dottie retrieved her mail, dropping an envelope with a handwritten return address that bore her maiden name. I handed her the letter. "That's my brother," she said and sifted through the stack, ticking off the senders: "Macy's, Con Ed, the bank." "Wait with me, will ya?" she asked. "I hope it comes," she said of the single elevator running that day. An out-of-order sign hung on the other elevator's dung-brown door. "There it is," she said. We gazed at the double row of illuminated floor numbers above the elevator door; 20 lit up cherry red. Dottie leaned on the ledge below the mailboxes while we waited. A young Latino man with heavy brows and a purposeful stride opened a second-floor mailbox with a brisk, efficient turn of his key. "Sorry," Dottie said and let him by. The man scooped up his mail without a word and headed to the stairwell. Dottie moved towards the elevator bank, though the illuminated floor indicator showed it stuck on 16. A Chinese food delivery man carrying a bulging plastic bag entered the lobby, trailed by a petite Black woman who appeared in her late 30s, wearing a knitted cap and shiny black jacket, hands dug in her pockets. A woman with a stroller and yawning child by her side followed. As our wait dragged on, more people packed the lobby, reminding me of the stateroom scene in the classic Marx Brothers' comedy *A Night at the Opera*, in which a motley crew of characters crowd into a closet-sized ship's cabin. The wheezing elevator finally arrived. Dottie headed inside first. The Black woman smiled at me, as if pleased that Dottie had company.

YOU CAN LEAVE, BUT IT'S GOING TO COST YOU

Cost weighed heavily in former bakery customers' considerations about where to gather. Many cited McDonald's affordability as a major incentive to regroup there. Specials such as two breakfast sandwiches for $3 and other monthly promotions reduced prices further. Senior discounts on hot beverages lowered the price to 94¢ per cup of coffee, less for tea. Dottie recited her impressive knowledge of dollar-menu items, saying, "I can afford everything there. Works for me." McDonald's prices discriminated against no one and gave abundant purchasing options. Even people who asked for change usually collected enough to buy something.

Unlike the sleeker coffee shop next door, The Art of Coffee, Pete's made no lofty claims about its brew. The coffee was good and cheap at

$1.25 for a small cup. Two center beams contained merry-go-round shelves that catered to a range of tastes and budgets, from single-serving packages of Oreo and Linden's cookies for $1 to more expensive Kashi brand cookies and other organic snacks. A salad bar housed hot and cold food, including salad, lo mein, sweet plantains, mashed potatoes, pineapple and cantaloupe wedges. Commercial refrigerators lined the right wall and contained numerous soda brands, along with cartons of milk and Tropicana orange juice. A separate refrigerator stored pricier, brightly labeled Odwalla fruit juices and Naked smoothies for $4.50 per fifteen-ounce bottle. But most former bakery patrons and I only ever drank tea, coffee, water, milk, Snapple, and canned soda.

The variety of stock was not accidental. Pete's served a cross-section of customers comprised of Hudson Towers building workers, moneyed residents of nearby market-rate apartments, and longtime older residents. The store's array of products also reflected its location, three blocks from the Hudson River. Retail spaces grew sparser and residential buildings predominated, including a mix of prewar town houses, the massive, block-long Hudson Towers complex, and newer condominiums closer to the river. Within this neighborhood context, Pete's also functioned as a small supermarket. In addition to prepared food, customers could buy staples like milk, eggs, bread and other household items such as dog food, paper towels, and cans of WD-40.

Pete's buffet of options for different income levels had managed to attract its share of former bakery customers. A comparison of Eddie and Sylvia's purchases at Pete's revealed wide variation in spending. Over four years, I never saw Eddie eat anything. In warmer weather, he drank a can of ginger ale for $1 and in winter sipped a small tea for $1.25. Meanwhile, Sylvia often ate dinner there, either salad or sandwiches in the $7 range. Over time, she bought more there, including paper towels, granola bars, yogurt, and milk. She knew that she paid more for these items and was able to tick off the lower prices of similar items at the supermarket around the corner. Her efforts to bolster

Pete's business also reflected apprehension about losing another neighborhood place. "I don't want to get evicted again," she joked a few months after the bakery closed. She shared concerns about a slowdown in Pete's business, noting the trickle of customers, and observed that the owner put less food in the salad bar because he couldn't afford to throw out what hadn't sold. "That's what the working people want to eat. The ones who labor need food to get them through the day," she said, worried about the effect of diminished buffet offerings.

At Pete's, Phyllis extended her role as arbiter of praiseworthy behavior and often endorsed Eugene's healthy eating habits.

"That's very good," she gushed, her eyes scanning the components of Eugene's dinner that evening. "Salmon, salad, avocado, tomatoes," she said, listing each item that garnered her approval.

"He always eats well," Lucy concurred, praising Eugene in the third person as though he were absent. "You always eat well. It's important," she said, turning to him and looking into his eyes. "Do you always drink milk?" she inquired, pointing to the empty pint-sized milk container on his tray.

"Every day. Always have," he said.

"That's good, that's good. More people need to do that, take care of themselves," Phyllis said. "Some people, you should see what they eat. Junk. That's why they get so fat. And they wonder why they get sick."

Phyllis started in with her own tale of virtue, a story she had told us more than once. She and a few neighborhood women went to an old-school Puerto Rican restaurant known for their generous helpings of such mainstays as rice, beans, roast pork, and flan. She asked them if they could make an egg-white omelet. "They looked at me like I was crazy. I felt bad and apologized," she giggled with obvious glee.

In the first few days of its opening in the old bakery storefront, Sylvia and I tried Loaf, the new bread bakery. She took a menu to show Eugene, who vowed not to go. I paid $4 for an iced coffee and Sylvia paid $2.75 for a small hot coffee. She had more financial security than many other bakery regulars and rarely complained about money stresses, though she admitted concern about her climbing rent. Mysterious fees appeared on her monthly bills, but she paid them without saying anything. "I don't want to make waves." That day Sylvia raised her eyebrows at the cost of her coffee and buttered roll. "They're [older people] not going to go for this." Surveying glass cases containing high-priced baked goods with Italian names, such as the "bambolonis," petite $3 doughnuts, she murmured, "This place is not for the neighborhood people. It's for a younger crowd."

For others, trying Loaf was not an option. As Sylvia and I sat, an older bakery regular named Juan, who lived in the housing projects, passed by without glancing over. Eddie also wouldn't venture in, due to his financial constraints and anger at gentrification's harm to long-time mom-and-pop stores. He often referenced his cost-cutting strategies, such as stocking up on canned soup and individual frozen pizzas on sale for $1 each. Years before he had trekked to two less expensive supermarkets fifteen blocks away. Unable to walk that far anymore, he waited until Wednesdays to purchase sale items in bulk with a 10 percent senior discount at the supermarket a block from his building.

Yet others, like Phyllis, visited Loaf more than once. She delighted in becoming a regular customer, mostly because the majority of the bakery's elder patrons had not frequented the new establishment, and she relished telling me about seeing "people from the co-op" (a euphemism for old people) complain about the prices. "They'll try it once, but they won't come back." She conceded the prices were expensive but claimed they posed no problem for her and raved about the new bakery. "I love it there." Phyllis also disclosed a private conversation with the new owner about his desired clientele. "He said he doesn't want people from the co-op coming," she said, elated at gaining the new owner's confidence and approval. Though she was a "person from the co-op," by confiding in her and gossiping with her about those less desirable customers, he distinguished her from other older people. Her patronage not only bought her higher-priced baked goods but helped secure her special status and some reprieve from the stigma of old age.

DIFFICULT BY DESIGN

Elements of spaces I categorize as "design," including decor, furniture, seating arrangements, and window placement, added or detracted from people's comfort and ease in socializing. For example, the bakery's seating arrangement alone hadn't guaranteed such recurring interactions, as observations at a nearby bagel store on a bustling avenue proved. Izzy's Bagels had a similar table arrangement but nowhere near the same level of interaction. The busy morning pace hampered the same spontaneous and leisurely banter. During quieter afternoons, people interacted more with technology such as computers and smartphones than with neighborhood acquaintances. This place drew fewer regulars, more tourists, and an overall younger crowd. People more often socialized as part of an established pair or group that had arrived and left together.

After the bakery closed, gathering required greater coordination to ensure others showed up to alternate locations. Whereas people could always find someone at the bakery, meeting elsewhere entailed making phone calls. Once there, physical features of the new spaces compelled greater commitment to interaction.

Phyllis called women that frequented McDonald's "the dementia club." She no longer went there as much. "You are what you are by who you hang out with," she explained. The women she was talking about preferred to sit near the entrance in an area surrounded by a railing painted the same fire-engine red as Ronald McDonald's hair. The section had a more intimate feel than the rest of the busy store and contained six tables with seating for twenty-four people—eight more seats than the bakery. Still, the layout felt more cramped, with tables for four instead of two. Greater distance between tables and ambient noise required people to sit *with* each other for any extended interaction rather than near each other. When the front tables filled, those in the spillover group had to seat themselves directly behind at the second table in the row. One day I discovered Jeannette sitting alone, trying in vain to insert herself into the discussion with people's backs towards her. She shouted to compensate for the distance. I sat with her, but after a few minutes I also felt left out of the larger group interaction and had to stand alongside the other tables to say hello and catch up with people. During afternoons, elders generally clustered here, while the after-school crush of teenagers held court towards the back of the store.

Eventually McDonald's roped off the teen area from the rest of the store, drawing these boundaries more firmly. Gladys, a Puerto Rican woman in her late 70s and former bakery customer, informed me about the purpose of the band stretched across this part of the store during a conversation about the prison-house origins of the teenage boys' baggy pants. "They [the kids] can't go past there," she said with a knowing nod. Carmen joked that the rope reminded her of a fancy night club. More dirty, retractable polyester belt than red velvet rope, it upheld a set of rules about entering this space. During afternoons, workers responsible for cleaning and unlocking the restrooms herded the after-school crowd behind the rope. Teenagers had to show a tray with their purchases to enter. Adults could also sit there with less scrutiny as I learned when I stepped inside without having bought anything. Though many former bakery customers complained about the teenagers' noise, many of them chose to sit in the back with them instead of in the front. They admitted missing the kids during their school breaks when McDonald's grew quieter and emptier in their absence. More than one person cited their preference for sitting in the back rather than near the store entrance because they wanted to avoid the old people there. Many elder customers in the front enclosed section predated the ex-bakery patrons, who had only recently started coming. A few integrated themselves into this preexisting group, such as Theresa, who befriended a 90-year-old woman who came daily with a middle-aged Asian woman who worked as her caregiver and assisted with tasks such as laundry and using the restroom.

For most people who came into Pete's Deli in the early evenings, the deli-cafe served as a grab-and-go place. Save for a handful of regulars, most didn't linger. Several darted in just to use the ATM. Others stayed briefly, like a young white woman with cascading brown curls in short navy dress. Her silver bracelet glinted each time she lifted the bottle of an aloe peach drink to her lips. She sat no more than fifteen minutes, her eyes trained on her salad while texting on her iPhone. Workers from surrounding buildings also hurried through. Their uniforms gave them away: the Hudson Towers doormen in blue button-down shirts with navy epaulettes and the porters and maintenance men in tan shirts with rolled-up sleeves and dark brown pants. These men usually left with plastic buffet containers or gobbled their food in a rush.

Pete's didn't promise an experience or atmosphere. In contrast to the coffee shop next door with its lime-green walls bathed in a golden glow from amber fixtures, long fluorescent bulbs flooded Pete's with sterile white light. After sunset this artificial illumination darkened the space, casting shadows on the exposed red brick wall and outdated wood paneling over the cash register. Crumbs littered the stainless steel table tops streaked with coffee rings. Lightweight aluminum chairs felt comfortable but not too comfortable. Eight tables and sixteen chairs squeezed near the entrance forced people to sit close to each other.

A sun-bleached poster reproduction of Van Gogh's painting "Café Terrace at Night" hung on an adjacent wall. The artist's rendering of outdoor tables and passersby on a cobblestone street underneath a twinkling sky reminded me of the slender thread connecting these public gatherings across time and space. When Pete's folding glass doors retracted in the warmer weather, the space opened to the street, transforming into an urban front porch. People stopped to chat with those inside seated at tables bordering the sidewalk. A couple in their late 40s who lived on the block always paused to exchange friendly words with Eugene while walking their dog, a Rottweiler mix named Ollie. "Hello Ollie," Eugene called with gusto. The dog trotted over to him, giving Eugene sloppy kisses as he hugged the affectionate animal.[4]

One day Eugene, Sylvia, and I sat at two tables jammed between the store entrance and the ATM. Eddie came in. He shot me a leery look as he passed behind Sylvia, his eyes darting down, then back up, as if to say, "What's she doing here?" He headed to the refrigerated case and paid for his soda. Upon returning, he had no choice but to take the last open seat beside Sylvia, across from Eugene, diagonal from me. In a loud, staccato voice, he told Eugene, "Get her outta here," pointing his right index finger at Sylvia. She raised her eyebrow at me and Eugene but said nothing. Eddie smiled, but it was always difficult to tell how much he was joking. Eugene, Sylvia, and I continued talking as if nothing happened. I'd grown used to Eddie's shtick, so this awkwardness also felt somewhat routine. Eugene continued an earlier thread of the discussion, about his ideas for patents and uncertainty about where or how to obtain one.

With Sylvia and Eddie present, interesting patterns of interaction emerged. Before Eddie's arrival, Eugene, Sylvia, and I participated equally in a three-way conversation. With the four of us together, Eugene and Eddie mostly talked sports and Sylvia and I discussed topics such as health, memories, and family. This gender division occurred not only in terms of discussion content but manifested in our positions at the table, as I faced Sylvia and Eugene sat across from Eddie. Because I spoke mostly with Sylvia when this quartet formed, I caught only snatches of Eugene and Eddie's discussion. Such interaction patterns reflected Eddie's avoidance of Sylvia, with whom he had never chatted in the bakery.

Other scuffles over space occurred at Pete's, most frequently between Sylvia and Lucy. Sylvia complained that Lucy thought of no one but herself. "She's in her own little world." She disliked Lucy's tendency to leave her folding cane lying on the floor. Even with the cane tucked beneath Lucy's seat, she cautioned in a high-pitched voice, "Lucy, your cane. Watch your cane." When Sylvia's warnings began, Lucy responded with a distracted, "What? Oh, okay." Later she answered with annoyance, "Yes, Sylvia, my cane, my cane, I know . . . ." Clashes also concerned table space. Lucy often paged through her copy of *The Daily News* and read the headlines aloud. Eugene quipped, "She's like our own mayor LaGuardia," referring to New York City Mayor Fiorello LaGuardia's reading of the funnies over the radio during a prolonged 1945 newspaper delivery strike.[5] Sylvia turned her face when Lucy held the paper open inches from Sylvia's cheek. "Uh, Lucy," she said batting the paper away. At the bakery, Sylvia had exchanged polite hellos with Lucy and sometimes engaged in small talk but rarely sat with her. In the four years since the closing, they sat together several evenings a week at Pete's. After one of these turf battles, Sylvia said exasperated, "Who is she? And where did she come from anyway?"

Of the neighborhood spaces I observed, Loaf proved the least old-age friendly and accessible in terms of design and layout. After its redesign, which gutted the old bakery's space, permanent exterior decorative coverings blocked parts of the window. Less natural light filtered through the downsized windows, and dimmer light fixtures darkened the new store, straining cataract-prone eyes. Heavy doors hindered entry for people with canes, walkers, wheelchairs, and reduced muscle strength. One woman waited patiently outside with her rolling walker until someone inside noticed and opened the door for her. The layout also posed new physical challenges. A table with milk and sugar for beverages stood several feet from the cash register and seating area. Eugene mentioned difficulty carrying his tray with his cane. Disappointed, he said that in the old bakery, the counter person had always put sugar in his coffee for him. Angelica and Dani had often brought items to the table for those who needed help. Other features, such as the tall pastry case, inhibited interaction with staff as people struggled to see over the counter. A long row of tables and chairs along one wall precluded the interaction possible between customers in the previous space.

I ALWAYS FEEL LIKE SOMEBODY'S WATCHING ME

Surveillance emerged as a primary consideration in the search for new gathering spots and helped explain why some places worked and others never attracted a following among those who had previously enjoyed low levels of monitoring.

McDonald's loose supervision helped make it the most reliable site to find former bakery patrons. The fast-food joint was a remarkably democratic space in terms of its unrestricted access, though perhaps too democratic for some. Persistent complaints stemmed from the place's chaotic and noisy atmosphere. Much of its appeal derived from the fact that "you could sit all day," as you could in the old bakery. Many didn't buy anything and imported outside food. This lax surveillance explained why measures like the rope caught me by surprise. While decals plastered on the entrance doors bombarded the entering customer with a laundry list of regulations (e.g., Restroom for McDonald's Customers ONLY; Only Food or Beverages Purchased in McDonald's May Be Consumed in McDonald's; No Loitering: 30 Minute Time Limit for Consuming Food), the staff inconsistently enforced these rules and few infractions, short of violence, got anyone expelled or even merited a warning. The place attracted people asking for money and those who appeared to suffer from mental health troubles. For example, most afternoons a middle-aged Black man sat by the window shifting in his green oversized puffy green coat while talking to himself, the passersby outside, or sometimes shouting at the empty space in front of him. But as long as people did not threaten or aggressively harass others, staff left them alone. Only once I saw someone kicked out after attempting to engage in a sexual act in the restroom. After a worker escorted her screaming from the restroom, she threw a tray at a cashier before the manager threatened to call police. Similar tolerance also extended to the teenagers who congregated after school, from roughly 3 to 5:30 p.m. in the afternoon. They may have acted rowdily (yelling loudly, play fighting, throwing cups and ice cubes), but as long as they refrained from violence, workers also left them alone.

Weeks before the bakery closed, a regular named Arthur arranged for regulars to regroup at a diner he and many others frequented a block and a half away. This arrangement lasted only a few days. People spoke of not feeling "comfortable." Advance word of the ground "rules" that governed space at the West Side Diner circulated: you had to buy something; you had to leave a $1 tip; you could only hang out in the section cordoned-off for former bakery patrons between 11:00 a.m. and 2:00 p.m. People disliked the waiters' presence and believed their true function wasn't to serve but to monitor. Days later, people migrated to McDonald's and Pete's. When people first decamped to Pete's, they felt the owner and staff watching. "I kept buying things," Phyllis informed me, "because we sat for hours."

While most people avoided regrouping at the West Side Diner, some like Maureen came regularly on their own. Two years after the bakery closed I ran into her there. She had established a new solo routine after Tom's nursing home admission, during the same afternoon hours they used to go to the bakery. A clear plastic tube looped around her nostrils from her portable aluminum oxygen tank. Through her wheezing she relayed a recent hospitalization for pneumonia: "I had a collapsed lung. I'm lucky to be here. And all those years I took care of Tom, I was so exhausted, and I didn't even know how much." Maureen died a little over a year after our meeting that day. She was 85. Tom passed the following year, at age 88.

As people like Sylvia and Eugene became morning regulars at Pete's, their self-consciousness faded and they felt greater liberty to linger if they followed the same golden rule that operated at the bakery—the necessity of buying something, anything. After Pete's owner left in the early afternoon, a more relaxed atmosphere prevailed, though not to the same extent at the bakery. The young Mexican men who operated the cash register, prepared sandwiches, grilled food, and made deliveries, cranked up the volume on La Mega 97.9 FM, a Spanish-language music radio station. They gave away free buttered rolls and prepared extra large sandwiches for regulars like Sylvia, whom they affectionately nicknamed "Corazón" (which translates to "heart" in English). Compared with nuisances such as a steady stream of aggressive panhandlers, well-behaved old people who wanted to sit for a few hours hadn't concerned these workers. And they looked out for their regular elder customers. Whenever Eugene failed to show up a cashier named Ricardo asked, "No Mr. Eugene today?"

ALL THAT YOU CAN'T LEAVE BEHIND

Landlords' demands for ever higher commercial rents limit places where less affluent older residents can socialize. My longitudinal observations find that place magnifies in significance for people in late life as declining health and mobility, less discretionary income,[6] and surplus free time in retirement keep them closer to home. Dwindling gathering spots disproportionately harm the lowest-income elders with the fewest of these resources, those who have the habit of forming neighborhood-based relationships rather than branching out through widespread professional networks in retirement. This finding has implications for long-term residents aging in place in gentrifying areas as direct and indirect displacement shape their possibilities for belonging, community, and attachment to home and place.

In cities undergoing gentrification, defined as the process by which higher economic classes come to dominate residential and commercial uses in an urban area, older adults must grapple with the practical and emotional consequences of a changing retail landscape, including indirect displacement from commercial gentrification. The loss of places may result in grief, as occurred in this study and as prior research has demonstrated. Sociologist Melinda J. Milligan's study of a university campus coffee shop's move to a new location reveals the employees' attachment and feelings of loss with displacement, defined as "an involuntary disruption in place attachment."[7] Similarly, psychologist Marc Fried's study of forced residential relocation in Boston's West End finds the majority of displaced residents experienced grief, with a significant percentage reporting long-term sadness and depressive symptoms.[8]

But while public places may promote gathering, limits exist on the community people can form. Interactions can simultaneously ostracize some and foster inclusion and cooperation for others. While in theory public places let everyone in, in practice they can exclude people as groups carve out spaces for themselves and create their own private and intimate zones.[9] Attachment can encourage people to take better care of spaces and their denizens, but too strong a sense of ownership can breed hostility, fear, and resentment in those impeded from full access.[10] Urbanist and sociologist William H. Whyte's study of "small urban spaces" such as outdoor plazas demonstrates how even seemingly inclusive places can shut people out. Due to worries that popular public places will attract the "wrong" people—"undesirables" such as people without permanent housing and those suffering from addiction—businesses may create spaces that no one with other options would want to spend time in. Such unattractive places usually lack seating and have features such as ledges with metal spikes, which discourage resting.[11]

Gentrification has both expanded and limited elders' use of public spaces, offering new establishments and increased safety while also threatening and closing longstanding businesses, thereby curtailing possibilities for belonging. Writing about neighborhood changes in early 1960s London, sociologist Ruth Glass defines gentrification as a process in which more affluent middle classes "invade" working-class areas and convert formerly shabby residences into expensive homes. She writes, "Once this process of 'gentrification' starts in a district, it goes on rapidly until all or most of the original working class occupiers are displaced, and the whole social character of the district is changed."[12] I use a similar working definition, focusing on the gentrification of commercial spaces and indirect displacement of lower-income patrons through exclusionary practices and processes that make them feel unwelcome economically, culturally, and socially.

As gentrification has remade cities in the United States and around the world, urban scholars have broadened their understanding of gentrification beyond direct residential displacement to include more indirect effects on neighborhoods and residents, many of whom remain amid drastic change. Geographer Mark Davidson argues gentrification scholarship has dwelled on direct displacement while devoting insufficient attention to more subtle forms of displacement.[13] Building on urban planning scholar Peter Marcuse's notion of "exclusionary displacement," which examines broader affordability pressures beyond the removal of lower-income residents in favor of wealthier occupants, Davidson identifies three forms of indirect displacement (economic, community, and neighborhood resource displacement) that help explain changes in the social character of a gentrifying neighborhood.[14] "Indirect economic displacement" occurs when a steady reduction in affordable housing and increase in upscale commercial and residential buildings draw affluent residents and edge out older residents and their friend and family networks. "Indirect community displacement" involves a loss of power for longstanding residents to define place identity, participate in local politics, and determine the provision of services with the influx of newcomers. "Indirect neighborhood resource displacement" refers to a process in which the replacement of community infrastructure and services leaves original residents feeling like outsiders, such as when new businesses cater to a wealthier clientele.

As the infusion of economic and cultural capital gentrifies an area and spurs new commercial and residential construction, consequences for remaining lower-income residents include growing discomfort, disconnection, and apathy. With the loss of power to define their urban spaces and with an eroded working-class clientele for modest businesses, longtime residents feel "out of place" amid the proliferation of products and aesthetics for moneyed neighbors. Out-of-reach prices for new goods and services compel some to travel to less expensive areas to accomplish essential errands like grocery shopping.[15] Although researchers may encounter difficulties identifying, measuring, and conceptualizing indirect displacement, Davidson urges recognition of its importance alongside direct displacement.

In addition to economic pressures, urban policy scholar Derek Hyra argues for increased attention to the social consequences of gentrification for longtime residents in areas undergoing transition. For example, participants in Hyra's study felt that new amenities such as bike lanes and dog parks were not intended for them and sent a symbolic message they no longer belonged.[16] Sociologist Sylvie Tissot's study of public places such as dog runs reveals how seemingly open spaces can also create exclusive social boundaries, allowing gentrifiers to espouse a commitment to diversity while also distancing themselves from less affluent neighbors.[17] In this context, dog runs become sites of power struggles in which the more privileged exert control and restrict access while projecting community inclusiveness. And urban geographer and sociologist Ryan Centner's focus on elite consumption practices of young, urban professionals flush with dot-com-era wealth in San Francisco demonstrates how subtle processes steeped in privilege can exclude. His concept of "spatial capital," defined as the social power to take over and make over place, surfaces in accounts of discomfort in formerly familiar places. For example, one interviewee spoke of feeling unwelcome in a neighborhood bar packed with new customers and temporarily relocated to other nearby establishments until the dot-com bust thinned crowds.[18]

Socio-cultural displacement and the dismantling of community infrastructure that Davidson and Lees describe have implications for elders.[19] Their discussion of the intimacy of place and home has special relevance for those who lose the "emotional geographies" that anchor identities and personal histories.[20] Dislocation often produces grief, which older adults may feel more acutely.[21] As Hyra finds, longtime residents may experience weakened attachment to place as they no longer recognize their neighborhoods. Slackened bonds may also lead to political displacement as old timers lose political power and disengage when newcomers join community boards, thereby relinquishing their say in future neighborhood developments.[22]

Recent scholarly work uncovers troubling trends about how long-term residents manage such sweeping neighborhood changes.[23] Potential negative effects for elders include higher housing costs, the loss of support networks, and the threat of eviction.[24] Indirect and commercial displacement burdens older residents who may have stable affordable housing but experience growing exclusion as the character of their neighborhood changes and makes them feel unwelcome.[25] In their study of gentrification in three London neighborhoods, Davidson and Lees found increasing social isolation, writing, "local place had often been reduced to home; collective existence now took place within four walls and extended little further."[26]

While gentrification bestowed benefits—in the form of safer streets, increased amenities, and upscale stores for those who could afford them—on longtime residents who managed to stay, the influx of younger, wealthier residents and visitors also set the stage for the indirect displacement of patrons from their modest socializing spaces. Limited choices forced those with the fewest resources to spend more time at a dwindling number of affordable and accessible places. The three major draws of McDonald's—low cost, loose supervision, and relative proximity—helped make it the most reliable site to find former bakery patrons. While some identified things that they liked about the space—the availability of its public restroom and inexpensive menu—many expressed dissatisfaction. As Phyllis's comments about "the dementia club" revealed, old age stigma tainted the establishment as elders competed for space with teenagers, another group with less power and status. People couldn't claim the same symbolic ownership of this public space as they had with the bakery, subjecting them to what I view as a "social eviction" as they contended with chronic insecurity about finding and keeping their places, making do with ones that no longer catered to them and their needs.

My study helps address sociologist Ray Oldenburg's call for research on the use and value of these "third" places to older people.[27] In the context of shrinking families and friendship networks, daily social interactions between strangers and "non-intimates" will continue to grow in prominence for urban residents.[28] My ethnographic data confirm the development of emotional place attachments and suggest that they serve as an important positive component of belonging for those aging in place.[29] Talk of the bakery among former customers following its closing revealed deep bonds to this place and its people. In the last days of her life in a nursing home, Dottie's daughter taped a snapshot of the bakery crowd to her dresser as comforting memento of home. Years later, people continued reporting sightings of former patrons in the neighborhood, reminiscent of how high school classmates, for example, remain forever associated. In the context of gentrification, such losses understandably result in a range of negative responses such as anger, grief, disappointment, and uncertainty. Long histories of patronage make certain places more difficult to replace.

Dottie's affection for the bakery reflected many former customers' feelings. Despite joking about the bakery's outdated decor and wobbly chairs, the cast of regulars mourned its loss for years. They spoke as fondly and vividly of the business as of people they had lost. Their attachment reveals how much the bakery had formed the center of their daily rounds and routines, echoing the observations of urban scholars such as Lyn Lofland about the transformation of public spaces into "home territories" that anchor people in neighborhoods and provide opportunities for repeated interactions.[30] For example, one older man who ate dinner alone at a nearby diner never lacked for company. He sat by himself at the same booth near the kitchen, beneath a flat-screen television ideal for viewing the baseball and basketball games he enjoyed. He chatted with the waiters as they dashed by, and they honored his nightly "reservation" by setting out a placard that read RESERVED to save his favorite seat.

For urban-dwelling older adults with multiple vulnerabilities, the accessibility of these public venues and the ability to make them their own provided crucial opportunities to connect. The elders I came to know cultivated genuine affinity for the staff and other regulars at these establishments, which they demonstrated with their continual "sightings" of former bakery patrons and reflections about how much they missed the characters who went there. I also felt the weight of their narrowed options as they struggled to cobble together some semblance of their old routines. As more businesses struggle with rising rents, the changing urban landscape will constrain options for those with physical problems and fixed incomes who remain in a neighborhood that meets fewer of their needs for social engagement. Indirect displacement and commercial gentrification have significant consequences for the well-being of long-term, older residents and deserve increased attention from scholars, policymakers, service providers, and community members.

6

THE STRENGTH OF
ELASTIC TIES

AT FIRST THE BAKERY'S COMMUNAL atmosphere and the closeness among its patrons evoked for me *Cheers*, a popular sitcom I'd grown up watching about life in a beloved Boston bar. As lyrics from the theme song describe in its memorable refrain:

> You wanna be where you can see, our troubles are all
>   the same
> You wanna be where everybody knows your name.[1]

But as I spent more time at the bakery and mined the sedimented layers of customers' relationships, I discovered that the complexity of their social ties far exceeded sitcom simplicity. A tension existed in these relationships. People craved connection, but they also wanted distance and often didn't know each other's names or personal details such as home addresses, phone numbers, or emergency contact information. Over years, I observed them develop closeness; they spent hours together every week and shared private information about their health and life's trials and tribulations. Nonetheless, they didn't identify each other as friends or confidants when I spoke with them directly about their ties. On the other hand, when people appeared to lack intimacy, an event or crisis revealed the surprising depth of their connections. This chapter focuses on understanding the blend of closeness and distance in these neighborhood relationships.

At Pete's, regulars such as Sylvia and Eugene engaged in animated discussion. This evening, like most, they ate dinner and sipped coffee at the two small tables sandwiched between the ATM and store entrance. "Anybody want?" Sylvia asked, pointing to her turkey sandwich slathered with spicy brown mustard. She usually offered everyone at the table a portion of her food. "You want half?" she asked again.

"No, no," Eugene answered. "Thank you."

I politely declined, but like a doting grandmother—though she wasn't anyone's grandmother, because she never had children— Sylvia placed half her sandwich in front of me. "Here. Take," she ordered. I knew better than to decline again and accepted with a smile.

On this chilly evening, Sylvia wore her honey-blonde-dyed hair piled atop her head and a navy turtleneck, dark slacks, and comfortable moccasin shoes sufficiently warm for the weather. Eugene sat catty corner with his back against the ATM, cane by his side.

Sylvia teased him, saying, "I notice you're leaning against the money machine. Is it keeping you warm?"

Eugene laughed. "Yeah, that's how I'm going to get the money," he said, wiggling his fingers as if to coax bills from the machine. More likely, Eugene sat at this angle, leg stretched, because of last year's hip operation.

"I went to see that movie about the computers. It was boring," Eugene said, curling his lips as though he tasted something rancid. He saw everything from art-house films to the most recent *Spider-Man* flick and offered us the first word-of-mouth reviews.

"What's it about?" Sylvia asked.

"Oh, well, there's this kid, at Harvard, and he starts Facebook with his friend. But then the friend sues him," Eugene said before trailing off, losing interest.

"What's Facebook?" Sylvia asked.

"It's where they can find you wherever you are."

"Oh, I don't want that. It's enough that I get, 'Where do you go?'" Sylvia's complaints referred to neighbors who asked where she went now that their old bakery hangout had closed. To throw them off her trail, she answered, "All over."

Eugene and Sylvia liked to laugh together and saw each other at Pete's most evenings and nearly every morning.

"The boss has been speaking to me lately," Sylvia said, referring to the middle-aged Korean storeowner. By evening he had left. "He asked me about you," she told Eugene. "He said, 'How do you know him?' I explained, 'Well, he's a friend and a neighbor.'"

Without missing a beat, Eugene added in a playful conspiratorial tone, "We met in prison." The three of us cracked up. Eugene squeaked with red-faced laughter and could barely finish a sentence. Sylvia laughed so hard she grabbed my arm to steady herself, and I teared up.

When the laughter died down and we had collected ourselves, Sylvia extended the joke, "We met at Rikers."

With a sly smile, Eugene said, "It was co-ed back then."

"Yeah, we were the last two at Alcatraz," Sylvia said.

The relationship Eugene and Sylvia had formed over ten years of face-to-face interactions suggested a deeper bond than an acquaintanceship or a "weak tie." Sociologists use this term to describe social connections that lack the intimacy of close friends and family yet move important information between networks with little or no contact.[2] Given their apparent closeness, I was surprised that they hadn't named each other when I used a popular survey question from the General Social Survey to ask them to list those with whom they had discussed "important matters" during the previous six months.[3] As with the connections among many former bakery regulars, Eugene and Sylvia's rapport revealed a relationship more difficult to classify. Their interactions fulfilled many criteria for "strong ties," such as mutual confiding, emotional intensity, frequent interaction, and reciprocity, but their accounts of this relationship suggested their connection would remain invisible in many network surveys.[4] Based on these measures alone, many people may appear isolated and without social support. When questioned, they minimized neighborhood relationships outside of close friends and family. But long-term ethnographic observations of their social interactions with neighbors revealed the presence of "elastic ties"—non-strong, non-weak relations between people who shared intimate details of their lives with others whom they didn't consider "confidants," close friends, or friends at all.

ELASTIC TIES

Though people typically didn't visit each other's homes or know each other's family or friends—sometimes they did not even know each other's first names—elastic ties provided social support that helped them organize daily life and feel socially involved. Their relations possessed intimacy and distance. People who didn't recognize each other as confidants nonetheless provided each other with the support and practical assistance typically seen in strong-tie relationships. Thinking of social ties as elastic rather than fixed as weak or strong better reflects the complex, shifting relationships people forged during informal gatherings with no explicit agenda other than spending time in public.[5] Like a rubber band, elastic ties stretched to accommodate the fluidity and spontaneity of social relations and people's need for autonomy and connection. The freedom to occupy indefinitely "in between" positions allowed people to reach out as much as they desired or could and, therefore, to keep their options open as they balanced autonomy with commitment. Distancing served a protective function, and strength came from ties' elasticity, allowing closeness with distance and the space to pull back. Associations that appeared superficial or fleeting demonstrated their strength when mobilized during everyday challenges and crises. Yet people who appeared close by strong tie criteria expressed ambivalence about "friend" labels and implemented distancing strategies, including not learning or remembering each other's names. Though elastic ties allow flexibility, if stretched too far, the bond, like a rubber band, can snap. Their more fragile sense of obligation can leave people stranded in a crisis if demands strain the tie. Depending on context, elements of closeness and distance could coexist in a single interaction or tie.

Old age provides an opportunity to examine this fluid relationship that rises in significance during late life and may have implications for others experiencing similar conditions. Elastic ties develop in response to opportunities and constraints associated with the transition to retirement; the changing relationship to neighborhood and to time; and the loss of spouses, partners, friends, and physical ability.[6] Features observed in other relationships, which I will discuss, coalesce under these conditions to form a type of elastic relationship that allows older urban residents to secure informal support while preserving autonomy. Given the needs of an aging population, we must understand how elastic ties complement other kin and nonkin support. These findings represent an important step towards understanding network transformation later in life and build on prior scholarship that examines ties beyond those defined as weak or strong. Sociologist Matthew Desmond described a related category of tie, a "disposable" tie characterized by high yet fleeting support.[7] In contrast, elastic ties also offer strong support, but their distance allows participants to sustain their assistance of others longer term. They subvert conventional wisdom on friendship, acquaintanceship, and the strength of ties and enrich our understanding of how people build support networks across the life course.

THE DISTANCE BETWEEN US

How did people maintain such "intimacy at a distance"?[8] People interleaved distance into social interactions in ways that were more subtle than simply shunning others. They often infused moments of closeness with distance, seesawing back and forth in different situations. They created personal space and downplayed their ties in four primary ways: not learning or remembering others' names, avoiding "friend" labels, gossiping and bad-mouthing, and temporarily pulling back.

Many tended not to learn others' names, and if they did, it would happen only months or years after first connecting. Most never learned last names. Early on, I assumed that closeness required knowing someone's name and that ignorance of someone's name implied they only had a "nodding relationship" (e.g., exchanging a "hi" and "bye"). Extended observations corrected that faulty assumption and showed me that people who seemed close often didn't know each other's first names, which became clear during conversations I overheard about other frequent customers. For instance, people referred to one bakery regular as Fran in her absence. I presumed these speakers were close to her, because they interacted regularly; they spent considerable time together; and they discussed personal subjects, such as financial and medical problems along with happy childhood reminiscences. One evening, Lucy mentioned a woman who matched Fran's description, calling her Shirley. I revealed my confusion, saying, "I thought her name was Fran." To my surprise, Lucy said, "So did we." Through gossip, I learned that not knowing people's first names was more common than I thought.

Martin illustrates the depth of connections that appeared superficial or fleeting. I had known him for years but had not seen him until two and a half months into formal observations, when he started to return to the bakery in the evenings. Martin's health had declined for months, but I noticed nothing amiss other than lower energy. His drooping eyelids and perpetually downturned mouth matched his baseline depressed demeanor. He always shuffled rather than walked, staring down at his chest. I last saw Martin the night before Thanksgiving. Dressed in rumpled brown slacks and a cream-colored shirt, his sparse brown hair neatly combed, he brought a watch band for Eugene as a small gift and sat laughing with him and Eddie. Days later, I learned Martin had died. I asked Eugene if he had heard. "Martin who?" he responded, looking perplexed. "I'm sorry, I don't know who that is." The next day, he confirmed that he had known Martin by face, not name, and expressed his sorrow. No matter someone's advanced age or poor health, many felt surprised when a regular suddenly vanished.

Five months later, in a one-on-one interview, Eugene described the surprising depth of his attachment, though he had spoken with Martin mostly in the bakery. As we discussed people he'd met there, he mentioned that many had died. I asked for names, which produced this exchange:

EUGENE: What was his name? Was it Murray?

STACY: Oh, Martin?

EUGENE: Yes, Martin. I was very fond of him. I took his death very hard.

STACY: Oh, did you?

EUGENE: Yeah.

STACY: How come?

EUGENE: Well, we used to chat a lot. He was into nutrition. And he was always saying, "Have you heard of this?" "Yeah, I've heard of that." I'm sure I've told you this story. One day, I said, "You know I've got to get a watch band. Mine is broken." And one evening just before it was closing, he walked over and had a big box full of trinkets, of watch bands, a whole box full of things. He had made a trip especially over there . . . He was a wonderful man. It really brought tears to my eyes when I heard about it [his death]. And you told me. I didn't know . . . and I didn't know his name.

After the bakery closed, people used shorthand descriptions to identify former customers instead of their first names, including "the woman who took care of her mother," "the guy who dances," and "the man who scratches [lottery tickets]." Many blamed not knowing names on age-related memory problems. Initially, I also attributed oversights to forgetfulness. For instance, one woman with worsening dementia called everyone "Pepper" because she could not remember names. But I have become convinced that people sometimes didn't retain names as a deliberate strategy, though I cannot know whether they employed this tactic consciously. A woman in McDonald's discussed an extreme version of this strategy during our first discussion when I asked her name. She refused and explained her reasons for not revealing hers or learning anyone else's. "Oh, I don't give my name because then I have too many people calling me. Names don't matter, it's what's in here," she said, pointing to her chest. "What matters is the heart." I'd never encountered a refusal like that and felt guilty for asking. To show goodwill, I told her my name. "Oh, I don't know names, just faces. Thank you, but I won't remember yours," she said. During this interaction, I wondered if Gladys and Carmen, also present, knew her name. They didn't. "We don't usually sit with this woman. She's strange. She won't give us her name," Carmen said. At Pete's, I asked Lucy if she had ever encountered this woman. She hadn't, but the no-name policy piqued her curiosity, which she considered unfair. "Sure, she wants to know all the dirt but doesn't want to give anything." More than six months of sitting together passed until she finally revealed her name to Gladys, Carmen, and Lucy.

In some situations, people used their status as old people with failing memories to explain why they or others didn't know a person's name.

Eugene recounted how he asked Joan, a woman in her early 70s, if she had seen Gladys at the senior center. He told her that Gladys had some health problems that might interfere with her ability to care for herself. Unlike most people I observed, both women regularly attended the center. "And she said, 'Gladys who?' Can you believe that? She doesn't even know her name," he said, raising his eyebrows. "Just a few weeks ago, she told me she [Gladys] was her secretary." He said that after Joan determined she knew Gladys, she promised to inform the staff that Gladys might need help. Eugene repeated this anecdote throughout the evening. Lucy attributed Joan's ignorance to forgetfulness. "See, this is what you get when you deal with seniors. No one remembers anything. Mamma mia! We're all falling apart." Perhaps this oversight resulted from forgetfulness, but the name issue may run deeper than what people often referred to as a "senior moment." Not knowing Gladys's name freed Joan from a deeper obligation to help, though she agreed to alert the senior center staff. Friends who know each other's names and histories demand more in terms of emotional obligation and practical assistance, such as serving as someone's emergency contact.

Although people used forgetfulness to explain losing track of people's names, such "memory lapses" had not impaired their ability to remember nicknames. People used nicknames frequently and often exclusively. Years after Martin's death, I mentioned him to Eddie, who had known him for decades but hadn't known to whom I was referring. After several attempts, he finally exclaimed in recognition, "Oh, little Marty!" Although people could have used proper names, their range of nicknames for each other hinted not only at group standing but at strategies for preserving distance.[9] Whether nicknames indicated affection ("little Marty"), admiration ("the lion"), or derision ("turkey neck"), they helped people limit intimacy that may have forced them to transform their elastic ties into strong ties. For instance, Eugene spent many years referring to the man who tried to befriend him by his nickname, "the photographer." But in recent years, he also invoked his proper name, T. J., in moments when he acknowledged his finer character traits and described how T. J. had helped him, betraying some warmer feelings: "T. J. is quite a pain, but he is always checking to see how I am, leaving books for me in the lobby, et cetera. You wouldn't know it, but he's really quite brilliant, reads a lot. He was a first-class photographer for *The Daily News*. With him, you can't get a word in edgewise, so he is quite a bore. But he has a good heart."

The majority of the bakery's older customers lived alone like Eugene, whose case illustrates how this place helped potentially vulnerable people avoid isolation and supported those without family nearby. But for him, such support hadn't translated into strong feelings of friendship or generated a roster of confidants. When interviewed, despite receiving camaraderie from regular customers, Eugene didn't identify close friends or people with whom he could discuss important things. To my surprise, he didn't even mention Sylvia. But whether he identified them as confidants or not, he benefited from his frequent associations and the social resources he accessed at the bakery and other neighborhood places. Although he readily called the bakery crowd "friends," when asked later in the interview about classifying people as anything "from pretty good friends to close friends," he responded: "I only have two close friends, Maggie and her mother. Well, Maggie and I have known each other twenty years or more. We used to sing together in a group. We would go to hospitals and nursing homes to give a performance. And we have mutual friends." At the time of interview, he estimated seeing Maggie once per month, but years later, saw her far less frequently. Three years after the completion of fieldwork, Eugene admitted he had lost all contact with his friend and said, "I don't know if she's alive anymore."

When I asked Eugene the important-matters question, he didn't mention Maggie, though he might have assumed he included her because he already discussed this close friendship. I asked: "From time to time, most people discuss things that are important to them with others. For example, these may include good or bad things that happen to you, problems you are having, or important concerns you may have. Looking back over the last twelve months, who are the people with whom you most often discussed things that were important to you?" He answered: "They [his family] ask me what's going on, and I keep them abreast. And of course, my agent. That's about it. Everyone else is dead or moved away."

Eugene wasn't the only person who hesitated to identify those with whom he socialized most as good friends or people with whom he could discuss personal things. During an interview with Diane, I asked if she considered anyone at the bakery a friend. Like Eugene, she had a chatty disposition and had interacted daily with other patrons for the previous three and a half years when she moved back to the neighborhood after two decades in South Carolina, where her second husband died. After hesitating, she applied the friend label, but the long pause beforehand suggested she had done so only under pressure to categorize people and acknowledge their closeness. Yet, when I probed further, she refrained from using the language of friendship to describe these associations. When asked if she made close friends at the bakery, she answered "no" without hesitation. I asked if she had close friends. The woman she named had been a friend for decades. Although she didn't see her nearly as often as the bakery people, only about three times per month, she fit into a definable friendship. These cases represent a larger pattern among people who define friends as relationships spanning several decades, more often sustained through sporadic in-person contact and phone calls rather than frequent face-to-face interaction.[10]

Gossiping and bad-mouthing also created distance yet did not prevent people from spending time with those they disparaged. For example, Phyllis criticized Dottie about her weight, poor diet, and lack of exercise. "She's enormous. And do you see what she eats? She sits all day at the bakery, eating, eating," she said, lifting her hand to her mouth several times to punctuate her statement. These critiques increased as Dottie began having more trouble leaving the house because of growing physical limitations, during her hospitalization for a heart attack and transfer to a nursing home, and even after her death. Phyllis repeatedly denigrated McDonald's as the headquarters of "The Dementia Club" and discouraged Lucy from going there, saying, "You are what you are by who you hang out with." Yet Phyllis visited Dottie regularly in the hospital and updated others who couldn't or wouldn't visit about her condition. Though she curtailed her time in McDonald's, she continued going and maintained a relationship with Dottie until her death. Lucy also spoke of wanting to avoid "broken-down" and "dysfunctional" people, whom she lamented finding "everywhere," including in her building, the supermarket, and the doctor's office. Like Phyllis, she identified McDonald's as a bastion of "falling-apart women." But these protestations had not kept Lucy away.

When the obligations of strong ties overwhelmed, people also temporarily pulled back. For example, Carmen confessed to not wanting the responsibility of escorting Ethel, 90 years old, home every evening from McDonald's. Theresa had walked Ethel home because she suffered from vertigo and had no one to accompany her. After Theresa moved closer to her brother in New Jersey because of worsening dementia, Carmen avoided McDonald's for weeks. She told me she felt so much pressure to take Ethel home that she stopped coming. Days later, Lucy revealed similar pressure and declared, "I didn't want that job."

THE DEMANDS OF ACKNOWLEDGED FRIENDSHIPS

During crisis, the obligations and stresses of declared friendships surfaced. In these situations, many either rallied around the person in need or withdrew. Some chose a middle ground, steering clear of deep involvement but helping more modestly. Even those who gave significant help incorporated distance into accounts of their participation. The cases of Gladys and Dottie illustrate the pushes and pulls most people experienced as they supported others in late life and why people may avoid acknowledging more people as friends.

At Pete's, Lucy informed Eugene, Sylvia, and me about Gladys. Lucy spent time with former bakery patrons at Pete's and McDonald's and often carried information between sites. One evening Gladys had an "episode" minutes before Lucy had arrived at McDonald's.

"They wanted to call an ambulance, but Gladys wouldn't go," she said. Gladys's friend Carmen asked her to stay with her overnight, but she declined.

Carmen's boyfriend had recently recovered from hernia surgery at her apartment. Eugene joked, "It sounds like an annex of St. Francis's hospital."

Lucy lamented, "I was just looking for some company, somebody to talk to and I get pulled into this . . . dilemma. Well, I don't need that senior group."

Eugene mentioned that Joan, another Pete's regular, knew Gladys through the senior center and suggested that someone there might intervene.

"Yeah, maybe she [Joan] can help her," Lucy said.

Three days later Lucy updated us on Gladys's situation: "Carmen said the place was a mess." Carmen later confirmed Lucy's account. She had checked on Gladys but that day she would not open the door. "It's a burden to be the only one going over there," she said, distress etched on her face. Her heart condition made the walk strenuous, though Gladys lived only three blocks away from McDonald's. As far as Carmen knew, no other friends, acquaintances, or neighbors had visited. She also said Gladys had feuded with her family for years, complaining that her nephew stole money and household items such as linens from her.

"But I think she loves him; he's the only one that helps," Carmen said, adding that his assistance had enabled Gladys to keep her apartment after the co-op initiated an eviction case against her years before. She didn't know his whereabouts or have his phone number. She informed the co-op's senior center about Gladys's situation but expressed frustration that they neglected to say how they planned to assist, leaving us wondering if, when, and how they would intervene. "I don't want to be stuck with this," she said, but she also felt conflicted about involving an outside agency. Her annoyance and motivation for the call surprised me. Given Carmen's status as a retired social worker, I expected she would say something more altruistic like, "Gladys needed more help than I could give." Years later, in early midlife myself and able to reflect on my own decades of caregiving, I came to better understand her need to draw boundaries and limit her giving.

I accompanied Carmen on her next visit. We met at McDonald's beforehand, and Lucy sat with us. Carmen asked if she wanted to come.

"No, that's okay," Lucy said in a clipped voice and soon left for Pete's.

Halfway through our walk to Gladys's, Carmen stopped suddenly and caught her breath. "I feel like I don't want to go over there." But after a few moments of consideration, she decided we would go. "I have a guilty conscience," she said, pressing on.

We rang Gladys's doorbell and strained to hear signs of life behind the steel door. After several long seconds Gladys cracked open the door and leaned on the doorjamb, eyes narrowed. Carmen asked if she had eaten.

"That's where I was going," Gladys sighed. Her natural olive complexion took on a grey cast, and she looked thinner but appropriately dressed in a black beret—her steely hair pinned into a ponytail—jeans, knit top, and lightweight jacket. Gladys searched for her keys, still leaning on the doorframe.

"Can we look?" I asked. She handed over her purse, but we found only an asthma inhaler, no keys or money.

"That's okay," she said and began to shut the door behind her. Carmen and I tried to persuade Gladys to locate her keys before leaving. She suddenly listed to her side, grabbed the chain lock, and pressed her face against the doorjamb. I proposed that Carmen go inside with her while I picked up a sandwich for Gladys from the closest deli, two blocks away.

When I returned I saw the full extent of the "mess" that Carmen had alluded to days before. The apartment looked like a scene from the television program *Hoarders*. Debris along the walls recalled wreckage from an earthquake or tsunami. Mountains of random items, such as unopened mail, jumbled clothes, books, loose batteries, stray dollar bills, and a pint-sized carton of expired milk from the senior center, piled along the foyer and left only a narrow path to the living room. I accidentally stepped on a cracked mirror lying in the hallway to the bathroom, further crushing it. Blotches that resembled dried blood, perhaps shoe polish, dotted the hardwood tiles, and a fine haze of dust permeated the stuffy air. I felt exhausted from surveying this mess when I found Carmen seated on the living room heating convector. She rubbed her eyes like a tired child at the end of a long day. I could only imagine her discomfort, given her heart problems, earlier anxiety, and the stress of seeing her friend in this state. Gladys sat on a cleared-off section of the beige couch beside piles of newspapers and books— the only free spot to sit in the entire apartment. Clutter buried every other piece of furniture, and crumpled newspapers littered the floor. Carmen knocked over a glass vase near the convector when she scooted over so that I could also sit. When Gladys spilled the Coca-Cola I'd brought her, while looking for paper towels, I discovered an empty, broken refrigerator and no working lights in the kitchen. She seemed overwhelmed by the task of eating.

"Just eat some of the inside," Carmen said, directing Gladys to the turkey sandwich gently but firmly. She remained silent and gazed listlessly at her cluttered bookcases.

"The center's giving cooking lessons. I should make dinner and have you over," Gladys said suddenly, trailing off into a different reality.

Carmen tried again. "If you can't eat the whole thing, just pick at the insides." After more prodding Gladys chewed some turkey. During the two hours Carmen and I spent with her, she ate nothing more.

The crisis reached a resolution when Gladys's nephew walked in two hours after Carmen and I arrived. We learned that he lived in Queens and had just returned from a trip. He had no idea of Gladys's distress but expressed gratitude for our help and left us his telephone number in case of another emergency. Before her nephew arrived, Gladys's condition and the household dangers had prompted Carmen and me to discuss with her the possibility of going to the hospital, which she refused; privately, we considered calling 911 if she continued to decline. Her nephew's unexpected entry saved us from these difficult decisions and our fears of exposing her to the authorities, given the prior eviction attempt. He promised to clean up. Carmen's involvement with Gladys demonstrated the stresses "friends" shoulder when an older friend had health problems and weak family support. While Carmen stepped forward to care for Gladys, at times she also resisted the language of friendship. "She's not a bad person," she gave as the reason why she helped someone she had known for twenty years and socialized with several times a week for at least the past five years but did not call a friend. By commonsense standards, she acted as a good friend nonetheless.

Lucy's involvement from the sidelines revealed how people negotiated their desire to join others, while also preserving the self against demands they considered threatening to their well-being. Despite complaints about older "dysfunctional" people, this situation hadn't scared Lucy away from McDonald's—she accurately and enthusiastically updated everyone with Gladys's deterioration and others' efforts to help. She even asked her therapist for a crisis hotline number to give to Carmen, who became the de facto crisis manager. Not claiming friendship with Gladys freed Lucy from deeper obligations. She avoided calling on Gladys's behalf and visiting her but still went to McDonald's to connect with the company she craved. She could socialize with "dysfunctional people" but not see herself as such or as responsible for other troubled people.

Dottie's connection with others saved her life the day she suffered a heart attack, more than a year after the bakery closed. When she failed to show up for a birthday party in her building's community room, a neighbor found Dottie collapsed in her apartment. She spent six weeks in the hospital, followed by two more in a nursing home before she died at 83 years old. Circumstances towards the end of her life mirror health declines that threatened many people's ability to live independently. Before she died, Dottie, her family, and her extended neighborhood network of social ties wrestled with tough questions about her future medical care and living arrangements. At this crossroads, Dottie confronted life-altering losses of physical ability. Her feeble condition worsened while she remained hospitalized indefinitely. When she finally moved to a nursing home, Dottie and her family confronted three searing realities amid great uncertainty. The physical consequences of the health crisis and the specter of death loomed first, followed by adjustment to institutional living with its concurrent loss of privacy and control, and finally the permanent loss of home and neighborhood.

Dottie's rapid deterioration tested the strength of people's ties. She received many regular visitors, but not everyone went. Some claimed that their own health problems prevented them. "My doctor said I'm not supposed to go into hospitals," Sylvia mentioned whenever Dottie's visitors updated the group at Pete's about her condition. Others provided no explanation. Though Phyllis had distanced herself from the McDonald's group, she visited Dottie regularly.

Lucy proved one of Dottie's most reliable visitors but accumulated stresses on her almost daily visits, such as emotional drain and fatigue from skipping dinner and getting home late. Nevertheless, she admitted, "It's hard to leave. I have a girlfriend who told me, 'You're not family; I'm going to time how long you stay there.' She's right." Lucy said that Linda, Dottie's only child, compelled her to visit more and stay longer. "I try and be there for Linda, but my day is right around the corner, and who's gonna be there for me?" Lucy said that she was glad when I visited because she could leave earlier and hypothesized about others' absence: "You know what, we're old people, and we don't want to see it, because we're getting old. It's scary. They don't want to see what's happening to Dottie. They told me so. They said, 'We're only gonna stay an hour.' Phyllis told me this, and Carmen only comes once in a while." Lucy explained how the group interpreted her frequent visits, adding, "You know, I'm considered Dottie's best friend." She didn't say whether she or Dottie agreed.

I also found these visits emotionally and physically exhausting. Dottie could barely lift her arm to feed herself and could no longer walk, so visits often involved tasks such as filling water cups, cutting food into small pieces, and communicating Dottie's needs to nurses and doctors. Her eyes remained unfocused, the lids puffy and dark, and without dentures her words came out garbled. Black, purple, and yellow bruises riddled her arms from IVs inserted daily for weeks. Though Dottie retained a gallows humor about her situation until the end, she became disoriented and less accepting of the fact that she might never go home. Her heartache at the prospect of losing her apartment stood as the final step in a more protracted process of loss that had started in earnest with the disappearance of the bakery. Once that gathering spot closed, she fell further away from the group of regulars that had anchored her and admitted feeling depressed about losing contact with people she used to see there. On Dottie's armoire, her daughter taped a picture I'd taken of the bakery crowd, alongside a treasured World Series photo of Yankees baseball player Derek Jeter clipped from the newspaper. "I always knew where I could find Mom," Linda said, referring to the bakery. A few days before she died, while in the nursing home, Dottie shared her plans for her anticipated homecoming: "When I get back, I'm gonna have you over, and we're gonna eat good. I'll get some cold cuts, and we'll have sandwiches and Entenmann's cake. We're gonna have a party, you and me." She begged for company and feared dying at night when fewer staff attended to patients. Dottie's tears and pleas to stay "just a little longer" made it difficult to leave and recover from these visits.

As Dottie faced a permanent move to a nursing home, people debated where she should go. Her neighborhood ties thought she should live near her daughter to make visits easier. "Linda wanted to put Dottie in a place closer to where she lives, out in Queens, but Dottie said 'No,'" Lucy reported. "She wants to be close to her friends."

"Friends? What friends? Three friends," Judy chimed in.

"That's right," Phyllis murmured in agreement.

But Linda presented things differently and suggested that she also wanted Dottie to be "somewhere where her friends can visit her."

Framing this issue around proximity to family or friends perhaps revealed genuine concern but also represented a strategy to ease the pressure of visiting Dottie for everyone. If Dottie moved to Queens, her neighborhood ties would have difficulty traveling and a valid reason not to visit. Linda's concern for her mother's friends underscored her interest in not moving Dottie close to her, as her visits would conceivably need to increase in number and duration. Dottie already complained that Linda didn't visit enough, though she never missed more than a day. Prior to Dottie's illness, Linda saw her mother once or twice a month at most.

DON'T BRING ME DOWN: MOTIVATIONS FOR DOWNPLAYING TIES

Why do these older people downplay their ties? Three possibilities emerge: avoiding relationship risks and responsibilities (and thus protecting the self), avoiding the difficulty of replacing lost ties, and avoiding identification. These motivations highlight the benefits of elastic ties for people at risk of isolation who seek connection but who also, for good reason, inject distance into their interactions.

Three-quarters of those I observed discussed the challenges of remaining independent, and one-third noted how the stress of others' problems interfered with caring for themselves. For example, Lucy's and Carmen's avoidance of a woman with whom they had interacted daily for a year and a half shows the burdens involved with closer relationships. If Carmen and Lucy recognized deeper bonds with Ethel and identified her as a friend rather than simply another person sitting with them at McDonald's, they might have felt guilt for not helping or obligated to rearrange their routines to assist her. Lucy often said, referencing life's everyday hassles, "I used to be a fighter, but I don't have the energy for that anymore." The majority of those I spoke with offered similar statements about diminished energy compared with their younger selves. Their accounts of feeling overburdened support prior findings about older adults' sense of precariousness and needing to slow down, pace activities, and prioritize activities of daily living, such as cleaning and self-care.[11] Such public statements may also deter others from seeking their assistance.

The theme of lost ties arose almost daily. Early in Eugene's interview, he reflected: "I have friends, not many . . . most are dead or moved away. No, seriously, most are dead or moved away. I can just think of so many that have passed. And of course, my parents are dead." During the Thanksgiving and Christmas holiday season, while surrounded by people with whom he had interacted for years and who appeared to be friends, Eugene said much the same when asked about his holiday plans. He would spend those days alone working because "all my friends are dead." These statements reveal older people's difficulty replacing lost ties, which echoes earlier findings,[12] and may explain why important-matters or close-friends questions elicit responses about kin ties or long-term friendships but not the relationships I observed in public places. Such statements recall what the priest at Dottie's funeral said: "Death is not the end of human relationship." In some ways, these neighborhood figures acted as substitutes for lost ties. But, unable or unwilling to absorb them into their pool of long-term associations, people thought of relationships developed later in life differently. Upon death, interaction ended, but people kept the dead alive through reminiscence and memory. Sylvia built relationships with people connected to those she had lost and had befriended her husband's younger college classmates and the children of deceased friends. Like Eugene, she counted these enduring relationships as "truer" friendships. Of those with whom she had interacted in the neighborhood for years, she said: "God bless these women, but they're not my world."

Disavowing ties also relates to identification—specifically, avoiding the stigma of aging. Attachment to longstanding relationships reflects a desire to remember oneself at younger ages and in roles that correspond to those time periods (e.g., wife, mother, sister, etc.), roles that dwindle with each lost tie. Embracing new ties requires a higher degree of reinvention and reimagining than people in my study seemed willing or able to undertake. Shifting networks over the life course can mean that with retirement and the death of relatives, the workplace and family diminish as sources of strong ties and the neighborhood rises in importance.[13] This shift may account for some downplaying of ties, because people do not fully recognize (or want to recognize) that their friends and associates have changed along with routines. Old people do not often think of themselves as old,[14] and distancing from other elders may help some avoid stigma, as Phyllis did when she distinguished herself from those who gathered at McDonald's by referring to them as the "The Dementia Club."[15] Downplaying such ties and being selective when identifying friends helps older adults protect their self-image, albeit through internalized ageism. When I asked Eugene why he avoided senior centers, he answered: "I hate old people."

When others overwhelm, elastic ties allow retreat without confrontation. When Sylvia had had enough of Lucy's venting, she announced she would "take a vacation" from Pete's for a few days. "Yeah, it's nice to have a change of scenery," Lucy said, unaware that she had motivated this break. Three days later, Sylvia returned. When comparing neighborhood women with her lifelong friends, she claimed, "I never met such a cruel group." Phyllis also revealed her need for escape from Lucy and Sylvia six weeks after she had stopped frequenting Pete's as well. She disliked Lucy's "negativity" and celebrity gossip and Sylvia's jealousy of her closeness with Eugene. "I've been through that before. There's one man around, and all the women get jealous," she said. Phyllis described her avoidance of Pete's as part of a larger positive development in her life. She had also cut other ties and quit playing bingo. "I'm going to museums now, learning things, doing things on my own . . . It's a new life for me," she said. Her previous break from McDonald's and return when Dottie became ill shows the forgiving nature of elastic ties. After we ate dinner across the street from Pete's, she proposed going there "for a few minutes to say hello," suggesting that as much as elastic ties offer easy exit, these attachments remain difficult to abandon. Three years after the completion of fieldwork, I ran into Phyllis on her way to McDonald's. Despite her latest complaints about her frailer age peers, she still maintained some, if a sporadic, connection to them. The complexity of how people act as confidants towards each other in different situations underscores the slippery nature of this relationship category and the limitations of understanding how people meet their social needs solely through self-reporting, which we must approach with skepticism.

MEASURE FOR MEASURE: NETWORK APPROACHES
TO SOCIAL CONNECTEDNESS

The discrepancy between the interactions I observed and people's reports of their relationships posed a puzzle for me that I wanted to solve, guiding me to prior research on social relationships and networks.

Surveys have offered an important cross-sectional portrait of people's social networks. For example, the General Social Science Survey (GSS) social network module provides valuable data on Americans' core discussion networks, asking interview respondents to list those with whom they discuss "important matters."[16] When social network researchers discovered a three-fold increase in people who claimed to have no one with whom to discuss "important matters" and a decline of nearly one third (or the equivalent of one confidant) in people's overall social networks between 1985 and 2004, their findings sparked new debate over isolation, prompting concern over the uptick in people with no one to talk to and skepticism from researchers.[17] Debate ensued about whether such a dramatic social change without explanation was genuine or an "artifact" that resulted from data collection errors.[18]

Previous studies have attempted to understand what the "important matters" question captures.[19] Scholars agree that this name-generating question best gauges people's strongest ties, including kin networks and relations such as best friends and romantic partners.[20] Such emphasis has consequences for measuring the strength of less central ties, such as neighbors and acquaintances, which I argue matter more for older people with fewer core ties.[21] Most network studies ask about ties to family, friends, and less often neighbors. This method of generating a network roster seems straightforward, but as my fieldwork uncovered, people discussed personal issues, such as medical conditions, family problems, and money concerns, at length with people for whom they could not provide a full name and in some cases could not even provide a first name. If a person does not know someone's initials and feels uncertain about how to categorize them, they may not mention them on a survey. Furthermore, people might not identify public places as appropriate venues for discussing important matters and thus might not volunteer ties there as close contacts. This omission could result from not recalling interactions considered superficial or from a reluctance, in the absence of family or friends, to name these contacts as confidants because of associated feelings of shame or self-consciousness about lacking such well-defined strong ties.

Eliciting names to create network rosters takes considerable time.[22] Some surveys, such as the National Social Life, Health, and Aging Project (NSHAP), have pieced together more complete respondent networks through extensive probing. The University of California Berkeley Social Networks Study (UCNets) also employs an extensive egocentric network approach, asking respondents seven name-generating questions about different social activities and exchanges to form a fuller picture of people's social ties.[23] Yet the main surveys of older adults rely on the important-matters question to generate respondents' networks.[24] Thus, the assembled network hinges on the identification of close, defined relationships. These surveys also collect minimal information about respondents' neighborhoods and time in public spaces.[25] Data collected from smartphone-based ecological momentary assessments (EMA) ask respondents to report items such as health symptoms and the presence of others when "pinged" throughout the day, offering another lens into unfolding interactions that may prove consequential for health and well-being.[26]

Only after years of fieldwork did I discover the discrepancy between people's accounts of their relationships and my observations of these ties. When I asked my interviewees the important-matters question and discussed their relationships during participant observation, I found that people who appeared close rarely called one another friends, named each other as confidants or conversation partners, or reported affective or emotional feelings about one another.[27] Divergence between their accounts and actions stands as a compelling "warrant" for using observational methods to analyze the kinds of social relationships I observed.[28] Ethnography can serve as a powerful tool for uncovering and explaining discrepancies between what people say and what they do.[29]

Although improved design, increased interviewer training, early placement of egocentric name generators, and additional follow-up questions may resolve some issues,[30] I argue that the best surveys still miss in situ action and offer responses divorced from context. Observational methods can help network analysts uncover social relations that fall outside predefined survey categories by providing a window into a form of intimacy that traditional name generator questions are not designed to pick up.[31] Although useful in revealing close ties, given the closed-ended nature of many survey questions, name generators obscure the finer qualities of indeterminate relationships, which are easier to overlook. The intimate qualities of elastic ties challenge core definitions and assumptions of what makes a relationship strong, raising the question, What is closeness?

THE SPACE OUTSIDE WEAK AND STRONG

Despite the attention weak and strong ties have received in network research, some scholars have examined ties outside these designations and take the contradictions of relationships as a starting point of analysis. Sociologist Georg Simmel used the figure of the stranger to illuminate "the union of closeness and remoteness involved in every human relationship."[32] The stranger's simultaneous insider-outsider position speaks to the desire to participate in relationships and stand outside them. Straddling the line of belonging grants the stranger a freedom that those in dense networks lack. In Simmel's words, the stranger illustrates how "factors of repulsion and distance work to create a form of being together, a form of union based on interaction."[33] And in the present day, contact with strangers in urban areas occurs more frequently than in the small village Simmel describes.

Scholarly work in this vein has focused on intimacy between people with similar vulnerabilities. As the concept of strong and weak ties draws from middle-class experiences, such as white-collar employment seeking, ties outside this binary tend to serve people who lack access to resources.[34] For example, sociologist Elliot Liebow has observed that many African-American "streetcorner men" who gathered in public had elevated what others may have considered passing acquaintances— men about whose personal history, present circumstances, or even sometimes a last name they knew little—to close friendships.[35] Modeling friendship networks on kin relationships resulted in "going for brothers," in which two men presented themselves publicly as family, thus heightening the obligations and loyalties of friendship. Despite accelerated intimacy, Liebow discovered the instability of personal networks, writing, "Attitudes toward friends and friendships are thus always shifting, frequently ambivalent, and sometimes contradictory."[36] Desmond's study of survival strategies among evicted tenants in high-poverty neighborhoods echoes Liebow's findings. They relied more on acquaintances than relatives for food, child care, and shelter. However, despite high support, ties proved fleeting and unstable; Desmond calls them "disposable ties."[37]

Studying ties forged through these kinds of interactions also has implications for understanding how people manage significant social transitions, such as divorce, job loss, or moving. Further, observing people's actions over time pushes debate about network measures and methods beyond interviewee fatigue and problems recalling information to consider the deeper limitations of "confidant" as a relationship category. Sociologist Mario Small writes, "People are far more willing to confide personal matters to those they are not close to than they are inclined to believe about themselves, than network theory would propose, and than social science is likely to uncover without expanding the way it studies networks."[38] And yet, although these conceptualizations have advanced sociological understandings of how people accelerate intimacy in seemingly distant relationships, none have theorized the inverse and focused on the active distancing that characterizes elastic ties.

CONCEPTUALIZING ELASTIC TIES

Despite advances in network analysis, relationship categories have undergone less interrogation. Questions remain about the dimensions of supportive relationships, the stability of relationship categories, and what happens during interaction between network members. In this chapter, I advance an alternative approach to classifying those relationships that possess qualities of closeness but defy classification as either weak or strong; I consider people's statements about their social relations alongside my observation of their interactions. In light of discrepancies between what I observed and what people said, I approached their accounts of relationships with skepticism and did not view them as an accurate representation of their social ties.

Are elastic ties merely a species of weak ties? I argue that we need to conceive of them as a separate form of tie. Elastic ties do not simply provide passing acquaintanceship, information, or bridges to other groups and networks as Mark Granovetter has conceptualized weak ties.[39] Perhaps they originate in these forms but rather than becoming traditional strong ties, they continue to exist outside weak and strong. Instead, elastic ties possess elements of both types, which combine to create a new category that offers people a third way to insert distance but retain intimacy. As Sylvia remarked about her relationship with

Eugene, "I know him, but I don't." Comparing elastic ties with other relations that merge closeness and distance may help clarify the significance of these relationships for the study of neighborhoods, networks, and social support for elders and others with vulnerabilities.

Prior network research has developed not only a middle-class model for social ties but one anchored in experiences pressing for younger people, such as career advancement and workplace connections.[40] Other scholarship has found "business-like but intimate" relationships rooted in structured community service.[41] Though these "intimate secondary relationships," as sociologist Peggy Wireman calls them, meld distance and intimacy, their middle-class participants typically engage in additional activities and avoid deeper involvement with others. As sociologist Lyn Lofland points out, those relationships tend to have a positive emotional tinge due to a lack of attachment and the ease with which people can withdraw from them.[42] Despite their stated wishes not to, many people I observed became deeply involved with each other. Difficulty disposing of these ties make them different from the compartmental tie that Mario Small theorized, which was maintained by organizations and thus perhaps easier to drop.[43]

Although many people belonged to multiple networks, numerous constraints in old age converged to render the neighborhood not simply one of several, equal bases of partial commitment in a "community of limited liability" but a site of deepening investment.[44] While urban sociologist Scott Greer saw a rise in the importance of local geography among home owners or those who were child-rearing, in this case its importance rose with greater physical limitations, losses of family and friends, and unstructured time in retirement.[45] Repeated interactions at different neighborhood places also heightened obligations, offering insight into why people retain network members whom they find demanding and difficult and how people use distancing as a tie management strategy.[46]

Ties remained elastic for elders because of their precarious position later in life, which compelled them to work within growing constraints to meet their needs for connection and support. Contrary to Lee Rainie and Barry Wellman's claim in *Networked* that "people have more freedom to tailor their interactions" because "they have increased opportunities about where—and with whom—to connect," people in my study faced less choice in their interactions.[47] Their gathering spots dwindled due to a changing retail environment that closed establishments and posed economic barriers to accessing their replacements. Many became "stuck in place," lacking the social and physical resources to comfortably age in place.[48] As physical issues arose and retirement ended old routines, people formed ties with people they never considered important before, such as neighbors. For example, Sylvia forged relationships with younger neighbors following her husband's death. A middle-aged gay couple next door helped with small but daunting tasks, such as programming her television remote control. Sylvia had family but relied on these extra-familial relationships to avoid overstressing kin networks. Fashioning ties with neighbors also supported her independence and helped her rebuff offers from well-meaning relatives to live with them.

The elasticity of these ties also mirrors the unstructured time that older adults confronted. The majority avoided formal organizations or institutions, such as senior centers and church.[49] For the few who attended, these activities supplemented rather than structured their daily routines. The public places where people formed elastic ties helped fill gaps of time that caused unease for some but provided fluidity that befitted their freedom from rigid work schedules.[50] Moreover, the spaces that facilitated the development of these ties provided a reason to leave the house beyond completing daily errands and attending medical appointments. The majority expressed the importance of going outside each day. As Sylvia explained, no matter how badly you feel, "You've got to get out of bed and put your lipstick on."

The emergence of elastic ties also corresponds to a changing relationship to the neighborhood upon retirement and the end of child-rearing responsibilities. Given her half-century residence in the neighborhood, I asked Phyllis once if she remembered the storefronts along an avenue one block past her apartment. "I have no idea. I never went there," she said. Working multiple jobs and rearing two sons had left little time to explore. She had no practical reason and few opportunities to familiarize herself with this area until after retirement. Similarly, others became regulars at neighborhood establishments upon retirement or, for women who did not engage in paid labor, after their partners had died and children had moved away.

The desire for closeness and distance in social relationships is not exclusive to older adults or any group of people. As we move through our lives, we encounter situations that blend intimacy and detachment. For example, when I accompanied Angelica to a surgical breast cancer consult at a large public hospital, a woman in the waiting room disclosed her HIV status to me. She had told few in her social circle and said, "I don't care if you know, because I'm never going to see you again." A similar type of deep and spontaneous revelation can happen in a bar or any context where alcohol and other substances loosen lips and inhibitions. Encounters that blend confiding with the fleeting exchange of minimal identifiers carry less risk given the limited time frame and anonymity.

Other contexts in which people betray closeness but maintain boundaries over a longer period include the workplace or organizations such as a day care center.[51] We even have a special word, *collegiality*, for camaraderie and cooperation between coworkers.[52] Support groups, such as Alcoholics Anonymous, mirror some of the conditions and setting characteristics of elastic ties insofar as participants create spaces where communication about sensitive topics occurs on the condition of confidentiality. People share painful histories and struggles with addiction, often enlisting individual sponsors who support them outside the meeting space, but adhere to rules, such as avoiding last names, that protect privacy and maintain distance. Unlike elastic ties, these examples of closeness and distance have firmer boundaries, occur in more organized spaces defined by purpose or activity, or involve shorter time commitments.

Older adults and others without work and family to impose structured support have more needs, greater vulnerability, fewer options to form ties, and less incentive to get too close for fear of incurring the burden and expense of strong ties.[53] Elastic relationships rise in salience in late life as older adults work within growing constraints associated with retirement; physical limitations; and the loss of spouses, partners, and friends to meet their needs for connection and support, while preserving autonomy. Despite the limitations of my small study sample, based on the conditions I have identified for elastic ties, we might expect to find similar ties among people constrained in urban spaces, with high need, low resources, and weak support, such as those struggling with a serious physical or mental illness, unemployment, or living on the street. Sociologist Forrest Stuart's finding about how Los Angeles Skid Row residents constricted their relationships with each other due to the threat of unwanted police contact offers a clue to other contexts in which people may rely upon each other, while also maintaining distance.[54]

Shifting from viewing tie formation as a deliberate process to focusing on contexts that offer people opportunities to create ties would help increase researchers' chances of capturing the elastic relationships I have identified.[55] This study offers promising avenues for future investigations into the personal networks of older adults and others with multiple vulnerabilities. Integrating a deeper understanding of barriers to tie formation and designing social-network items to collect detailed data about respondents' time and place usage and daily routines would increase the likelihood that researchers might discover these less easily categorized, yet vital, relationships formed in response to multiple needs and constraints.

This chapter has presented an alternative conceptualization of social ties that defy categorization as either weak or strong—the predominate classification in most social-network research to date. Elastic ties more accurately convey the ambiguous relationships people forge in face-to-face interaction with others who fall outside the traditional parameters of close friends and family. They challenge conventional wisdom that weak ties provide information and strong ties provide support. Elastic ties incorporate elements of both as people with reasons to resist the commitments of deeper friendship but want to avoid isolation find a third way to feel connected but not stifled.

This strategic fashioning of ties recalls classic social theorist Georg Simmel's writings on the stranger and urbanist Jane Jacobs's celebration of the supportive but delimited social bonds that vibrant urban public spaces foster.[56] Despite their familiarity and regular interaction with others with whom they shared elastic ties, those I observed strived to occupy something of a permanent stranger status and longed for the freedom that came with distance. Elastic ties' mingling of distance and intimacy explains how a person who may claim to have no friends could still avoid loneliness or social isolation. My findings suggest that researchers may miss many nuances of social relationships if they neglect the fleeting and spontaneous interactions that form the backbone of elastic ties. At best, survey measures of social networks and isolation such as the important-matters question provide a partial picture of a respondent's social ties. At worst, they may distort social connections and the myriad ways people derive social support and organize everyday life. In situ observations of people's relationships provide a check against their own accounts and the static character of large surveys, which can only capture respondents' decontextualized claims about their networks at a single moment, thereby glossing the complexity of ties formed in daily interaction.

7

I SING THE BODY ELECTRIC

I have perceiv'd that to be with those I like is enough,
To stop in company with the rest at evening is enough,
To be surrounded by beautiful, curious, breathing, laughing flesh is
  enough,
To pass among them or touch any one, or rest my arm ever so lightly
  round his or her neck for a moment, what is this then?
I do not ask any more delight, I swim in it as in a sea.

There is something in staying close to men and women and looking on
  them, and in the contact and odor of them, that pleases the soul well,
All things please the soul, but these please the soul well.
—WALT WHITMAN, "I Sing the Body Electric"

IN OUR EARLIEST CONVERSATIONS EDDIE spoke of wanting to return to construction work due to boredom and financial need. But as he grew older and turned eighty, he dropped those discussions. His physical problems in the early years of the study worsened, and new issues emerged. Disabling pain and swelling in his ankles and knees immobilized him for days. Episodes of home confinement increased in frequency and duration, from every few months to every few weeks, and from a day or two up to a week. More recently, he also had an unexpected surgery, followed by a ten-day hospitalization, but would not reveal details of the medical condition that prompted this intervention. Despite these challenges, he ventured out as much as he could, while factoring in the physical consequences of shorter and long-distance excursions. For example, a rare trip to the United Kingdom to visit his son, daughter-in-law, and two granddaughters, exacerbated his knee pain due to sitting in the same cramped position for the seven-hour flight. Soreness and fatigue from the active time with family required a lengthy recovery of several weeks afterwards.

Examining the physical experience of late life is paramount to understanding how the increasing severity of bodily challenges pattern and often constrain older people's social worlds, their possibilities for interaction, and their experience of neighborhood and place. This chapter considers the ways that people in my study managed the physical and social self in the face of cultural pressure to eschew dependence and maintain autonomy. As the body's functional abilities deteriorated, people developed strategies to absorb these changes and assuage the threat not only to their sense of self but also to their relationships with others in the neighborhood, which suffered when mobility declined.

Elders vulnerable to isolation due to living alone and health and mobility problems cultivated a rich network of neighborhood connections in public spaces. In these third places they consulted each other about health-care decisions and frustrations they encountered in formal medical settings, receiving assistance evaluating their options. Underlying narratives of positive and negative experiences with the medical establishment was the desire to build trusting relationships with providers and to be known, seen, and cared for. This chapter also highlights how elders creatively patched together practical and emotional support when their needs went unfulfilled in other venues they found stigmatizing and ageist.

After the bakery closed Eddie never found another spot he frequented as much, but he dropped by Pete's a few times a week. Over the study's last two years, more often than not he declined to come, especially with increasing trips to the VA Hospital for tests, doctor's appointments, and physical therapy sessions. By the late afternoon he was exhausted and in pain from excursions to the clinic or shorter neighborhood outings, such as a two-block walk to the bank. He called to cancel, his voice heavy with apology, "I thought I could make it, Stace, but I can't do it." Eddie's name came up in discussions when people mentioned not seeing him in a while and wondered how he fared. I updated the group on any new information I'd learned from our telephone calls. Occasionally someone shared a recent sighting of him at Key Food Supermarket, Johnny's bodega, Good Neighbor Pharmacy, or by his building's mailboxes. Lucy mentioned seeing him "bent over" and bowed to illustrate the severe angle at which he hunched forward.

"He looks horrible, horrible," Sylvia said. "But he still has his quips," she added, unsmiling.

"Yeah, he looks real bad," Lucy agreed.

When Eddie finally arrived later than usual one evening, about 6:30 p.m., he joked about his absence. "Listen you ancient wimp, be there or incur my wrath," he said in our direction with a chuckle. He repeated the line again, laughing, and told Eugene that I'd scolded him with this command on the telephone earlier.

Eddie's physical hurdles surfaced when leaving Pete's. Getting up from his seat began a drawn-out process that lasted a good half hour to forty minutes. Eddie liked to walk out with me, prompting me to give him advance notice if I had to leave by a certain time.

"Okay, Stace," he agreed and turned his body sideways, away from the table, seeming to contemplate the infinitesimal steps of the procedure ahead. First, he grasped his empty soda can and rested his palm on the tabletop, then twisted his body in his seat, shifting side to side. Just as he appeared ready to get up, he began talking sports with Eugene before segueing into other subjects, such as local politics or other neighborhood happenings.

"In more important news," he said, looking at Eugene, "we're half a game behind in the American League." He described a television program he watched on ESPN, ribbing Eugene for not having cable. "Somebody here thinks he's too good for it," he said, turning to me and half covering his mouth as if telling a secret, though Eugene sat beside us.

Eugene played along. "Somebody's working," he said with a whiff of superiority, speaking of himself in the third person.

"Okay, let me educate you, then," Eddie said with a sly smile. He told us that the show ranked the most hated people in sports, with the top six on the list currently playing. "Number one was Michael Vick, followed by Tiger [Woods], Kobe Bryant, two NFL guys, both in Cincinnati, and Lebron James."

"I'm surprised to see Tiger so far up the list," Eugene said.

"Yeah, me too," Eddie said. "For all their talent, they all have big mouths."

Small talk appeared to distract him from the task of hoisting himself from his chair, and he suspended his efforts while chatting. Instead, he leaned back and settled in his seat. I felt frustrated when in a hurry, my patience wearing thin with Eddie's stop-and-go progress. Just as he seemed close to getting up, he stalled like a sputtering car engine. I stood throughout this process, concerned that sitting would encourage him to prolong his chitchat. But I also realized that my annoyance was illogical and could only imagine his own frustration and other emotions. He used conversation lulls to recommence his efforts and placed both palms on the table to steady himself, growing quiet and fixing his gaze on an invisible focal point on the tabletop. After a few minutes of concentrated focus, wincing in pain between the slightest movements, his shoulders relaxed and his efforts ceased. He continued with the sports thread and launched a discussion about football players that skipped college classes or majored in "dummy subjects" like "playground" [playground administration]. He told us about one player who studied this subject and landed on the dean's list. "And meanwhile, you got a gal who also made the list and is studying astrophysics." Then Eddie and Eugene talked about young athletes who spend their money on extravagant purchases.

"These young guys can't handle making all this money all at once," Eddie said, mentioning a news item about a young football player who lost an earring worth $50,000 dollars during practice. All of us laughed at the idea of groundskeepers bringing out metal detectors in hopes of finding the missing treasure.

"That's a year's salary," Eugene said.

Chitchat served as the connective tissue between these bouts of physical effort. Eventually Eddie gained enough momentum to eject himself in one brisk movement from his seat. His talking strategy allowed him to save face and distract from the time and effort he required to complete this physical act. Intentional or not, chatting may have also made this protracted process more bearable and blunted his pain.

Like Eddie, most people experienced emerging physical issues over the study's five years. Many of those I came to know juggled coexisting chronic illnesses, such as arthritis, diabetes, and high blood pressure. They often had sensory problems with hearing and eyesight. Some used hearing aids and many used reading glasses or wore glasses all the time, but a considerable number carried on without these assistive devices. This absence of helping equipment sometimes interfered with interaction when one party could not hear, read, or see something the other person wanted to share. Many had undergone cataract surgery. Most had experienced a serious health event such as cancer or a heart attack or endured at least one major surgery or hospitalization in their lifetimes.

Trouble walking presented one of the gravest challenges to independence and a major impediment to accessing the social world. People faced a range of walking-related problems, including balance, endurance, and pain from arthritis and other foot problems. Many relied on a cane for support and had a history of falls. At least four people mentioned a past accident that continued to affect their walking. Over time many couldn't maintain a brisk, steady pace, stretching a walk of a few blocks into a half-hour or forty-five-minute journey. They also accounted for external hazards that aggravated their already compromised balance, such as inclement weather, cracked sidewalks, bicycles and skateboards, and momentary attention lapses from everyday street distractions. Even the raised bumps at crosswalks, intended to provide a no-slip surface, created an obstacle.

People retained a modicum of independence through simple gestures. For example, at Pete's Sylvia often bused the table for herself and others, piling everyone's garbage onto a single tray. She took careful steps to avoid dropping any teetering items, such as Lucy's discarded candy wrapper and Eugene's empty Snapple bottle, as she carried everything ten feet to the trash bin. Sylvia insisted on performing this task every evening. At first, Eugene resisted.

"No, no, that's fine. I'll do it," he said softly but firmly.

Within the last year he had protested far less. Most times when Sylvia or I offered to take his trash, he allowed us to. We joked with her about her insistence on this chore. She called clearing the table her "job."

"Where's my tip?" she said with a wink. "I need tips," she kidded often, referencing the high cost of living. "My rent's not going down."

Whenever Eugene or Sylvia treated me to coffee and cookies, I noticed their determination to complete this undertaking from start to finish. Had I ordered my coffee at the register and plucked the cookies from the shelf myself, I'd have spared them extra effort, leaving them only to pay at the end. But they insisted on carrying out these steps and serving me while I remained seated. I called my order to Ricardo behind the counter, as Eugene or Sylvia pointed to me to indicate that he should make the coffee according to my usual specifications. From my seat I shouted the brand of cookies I wanted, raising my voice because they had trouble hearing from a distance. As they brought them to me, I felt somewhat guilty about two octogenarians with mobility issues waiting on me. But I realized the significance of these tasks for them, respecting their desire to complete them.

What did old people gain through these simple gestures? The benefits far exceeded the inefficiency and time required to accomplish them. They not only revealed the importance of routine but may have helped them develop greater efficacy, providing tangible evidence of continued physical functioning.[1] Such routines structured time and imbued daily neighborhood interactions with purpose. But they may have also reinforced people's awareness of tasks awaiting them outside and ingrained a sense of obligation to meet those demands, helping them achieve the goal of leaving home each day, which many mentioned as critical. The potential value of this subtle pressure supports the "person-environment fit" theoretical model of aging that argues that making things too easy for older people, such as in a hospital or nursing home context, can disadvantage them over time. A certain level of challenge and discomfort is necessary and perhaps beneficial,[2] otherwise they can become physically dependent on others and lose the ability to execute activities of daily living (ADLs) such as grooming, bathing, and dressing. This principle explains why, after a surgery, medical staff force a patient out of bed to walk right away even if it feels like torture and the last thing a person wants to do after awakening. The older people in my study seemed to intuit the necessity of pushing themselves to meet these challenges. They may have also learned from prior experiences watching their peers, so-called negative examples, who lost functional ability. And they may have also derived satisfaction from accomplishing tasks that someone with greater physical ability may perform without thought, which therefore held special significance for those who had lost some functioning.

TALKING BODY

Managing the body often involved talking about it, and almost every conversation contained on-ramps to discussing the body and health. Visits to health-care sites loomed large in most people's lives, especially those with multiple chronic illnesses. Some received primary care at one of two clinics located a few blocks from their homes, including one devoted to geriatric medicine. But many also traveled outside of the neighborhood, especially for specialized medical care. When someone gave a play-by-play account after returning from an appointment, regulars often joined in the post-game analysis. These interactions provided a chance to vent their own frustrations and compare health problems. After Eugene returned from the VA Hospital's geriatric clinic, along with medical updates, he always came armed with stories of how the staff had condescended to him. His accounts gave people the opportunity to opine about his treatment and share their experiences. He voiced his distaste for the protocol that staff followed to assess his physical status and mental acuity. They asked him if he could tell them the day of the week and to explain how he traveled to the clinic on his own. Once they took their assessment further; they removed Eugene's shoes and asked him to demonstrate that he could put them back on without assistance. Afterwards Eugene wrote a complaint letter to the VA hospital director and received a written apology.

"When I go to the doctor, it's always the same thing, 'What day is it, here are three objects, an apple, a dog, an airplane,'" Eugene imitated in a sing-song falsetto. "Then they walk away and quiz you later. Do you know how many times I've drawn a clock with its hands at ten of twelve?"

"Oh yes, I hate that one, when they leave you sitting there and walk away," Sylvia said, of the first cognitive assessment. "Uh huh, and what if you forget one of the things? What then?" she shuddered. "And the other one, where they write the letters, that's a tough one." She described another of these "tests"—her pejorative term—in which a doctor instructed her to close her eyes while he traced an alphabet letter on her open palm, then asked her to identify the mystery letter.

"Here, like this," she said, when I asked her to demonstrate. She traced the outline of an alphabet letter on my open palm while I kept my eyes closed. I flunked, unable to identify the mystery letter.

"What was it?" I asked.

"Q."

"Well, here's the deal," Eugene continued. "What I don't understand is, if they want to make sure I'm not senile, why don't they discuss current events with me, ask me what's going on in the world or if I've read the newspaper? I'm the author of over fifty books."

Sylvia confessed that these "tests" made her nervous and that she also hated them. "But what choice do I have? They need to check for certain things," she said, knocking on the table to ward off ill fortune and looking up at the ceiling, or to a God she admitted doubting existed.

Eugene rolled his eyes. "Well, I don't have to take it," he said, raking his fingers under his chin and flicking them in his favorite defiant gesture, which he directed at reckless drivers, condescending medical personnel, and anyone else who disrespected him or pissed him off.

"I don't like to make waves," Sylvia cautioned. She invoked the same phrase when talking about her building management, another entity that could jeopardize her physical and emotional security if rocked the wrong way. She was a vocal proponent of following doctors' orders even when skeptical of the message. She also encountered ageism during medical appointments and claimed that elders received dismissive treatment "when they see that number on the form, when you get above a certain number." When speaking with Eugene about his health, her voice contained a wellspring of concern. She sounded fearful of the consequences if he argued with the VA staff, as when he refused to take his medication after his heart attack. Sylvia counseled him to accept the treatment he detested, acknowledging its less-than-ideal qualities but arguing that they must follow doctors' recommendations if they wanted to live. Eugene and Sylvia rarely agreed. He admitted to postponing and canceling appointments to avoid interacting with clinic staff and described the latest indignity.

"They showed me pictures of a giraffe, a rhinoceros, and a lion, and asked me to name them. Can you believe that?" he said, with a look of disgust. His forceful breath betrayed a mix of humiliation, annoyance, and anger.

Eddie arrived later and shrugged his shoulders after listening to a quick recap of Eugene's frustrations. "Look, it's the geriatric clinic. This is what they do to everyone," he said with resignation, which stemmed from his own experiences at the VA hospital. "It is what it is, when you get up there in years."

Eddie's acquiescence reflected his typical response to these complaints. He believed that Eugene's doctors looked out for his best interests, performed their jobs to their best ability, and that Eugene should rein in his frustrations. Eddie and Eugene offered a potent contrast in the degree to which they accepted medical intervention, kept appointments, and adhered to medication regimens. Despite his blustery public demeanor and stubborn "fuck off" neighborhood persona, Eddie vigilantly took every pill and test that his physicians prescribed. Eugene often claimed to know more than his doctors. He used past negative experiences, such as an error or bad side effect, to justify his pick-and-choose-buffet approach to health maintenance and dealing with the medical establishment. Though Eugene had a more genteel, affable air, he resisted accepting without question anything his doctor recommended. As the author of numerous published books on nutrition, he possessed vast knowledge about medicine and health. He felt that, because of his education and writing on medical topics, he had sufficient expertise to evaluate and dismiss parts of the treatment plan. Unlike Eddie, who had completed some college but never finished, Eugene obtained his bachelor's degree. These contrasts may reflect some differences in class and education, with Eugene showing a greater desire to challenge medical authority while Eddie felt more comfortable confronting neighborhood figures but deferred to professionals in charge of his care. They may also tell us something about the ways older people, and men in particular, challenge ageism while also coming to accept how authority figures treat them based on their advanced age.

STAYIN' ALIVE

For older adults living alone, third places served as important physical sites to receive informal care and advice as they shared struggles and decoded information from physicians' offices. Lucy had a history of arthritis and temporomandibular joint disorder (TMJ), which causes chronic pain in the joints and muscles responsible for jaw movement. Years before I met her she had broken her shoulder by tripping on a cracked sidewalk while dashing to the bus. Despite her fatigue and chronic health issues, Lucy's body allowed her to maintain her routines and social interaction in the neighborhood, making it hard to imagine how frenetic her life would look if she had the energy she longed for and less physical pain.

When Lucy finally arrived at Pete's in the early evenings she inventoried a typical day's comings and goings, including gossip from McDonald's, updates from her medical appointments, and other daily frustrations. She described the minutiae of her life with such exquisite detail and heightened emotion that I felt almost as if I'd sat beside her when she haggled with cable customer service representatives about a faulty remote, disputed billing errors with her health insurance company, and resolved a problem obtaining a prescription at the pharmacy.

A simple trip to the store sounded more like an epic contest of wills. "I used to be a fighter," she said, unaware of how the battles she chronicled showed how much fight she had left. Her penchant for hyperbole not only reflected her distress but also evinced a larger observation about late life. Many people described their daily experiences as depleting, requiring energy they no longer had; they were tests of physical and emotional endurance.

Often Lucy's tales involved a show-and-tell component. In her younger years she had mostly ordered glittery jewelry, which she still wore, from the home shopping channel QVC but now had graduated to a different class of purchases. She reached into her purse like a magician pulling a rabbit from a hat and surprised us with her latest medical or assistive device. Sometimes she displayed the item for us to admire or to solicit our opinions. Other times she needed help inserting batteries or deciphering directions. One evening she brought a leftover acupuncture needle from an earlier appointment and the next day produced a magnifying glass with a built-in flashlight for reading small print. On another occasion she showed us a pendant on a chain designed to sound an alarm and alert her friend to an emergency, such as a fall in her home. Once, while Sylvia and Eugene watched and munched on a sandwich and fig newtons, she had difficulty fitting a dental guard for jaw pain over her teeth. After some fiddling, she positioned it correctly. Sometimes Lucy purchased these items upon a doctor's recommendation, but mostly she had decided independently that they might solve a problem.

Perhaps the most elaborate gadget she unveiled was an inflatable neck brace. Lucy unpacked the box's contents and tossed the packing material onto the table. She pulled out what looked like a deflated beach toy, with two thin tubes hanging limply, and explained that this device alleviated arthritic neck pain.

"How do I do this?" she mused to herself, then looked to us for pointers.

"Put it around your neck," Eugene offered.

"Like this?" Lucy asked, fumbling with the awkward plastic.

"No, maybe you should blow it up first."

Lucy set the item on the table. Eugene squinted and turned it over in his hands, pondering the best strategy. He unfolded the instructions like an accordion. "Here, you squeeze these things first," he said, gesturing to the pumps attached to the tubes' ends, "and once you pump it full of air, you put it around your neck."

Lucy pinched the tear drop–shaped pumps, placed the half-inflated tube around her neck, and continued squeezing. Soon she overfilled the contraption so that she could barely move her neck, immobilized by the taut tube.

"No, no, no," Sylvia chimed in. "You got to get rid of some of that," she said, waving her hand towards Lucy's neck to indicate she should remove the brace. Lucy pressed her forearm on the piece to release some air, to no avail.

Eugene looked at me with a raised eyebrow. He smirked in seeming disbelief, as she struggled with the brace, oblivious to his amusement.

"I think you need to let the air out of here," Eugene suggested and identified the escape hatch for the trapped air.

"Ah," Lucy murmured with relief. "Thanks." She adjusted the piece on her neck until comfortable. "I don't know. I think I'm going to send it back."

Though Lucy had confronted her share of health problems, they hadn't yet impeded her ability to socialize at local businesses, and she had never lived as a shut-in. She served as a gossip, reliable messenger, and roving reporter rolled into one. When we consider the downtrodden image that American culture attaches to the older person at risk of isolation—with no visitors on holidays, locked in darkened apartments, buried under possessions like the notorious hoarding Collyer brothers were—we don't think of someone like Lucy.

Lucy circulated throughout the neighborhood, and every corner seemed touched by her as if by a syrupy substance or dew. She floated from place to place like a bee landing on a flower and pollinated each daisy center with her presence. Lucy also carried information from one group to the other. For example, when she discovered someone had a problem, she usually shared the situation with others. The newly informed often dispatched assistance or offered suggestions that Lucy brought back with her. In social network terminology, she acted as a bridger, or as the network member that tied different clusters of people together.[3]

Whenever Lucy returned to Pete's with stories from McDonald's, Sylvia did not pass up the opportunity to distance herself from the stigmatized space.

"I don't know any of these people," she said. She admitted that she knew a bunch of the women who used to go to the bakery and now went to McDonald's but repeated her usual refrain, "I haven't been in there in years." She traced the last time she went there to twenty years before when her husband was still alive. "I used to run in and out, when Irv was still here, but I haven't been in so long."

Lucy took umbrage. "We know, we know. You haven't been there in years," she said, exasperated.

As much as Sylvia and Lucy had clashed over the years, Sylvia articulated begrudging respect for Lucy. "She's a single lady, on her own. She deserves a lot of credit." Lucy never married, while Sylvia was widowed. At this point in the life course they shared some similarities, such as living alone, though Sylvia had resided with her husband until he died. Lucy lived alone most of her life, ever since an irascible house guest decades earlier had refused to leave, forcing her to remove her in court. By recognizing Lucy's history as a lifelong single woman navigating that challenging terrain while most of her cohort had married, Sylvia acknowledged, rather than blanketed over, the differences between them that were important to Lucy.[4] Sylvia's respect for never-married older women's independence also extended to Helen, a petite wisp of a woman who frequented the bakery, Pete's, and McDonald's. Her solid silver-white hair gleamed in the sun. She spoke softly, sometimes barely audible, and favored pastels and pale greys to Lucy's bold black and red ensembles. Sylvia admired Helen's "strength" and "toughness," an inner core of steel at odds with her timid persona.

Ultimately a series of falls proved the biggest challenge to Lucy's autonomy. She fell one afternoon not due to an external hazard such as a cracked sidewalk, snagged carpet, or errant extension cord lying across her living room floor but at the supermarket while standing still. "I just went down," she said, perplexed at the cause. A month later she fell again at home, with no straightforward explanation. She saw a neurologist, who ordered a brain MRI. Lucy told the group that the doctor hadn't found anything. But Eugene said she had shown him the MRI films and radiology report one day.

"She had a stroke, a small one," he said. Lucy didn't confirm this information.

After her first big fall she began using a cane to strengthen her sense of security and protect against the potential catastrophic consequences of future falls. Geriatricians have long identified the fear of falling in older adults as a public health problem linked to elevated fall risk.[5] "I felt like I was gonna die," Lucy repeated often.

Despite her falls and the dread that accumulated as snow piled on the sidewalks that winter, one of the coldest and snowiest in twenty years,[6] Lucy continued visiting Pete's and McDonald's. She arrived bundled in her faded black 1980s puffy coat with the turtleneck collar buttoned tight. Following a major snowfall she avoided Pete's for a few days. But as winter turned to spring and bright green buds reappeared on tree branches, Lucy still stayed closer to home, even with the sidewalks free from slippery ice and slush. Instead of heading to Pete's around 6 p.m. as she had in preceding years, she remained at McDonald's and whiled away the nighttime hours with the regulars there. Pete's stood three and a half blocks away from her home, compared with the single, long cross-town block to McDonald's. Eugene's camaraderie hadn't proved enough to lure her to Pete's, though she showed up occasionally, with several days and sometimes a week between visits. Lucy's drop-off surprised people, given the steadfastness of her presence over the years and her fondness for Eugene's company. She had often stayed at Pete's with Eugene for hours after everyone else had left.

Lucy's final fall in late spring resulted in a broken ankle. Still, she persevered despite a drastic drop in the frequency of her outings. After several weeks she returned to Pete's but never regained her prior levels of attendance. She mentioned getting depressed when stuck in the house, having lost any reason to put on makeup or dress up. Usually she styled her hair at the salon every few weeks, varying the shade from dark honey to blinding platinum and the texture from fluffed to sleek. Her frequent references to her isolation showed how profoundly the bad weather and injury had affected her morale.

"I didn't see anyone. I had no reason to do myself up," Lucy said.

"And you're usually dressed to the nines," Eugene said.

"Yeah, I know," she agreed glumly.

Lucy's trajectory during this season provides a longitudinal glimpse of the interaction between physical deterioration and hazardous weather.[7] The impediment of snow had threatened her ability to care for herself and stymied her usual access to the neighborhood, making nearby places seem further away. Despite the psychic toll of this externally imposed isolation, Lucy soldiered through that winter. We saw her regularly despite gaps between outings, and she relied on neighborhood venues to commiserate about new physical problems and the weather's stresses. Her tenacity in seeking out support despite increasing challenges reflected the predicament that ensnared many of the elders I encountered who fought physical wear and tear to commune with others about their suffering bodies.

MY WAY

Most people accepted that they must maintain their bodies by going to numerous medical appointments if they wanted to continue to live and live well. Eddie, Sylvia, and Lucy acted in the most traditionally responsible way about their medical care. They attended doctors' appointments and followed orders without much modification, despite hurdles to complying with a prescribed treatment, such as high out-of-pocket costs. Their compliance didn't preclude complaints about aspects of their regimens. But after discussing their concerns or questions with family, friends, and assorted neighborhood people, they either consulted their doctors and agreed to abide by their orders or otherwise reconciled themselves to the treatment.

A few identified bright spots in the morass of health-care services. Sylvia pointed to her physical therapist and Lucy to her acupuncturist as attentive exemplars. They praised these providers' patient listening and the time they spent with them to understand the connections between various symptoms. Unlike some specialists, they treated the body as a system rather than a disconnected collection of parts. Other people resisted treatment, taking only some prescribed medications and only attending appointments and medical tests they deemed necessary. Eugene remained ambivalent. He saw his physicians but modified his regimen and lapsed in the continuity of his care, postponing and canceling appointments due to condescending treatment at the VA hospital until they refused to refill his medication. Yet, despite Eugene's resistance, consultation with other elders and their subtle peer pressure helped him comply with more of his medical regimen than he might otherwise if he had nowhere to air his dissatisfaction.

Another contingent avoided doctors for years, until a crisis forced them back into the health-care system after a medical emergency. Joan and Dottie evaded medical care for years. They developed serious, life-threatening complications as a result of medical problems that barreled out of control without earlier intervention. Both women attracted commentary from peers for their self-care practices, or in the eyes of critics, for their self-neglect. Their visible physical problems exposed them to greater public critique.

Joan, a retired choreographer in her mid-70s, faced severe mobility limitations and could not walk more than a few paces without struggling. As her legs worsened, Eugene and Sylvia criticized her for not taking better care of herself.

"She needs a surgery. She has top of the line insurance. She could have it for free. Why doesn't she have the surgery? She can barely walk," Eugene wondered aloud.

"Ah, who knows," Sylvia sighed, indicating that deciphering Joan's behavior was a lost cause. "To have it [the surgery], they would have to break her . . ." she trailed off, suggesting that she somewhat understood Joan's rationale for avoiding the procedure's potential torment. Joan spoke openly about dodging medical care. The previous autumn she prepared to return to the doctor and told me that she had not seen a physician in four years.

"What kinds of questions do you think they'll ask on those forms?" she asked in a wavering voice. "I think that's a good clinic. A lot of seniors go there," she said of the geriatric clinic a few blocks from Pete's. "They take my insurance." She admitted anxiety about returning to medical care after such a long hiatus.

An incident occurred one night at Pete's in my absence, a few weeks after Joan had made plans to see a doctor again. She tripped on an unsecured corner of a carpet intended to track dirt and prevent falls. For weeks I'd observed people stumble on the curled-up mat. According to Eugene and Sylvia, Joan screamed out in pain and could not get up. An ambulance whisked her off to the hospital, forcing her into sudden contact with the health-care system again. Afterwards no one saw Joan for months. When she finally resurfaced, her appearances at Pete's dropped off significantly to less than once a week.

For those who withdrew from health-care settings altogether, third places arguably provided even more support. Dottie's health problems attracted attention as she had difficulty walking more than a block. She caught flak for her perceived unhealthy habits, such as eating sweets, and her weight drew extensive concern and disapproval. But unlike Joan, Dottie hid her avoidance of medical care from friends, family, and neighborhood ties. Before her primary care physician retired, Dottie talked about seeing him regularly at his office two blocks from her home. The only other doctor she mentioned visiting was her longtime podiatrist, Dr. Gurvits, whose office stood across the street from her apartment building. She remained under his care until he also retired. They had built such a close relationship that he gave her a copy of his apartment keys in case she ever needed to stay with his family in an emergency. Dottie never informed regulars at her neighborhood hangouts about her lapsed medical care. After her heart attack and subsequent hospitalization, we discovered from her daughter Linda that she had not seen a doctor besides her podiatrist for years. "The only person she was seeing was Gurvits," Linda said, when I asked if her mother told her she had seen other doctors. "Lies, all lies," she huffed. "After Gurvits was gone, she didn't see no one at all. No medication, nothing. She weighed down that cart with a bunch of phone books," she added, clarifying how Dottie had managed to fashion her cart into a makeshift rolling walker. She said she had offered to accompany her mother to medical appointments, but Dottie had declined. Despite these gaps in care, Linda identified the bakery as the one reliable presence in Dottie's life.

Research on heterosexual couples has found that women bear more responsibility for tending to their partners' health and their own. When wives die, their surviving husbands' health typically suffers. Due to this more active role in partnerships, divorced and widowed women have lower remarriage rates and often hesitate to remarry due to fatigue from extensive caretaking, compared with men who remarry at higher percentages. For example, one study showed 64 percent of men 55 and older had remarried compared with 52 percent of their women counterparts.[8] Among elders in my study—most of whom were uncoupled when I met them—I encountered both men and women who fully complied with doctors' recommendations and initiated appointments to monitor chronic illnesses and new symptoms when feeling unwell. I also met men and women who abstained from consulting doctors entirely, concealed growing health problems from friends and family, and disregarded medical advice. Given my small study sample I cannot make strong claims about gendered patterns among men and women's health-related behavior. I observed a mix of approaches to managing the body. Men often acted just as responsibly as the women, if not more so in some situations, perhaps because they could not rely on a partner or anyone else, and thus had learned to care for themselves.

Sylvia also bumped up against her limits when it came to following doctors' orders. Despite affirming the importance of regular medical care, she resisted certain interventions. She had experienced two separate life-threatening events, a heart attack and a subarachnoid brain hemorrhage. "I shouldn't be here," she often said. Her friend had saved her life when she suffered the hemorrhage, calling an ambulance after discovering her collapsed in their hotel room while on vacation. "I don't remember anything. Woke up in the hospital five days later." In addition to arthritis, she faced two major medical issues that had marred her recent quality of life. She had lost a significant amount of peripheral vision in her left eye due to an untreated cataract. Despite a successful operation on her right eye years before, she had gone from delaying the procedure on the second eye to refusing it altogether. When her eyesight first began to deteriorate, she would talk of "losing vision." Later on, with stark acceptance, she pronounced that she would lose sight altogether in her left eye: "I'm going blind." She offered opposing reasons for rejecting the surgery. At first she said her doctor told her she "couldn't" have it due to nasal polyps that would obstruct her airway if she lay on an operating table. Over time, she opened up about the daunting nature of the procedure. "It's too much at my age." She also explained her refusal to have her nasal polyps operated on, which caused ongoing breathing problems. "They'll have to knock me out."

During more recent discussions about Sylvia's cascading health concerns, she expressed interest in assisted living. "There are people there," she cited as the appeal of a facility with medical personnel on site in case of emergency. Before she'd warmed to the idea of a retirement community, she had also suggested the possibility of living with relatives in New Jersey. Eugene cautioned against giving up her apartment, though Sylvia had merely floated the idea and had not seriously discussed it. Years before she had fiercely resisted the idea of moving in with family.

"What will you do there? You have everything you need here," he argued.

"It's getting harder," she said.

"Yes, but it's going to be hard out there. What will you do without the Galaxy Diner?" he smiled gently, bolstering his argument with a teasing reference to her favorite nearby diner.

Sylvia had devoted significant energy and time to persuading Eugene and others to comply with professional medical advice, and as she grew older, she received similar encouragement from those she'd nudged over the years. In the weeks after Eugene's heart attack, she spent many hours trying to convince him to take his cholesterol drugs and other prescribed medications. A few years later Eugene took the lead in urging Sylvia to reconsider her stance on the polyp and cataract surgeries. Though Sylvia never reached the same wholesale rejection of medical care like others did, her example shows how anxiety can lead to refusing more and more tests and procedures until developing fierce opposition and abstaining altogether. Her case also pointed to a common occurrence among elders I observed. The same people who voiced their misgivings or intentions to decline a procedure or medication often cajoled others into following doctors' orders. In addition to trying to persuade Sylvia to get her nose polyps removed and undergo cataract surgery, Eugene also attempted to convince Lucy to allow her physician to implant a device to decrease stroke risk.

"I don't want to be a guinea pig," she said. "I don't know what he wants to do," she added when I asked for clarification about the procedure. "To tell you the truth I don't understand the whole thing."

"Well, if it's a stent, you should have it done. I had it and watched while they put it in." He reassured her of the safety and ease of stent implantation by summarizing details of his own procedure.

Eddie talked to both Eugene and Sylvia about their qualms concerning different procedures. Eddie required scant convincing. For all of his gruffness and stubbornness about other things, he complied with medication regimens and doctors' suggestions. Through these discussions everyone received support or encouragement to care for themselves, even when they eschewed their own physicians' recommendations.

Talking about health allowed people to gain a sense of their relative standing and discover if others had similar, worse, or better health outcomes. Comparison helped them evaluate their own physical experiences and offered a yardstick to measure how they fared in relation to their age peers.[9] They also received a glimpse into different treatments and collected data on others' experiences of improvement or decline. Comparing treatment regimens encouraged sharing information and resources that helped people amend their own regimens with practical suggestions from those with similar experiences, such as asking physicians for a medication with fewer side effects or a lower cost. Some expressed greater confidence in their own treatment after exposure to these comparisons.

Venting with others also offered emotional release and helped people confess their fears and unburden themselves of anxiety, especially important for those with little support from family or close friends. Even those who mostly listened gained something valuable from these discussions. For people who felt uncomfortable sharing sensitive health information with relatives for fear of losing independence or to avoid the pressure to live with them or move into assisted living, venting among neighborhood contacts offered a safer way to confide with lower risk of adverse consequences for their autonomy.

Though they may have faced modest judgment or pressure to choose a specific approach, the urging they received was mostly supportive. After a discussion about someone's treatment options, they may have asked which path they selected at the next opportunity, but this laid-back inquiry comprised the extent of the follow-up. Recommendations fell into the category of "gentle nudging." I also experienced concerned querying when I encountered my own health problems. Sylvia diligently tracked people's upcoming medical appointments and the outcomes of different procedures or tests. Somehow she managed to solicit this information in a caring way that never seemed bullying or intrusive.

On the surface, such check-ins may appear to be a pastime for old people with limited options for filling time. Many elders lamented hearing their counterparts "talk all day about their aches and pains." People could also interpret these chats as invasive and prying. But monitoring others' health status and progress also revealed concern. By this age everyone had lost someone close to them whom they loved and missed. Somewhere in this talk they wanted to ensure the well-being of those who remained. Even in situations when people persistently discussed someone's physical situation and criticized them for ignoring health problems, such as Joan, who received significant criticism for her poor physical shape, a desire to prevent needless suffering underlay the rebuke.

GENTRIFICATION EMBODIED

Exiled bakery customers got to know Joan at Pete's. She had lived in the neighborhood for multiple decades but was never a bakery regular; she had just dropped in occasionally over the years. Sylvia recalled a deceased friend getting into a row with Joan on one of the many occasions when she complained about living in New York and sung Toronto's praises, gushing about her preference for her home country, Canada.

"'Well, if you like it so much there, why don't you go back,' my friend Elsie went and walked away," Sylvia laughed. She reenacted that long-ago scene for us as she had throughout the years whenever the subject of Joan's origins and her prickly demeanor came up.

Rather than spend long hours at the bakery, Joan frequented the city-run senior center located in a large housing project complex six blocks from Pete's and approximately ten blocks from her home. She participated in the center's advocacy efforts, meeting with legislators and traveling with other center members and staff to protest budget cuts at the state capitol in Albany. To reach the center, she took two city buses. Pete's served as a convenient pit stop for rest and food.

From the day I met Joan at Pete's she appeared in rough shape. She usually wore a skirt, faded sweatshirt, white tube socks, and black sneakers, with her tousled salt and pepper hair pulled into a messy ponytail. Her physical condition belied her work history as a professional choreographer. At 75, though one of the younger elders, Joan faced among the severest mobility issues. She complained about knee pain and divulged that some physical troubles originated from a car accident years before. She had considerable difficulty walking to the cash register, only a few feet from the table and chairs, and depended on a cane. Given her unsteadiness, bowed legs, and immense strain walking, I wondered why she had not used a wheelchair. Minute undertakings required Sisyphean effort, and I felt exhausted watching her.

Joan readily accepted help but also barked orders at Pete's staff to wait on her or give her an extra plate, napkins, or utensils. She shouted monosyllabic directives ("fork" or "water") from her seat without saying "please" or "thank you," seemingly oblivious that her demands were rude and that she was disrespectful towards workers.

Many conversations between Pete's customers and Joan focused on her housing woes. A changeover in her building's owners and ongoing construction during the past few years had led to uncertainty about her living situation. Before her building was sold twice between 2011 and 2013, the residence had long fostered an environment sympathetic to artists—for example, allowing them to fall behind on rent without penalty. Changes in building ownership prompted Joan and other long-term tenants to band together and consult an attorney to protect themselves from future eviction attempts. Despite her thorniness and although Eugene complained that she had not listened to any of them, he and Sylvia listened to her often and offered suggestions.

"She has to get her own lawyer," Eugene insisted to me, during an uncertain autumn when she negotiated the terms of moving to a lower floor as building construction commenced.

"But we have a lawyer," Joan countered with a stubborn pause between each word. "Through our tenants association."

"That's not enough," Eugene said, wizened from his own battles with a building management company eager to remove him.

The new building owner seemed less hostile towards the long-term residents, and for the most part Joan approved of the plan to move her to a lower floor since it was easier for her to access physically. She contended with construction dust, noise, and disarray, taxing even for those without significant health problems. To some extent she still felt her home was under threat, evident in her habit of carrying bulky cloth bags at all times, perplexing everyone who interacted with her at Pete's. The heavy belongings would weigh down even those in excellent physical shape. Eugene suspected she carried all of her valuables with her.

Joan admitted that she avoided leaving important things in her room due to her mistrust of construction crews passing through during ongoing renovations. Upheaval with the building owners had left her wary. Wandering the neighborhood with her belongings added another burden.

One evening I observed how Joan struggled when navigating the terrain beyond Pete's. As I looked onto the sidewalk from inside the West Side Diner, the image of her limping entered my field of vision. She leaned on her cane, with a bag slung over each shoulder, and held onto the diner's windows to steady herself. She didn't notice me as I watched her outstretched palm graze the store's glass panes. Once past she grasped other buildings' walls and lurched towards the bus stop. A half-block remained between the bus's drop-off point and her building's entrance. In her condition I couldn't imagine Joan walking the entire one and a half crosstown block between Pete's and her home.

Despite her precarious housing situation, physical obstacles, and a changing neighborhood that catered more to newer affluent arrivals than to older, poorer residents, Joan derived great esteem from her residence. "She can't imagine living anywhere else," Eugene said, after one discussion about Joan's unsettled tenancy. The building had not only housed her for more than three decades but provided a personal and professional anchor to her former artistic work and to her late husband, who had died fifteen years before. Joan regaled anyone who would listen with stories of her gloried past and enjoyed talking up her perceived status markers, such as her activities "helping" others at the senior center. She boasted of "connections" at businesses on her block that gave her special treatment, including free movies at the theater and discounts at a trendy doughnut shop where she mingled with an international tourist clientele. Sylvia recounted how Joan bragged that her connections helped her obtain Meals on Wheels, a meal delivery service available to elders, which saved her money and strenuous trips outside during a bitterly cold winter.

"Connections? What connections? 'You don't need connections,' I told her. Anyone can get that. I could get that if I wanted to," Sylvia scoffed.

Joan envisioned one bleak alternative to living in her building—the public housing projects that rose up on the neighborhood's western edge. She spoke often about her fear of having nowhere else to go if she lost her apartment. Eugene told her she would be lucky to get into the projects, with their long waiting lists of several years. But this reality hadn't assuaged her worries.

WE'RE NOT GONNA TAKE IT: AGEISM IN HEALTH CARE

Older adults mostly receive health and medical services in organized settings, such as hospitals or neighborhood clinics. Since they tend to use medical services more frequently, they face a greater likelihood of negative interactions in a health-care system permeated with ageism.[10] Scholars have found that ageism in the health-care system lowers older adults' willingness to seek professional medical help, reducing their access to health supports for aging in place.[11] Ample literature has documented ageist comments by medical trainees and professionals.[12] Geriatrician Louise Aronson describes one incident in which a reputable surgeon asked a medical student which specialty she wanted to pursue. When she answered "geriatrics," the surgeon laughed and raised his voice while imitating older patients complaining about constipation.[13] Studies also reveal implicit ageism. For example, health providers tend to baby talk with older patients by speaking loudly and slowly, acting overly polite, and repeating simple sentences.[14] These practices cast older adults as less cognitively and physically capable of communicating than younger adults.

Negative stereotypes also lead health-care professionals to provide unnecessary assistance to older patients.[15] Prior research has found that providers interact with elders in ways that make them feel incompetent, such as discussing their conditions with a family member instead of them.[16] Some mental health therapists have expressed reluctance to accept older women clients due to stereotypes of them as overemotional.[17] Researchers have found some physicians act more egalitarian and responsive to younger patients.[18] Physicians may also attribute older adults' symptoms to age rather than underlying disease, leading both to delayed or undertreatment of pain, fatigue, depression, anxiety, and cognitive impairment and to overtreatment with excessive tests, procedures, and surgeries.[19] Elders face increased depression risk and delayed diagnosis or treatment in part because health-care providers may mistake depressive symptoms as natural aging.[20] Older adults with higher social and cognitive functioning especially find such ageism condescending, disrespectful, and humiliating.[21]

As growing numbers of older adults live longer, they will need to seek a range of support for health-related challenges. My findings suggest more will rely on company in informal spaces as a supplemental, and in some cases primary, form of support as they age in their communities. In line with prior scholarship that has found ageism in health-care settings, greater mistrust of the medical system among racial and ethnic minority elders, and dislike of age-separated institutions like senior centers, these findings suggest a greater need for understanding elders' options for alternative spaces and for further research on how elders reach beyond formal settings to remain healthy and independent.[22]

These vignettes show how and why people avoided or preferred other spaces outside those that traditionally serve older adults, like senior centers, and the shortcomings of medical infrastructure. Even those who participated in formal settings had mixed experiences that may have prevented them from taking full advantage of available services. Often people felt unheard by medical staff and resisted identifying with the stereotypes they encountered of older adults as dependent and deserving pity. Yet, they also internalized larger cultural messages about the devaluation of older adults, and these ageist beliefs surfaced in their reasons for avoiding institutions and organizations geared towards elders. Under conditions of their making, despite their dislike of age-separated settings and hierarchical distinctions drawn between different older people, they enjoyed the company of similarly aged peers. We can draw implications from these observations for practice, policy, and future research to enhance exchanges between health-care providers and older adults so that they feel recognized, respected, and cared for, which would improve health-care outcomes.[23]

8

AT HOME IN THE CITY

ONE EVENING, EUGENE SHUFFLED into Pete's. "I have a story to tell you," he promised Lucy, Sylvia, and me, before heading to pay for his coffee. We continued chatting about Lucy's arthritis woes, never expecting Eugene's bombshell. "As I said, I've got a story for you. I just got back from the VA. I had a heart attack," he said. His nonchalance heightened the dramatic effect. He waited for our reactions.

Lucy stood up from her seat across from Eugene as she exclaimed her shock, "You what?" As her voice reached higher octaves, I almost feared she would bring on a second heart attack.

"My God," Sylvia said softly and leaned back as she touched her hand to her chest, her lips pressed into a serious line. "Are you all right?" she asked, patting his arm.

"Yes, I'm fine." Eugene explained that he had the attack yesterday while at the clinic for a routine checkup. He admitted feeling weak but enjoyed his storytelling, smiling as he described watching the monitor show his heart beating during the angioplasty.

"I saw the whole thing," he said, mimicking the swooshing sound of his pounding heart on screen. When Eddie walked in ten minutes later, he began the story anew and repeated details of his ordeal, how the hospital lost his clothes and "billfold" and how he had to wait two hours while they searched for his things.

"Is that right?" Eddie murmured. He saved his usual zingers and instead turned to me and chuckled, "We're seeing a ghost."

"I guess I'm indestructible," Eugene said.

"Well, how about that," Sylvia said with awe and reverence. Before leaving, she pulled Eugene's face toward hers and kissed his cheek. "I don't want to hear you're in the hospital again unless you're having a baby," she said with an affectionate laugh.

Despite the challenges of recreating the arrangement that they had enjoyed at the bakery and their desire to maintain distance amid the closeness of elastic ties, displaced elders persisted in gathering and offering emotional and practical support. People regrouped much like a flower transplanted to new soil, adapting to ensure the mature plant's survival. They continued seeing each other several days a week, four on average, and spent hours together. The experience of time changed depending on the mix of those who lingered and those who passed through. Even with the most entertaining personalities, discussion eventually dragged. But each additional person eased the burden of keeping conversation alive, and time seemed to pass faster with a larger crowd. People watching served as an important source of entertainment and confiding helped elders carry on relationships. As in the bakery, they gave concrete help when a challenge arose and mobilized resources when they learned of someone's emergent problem. They discussed a range of topics, increasingly health and their interactions with the healthcare system, and shared strategies to assist each other in making informed decisions to manage bodily declines.

Relationships continued, and new ties emerged as former customers negotiated spaces that no longer catered to them as older people to the same degree the bakery had. They discovered less than ideal conditions, such as chronic noise or cramped seating, which complicated interactions. As they adapted to less desirable spatial features, they encountered new social tensions and rivalries. At spots like Pete's, old tensions flared. At McDonald's, former bakery patrons managed relations with multiple factions competing for space, including elders that preceded their arrival and younger people who hung out after school and were confronting their own limited socializing spots. Still, despite clashes and dissatisfaction, older people enjoyed what neighborhood places they could. This chapter examines how they made do with their constraints, resisting the potential isolation of being "stuck in place." Despite sometimes reluctant company, they forged a home in the city that nurtured interdependence with life- and spirit-sustaining moments of pleasure, fun, and laughter.

SAVE A PLACE FOR ME

Despite the spatial and logistical challenges of regrouping at McDonald's, people continued supporting each other there through regular socializing. A few weeks after the bakery closed, Jeannette and I chatted while waiting in line one afternoon around 3:30 p.m. She had difficulty finding people in McDonald's, owing to greater foot traffic in the larger, more crowded space. When I arrived, a group consisting of Carmen, Marlene, and Diane sat at a table along the back wall. Theresa soon followed and beelined to her favorite table by the entrance, in the enclosed section along the railing. She motioned for the group to join her and placed an extra chair along the table's edge. No one migrated over. She finally relented and took a seat with them. Two teenage girls quickly snatched up her abandoned table.

More people trickled in as the afternoon grew long, and the late-in-the-day crowd coalesced. When Bernice came a little while later, Theresa complimented her lavender chiffon blouse. "You look stunning."

"Why, thank you," she said demurely, twirling to show off her ensemble.

Arthur's friend Pauline followed, dressed in her trademark pearls, wool slacks, and white cashmere sweater; her fluffy brown shoulder-length hair was perfectly coiffed. In a change from her bakery socializing patterns, she joined the group at McDonald's in Arthur's absence, traveling from her home a little over a mile away. George came at 4 p.m., sliding into the seat beside Diane, which she always saved for him. With no more spots left at the table, Jeannette and Gladys sat together in a booth across the aisle. Carmen motioned for Gladys to come over, but she shook her head.

During a quiet lull, a trim man in his late 30s with a bronzy complexion and slicked dark hair, who was well dressed in a fitted periwinkle suit, strode past to the bathroom.

"He's cute," Carmen said, half to herself. She peered at me to gauge my agreement. Absorbed in my observations of all the moving parts, it took a few seconds for me to pick up on her appraisal.

"Oh, you don't look," she said to my initial lack of reaction.

"Oh, it's not that," I said, explaining my distraction.

"I enjoy flirting, especially now that I'm older and men aren't looking at me that way," she said with an impish smile. "I've been with my boyfriend ten years, but I still have fun."

"On the subject of flirting, my boyfriend's coworker told him, 'I'm married, but I'm not dead,'" I said. We both laughed hard.

Gladys walked off abruptly and left at 4:05 p.m., earlier than usual. The group parsed her exit. "She does that all the time," Diane said.

"She's feeling under for the last few days," Carmen said, referring to Gladys's depression. "I know how that feels, to be down like that," she said and shared how recently she'd also felt low for a few days.

"She's mad because she doesn't like me," Bernice offered as an alternate explanation. "She said to me, 'I don't like you,' but used different words. She told me, 'I never saw you before.' And I said to Gladys, 'Well, I saw you.'" Bernice complained that Gladys had dismissed her for years—at the senior center, at the bakery, and now at McDonald's. "I don't want to see her, and I'll move away if I do."

"She was okay with me," Jeannette said, eager to point out her lack of friction with Gladys. "She talks about Pauline, that she thinks she's so much better because she worked on Wall Street." By this time, Pauline had left, having taken a cab to her home in a wealthier neighborhood across town.

"Well, she doesn't come every day," Carmen said.

After Gladys's departure, Jeannette moved to the main table. Theresa upgraded her position and relocated to Pauline's vacated center seat. Lucy arrived later, at 5:20 p.m., explaining that, because she needed a taxi to get to the McDonald's, Dottie couldn't make it.

STUCK IN THE MIDDLE WITH YOU:
A RELUCTANT COMMUNITY

While friction occurred between old and young at McDonald's, multiple clusters of old people mingled and sometimes bumped up against each other. Nevertheless, relationships of mutual need persisted.

One morning around 10 a.m., I ran into Spiro at McDonald's. He wore jeans and bright white sneakers in contrast to the dressy club-going attire he usually donned by afternoon. "Yeah, the guys go here in the mornings," he said. Despite the fact that they had sometimes pushed him to the periphery of bakery interactions, Spiro didn't mention their prior slighting and still sought their company. By that hour, most of the older men had departed. The photographer straggled out last that morning, dragging his cane and wearing a light beige baseball cap, baggy blue jeans, and a black bag slung over his shoulder. "I'm going to buy a ticket to see my cousin in Islip who does my taxes. I don't think I'll get anything this year," Spiro said. Despite the hassle of traveling to Long Island, at least he trusted his relative and saved on the tax preparation fee.

In the afternoon, Dolores left just as I arrived. She had to return home before her son's home health aides departed for the day. Bundled in a warm red coat, her pocketbook dangling diagonally across her chest, she pushed her cart slowly as she limped with a stiff right leg, grasping her thigh in pain.

Carmen stopped in 4:15 p.m., breathless. She climbed out of the heavy white coat that swallowed her petite frame, requiring her to peek over its collar. Dottie, Diane, George, Pauline, Theresa, Jeannette, Carmen, and Gladys occupied two tables along the wall in the elevated section near the entrance. Jeannette discussed lifting dumbbells at home and her desire to start working out at the local recreation center. "I want to get rid of my old lady arms."

"Who cares?" said Dottie, with a hint of disdain.

"I care. I want to be the best-looking old lady around."

She and Carmen returned to the subject of the attractive man they had previously spotted. "Remember that good looking guy that went into the bathroom last week," Carmen started.

"Yeah, I would have jumped him," Jeannette said.

I complimented Carmen on her silken royal blue blouse. Theresa joked about its "daring" neckline.

Dottie told us that she and Dolores had gone to the West Side Diner earlier. "We both ate the same thing: scrambled eggs, toast, and mashed potatoes. Split a strawberry shortcake. I told her my legs hurt, and she said hers hurt too, so we shared a cab from the diner to McDonald's." Dottie mentioned that she hadn't seen Sylvia in a long time, but sometimes Phyllis and Judy came to McDonald's in the late afternoon or early evening after eating elsewhere.

Throughout the afternoon Dottie asked about the blister on the side of her face. "It doesn't look bad, does it?" she wondered aloud.

"No, it looks fine," Carmen assured her.

Dottie solicited my ideas about her blister's cause and treatment options. She would return to this conversation thread three more times and talk at length about it when I walked her home. I suggested asking her doctor for advice, noting my father's skin cancer. She identified stress, anxiety, allergies, and sugar as possible culprits.

All of a sudden, Carmen's soda spilled. Amber liquid ran across the table and onto the floor, outracing our efforts to sop the spreading mess with napkins. Carmen grabbed a mop stored behind a nearby garbage can.

"I might as well use the mop here, because I never do at home," she said, smiling.

"But, Carmen, your house is so clean," Theresa said.

Carmen said, with a laugh, "Well, I have a cleaning woman."

Shortly afterwards, sparks were flying between two women seated by the window. They had gathered in that spot for years. All eyes at our table seized on the pair as the woman in a red turban-style hat and blue coat yelled at her table companion with a black felt Fedora atop her silvery shoulder-length hair. "Go to hell," she said.

Gladys murmured, "An old lady fight."

"They always fight. They fight like hell," Jeannette said. She turned to Dottie. "What would you do if someone told you to go the hell?"

"Jeannette, why would anyone say that to me?" Dottie said, pursing her lips in frustration.

"I hope we don't get like that when we're old," Jeannette said, looking around the table. "I wonder what we'll be like in another 20 years, when we're 90."

"I won't be alive in another 20 years," Carmen said, amused as she ruffled her hair.

Towards the end of the afternoon, Dottie had grown more annoyed with Jeannette. She rolled her eyes when Jeannette spoke in gross detail about her toenail problems and indigestion, claiming that lifting dumbbells helped rid her of her gas. "Sometimes that Jeannette drives me crazy," Dottie said, readying herself to leave, around 6 p.m. I offered to walk her home, but she said Jeannette would accompany her. Theresa expressed disappointment at Jeannette's imminent departure. "Oh no, stay," she implored. Jeannette lifted her bowed head and looked to Dottie for approval. "You should stay," Dottie said.

I walked with Dottie instead. "You and me, we go way back," she said as we exited. During our stroll, she confessed her exhaustion when cleaning the bathroom but didn't feel comfortable having strangers working in her home. Her daughter helped with chores instead. "My daughter finally found a job, after looking for so long. So she said, 'Ma, you're going to have to wait till Saturday.'" Despite growing aggravation with Jeannette, their connection enabled Dottie to reduce dependence on her daughter and other family for help with day-to-day tasks. Through her assistance, Jeannette gained access to a reliable social connection, a sense of purpose, and pocket change that allowed her to partake in eating out with other regulars at neighborhood eateries. Their symbiotic relationship fostered a delicate interdependence as they found themselves stuck in place and with each other.

WITH A LITTLE HELP FROM MY FRIENDS, NEIGHBORS, AND STRANGERS

Elders stitched a patchwork quilt to meet their needs for technology assistance, social connection, and safety, while feeling increasingly vulnerable as they grew older in the city. They derived support from expected and unconventional sources including friends, neighbors, and strangers. Their hangout spots formed an important milieu that allowed them to pull together these various forms of help.

Sylvia stopped into Pete's at 6 p.m. one evening, dressed up for Yom Kippur.

"How are you?" I asked.

"Well, I'm alive," she said with a faint smile.

I complimented her navy cotton dress with braided collar, underneath an oatmeal wool cardigan. "I got it while visiting my niece," she said, explaining that she took her shopping at malls near her home in New Jersey. Sylvia liked the dress so much she purchased the last two. "If I see them again, I'll buy you one," she offered.

"I'll pay you, of course," I said.

"And it's organic," she said, patting the fabric.

She mentioned recent trouble with her cell phone, which she'd obtained through a friend who had added her to her phone plan. The friend, Natasha, a younger woman in her 40s, accompanied Sylvia to the store for technical support, but problems continued. I pulled out my prepaid Nokia brick phone to show Sylvia the advanced features on her newer flip phone. Old people often asked me for help with their phones, forcing me to confess my lack of technical savvy compared with most younger people. As an old woman I met once in the bakery assessed, "So, you're as stupid as me."

"Yep," I agreed.

I asked Eugene if he had resolved his computer problem. "Oh, that fucking computer," he said, frustrated. "I don't know what I'm going to do. I can't send emails." He updated Sylvia on his computer woes. She nodded in a polite, abstract way, not having her own computer or any experience using one. I asked if he tried my CTRL+ALT+DELETE suggestion. Pressing the keys restarted the programs, but he still couldn't sign into his email. "The cursor keeps spinning," he said. I suggested calling his Internet provider, AOL, for assistance.

Sylvia then called the attention of a man who appeared in his early 60s, standing by the cash register. "Aaron!"

He turned towards her, "I was just thinking about you."

She stood alongside the table, while Eugene and I sat. "I was thinking about *you*," she said. "These are my friends, Eugene and Stacy." To us, she said, "This is my neighbor, Aaron. I have the best neighbors."

"No, I have the best neighbor," Aaron said, apologizing for leaving early to change for temple, despite already wearing a neat dress shirt, slacks, and blazer. "I have to go to temple to repent, like a good boy," he said, joking that he had too many sins and not enough time to atone. After his departure, Sylvia again mentioned the excellent neighbors on her floor. "If I have a problem—and I've had problems—I can call on them, at least Aaron." On a down note, she repeated a common refrain, "But they're all younger. And they're never there. They live in a different world."

New York City's fast pace and crowding has always challenged older adults and people with disabilities. Among the elders I came to know, the hustle and bustle of areas like Midtown Manhattan dissuaded them from leaving the neighborhood unless necessary, such as for a doctor's appointment. Difficulties navigating subways and stairs and jostling from hurried and harried New Yorkers made traveling to another part of the city seem like a much longer, more arduous journey. Many provided detailed dispatches about physical hurdles they encountered on distance trips. Sylvia recounted her disorientation earlier that day when trying to get through a subway turnstile with a malfunctioning metro card reader during rush hour. Eugene tried to defuse her distress by joking about how a man had tried to "pick her up" in the subway.

"No, no," she protested, with anxious recollection on her face. She explained that she swiped her MetroCard several times but couldn't pass through the turnstile. "There was no one around," she said, citing the absence of "token booth clerks" on duty, though token sales had ended several years before. "'Help, help!' I said, but no one stopped and kept going through the turnstiles. They ignored me," she said, her voice melancholy. "Pushing, pushing." Finally, a middle-aged man swiped her through. "He was the only one. The only one." She tried to give him the fare in cash. "But he said, 'I don't want your money. I don't want your money,'" she said, imitating the man's adamant hand wave declining her offer. They rode the subway together and lamented the loss of station clerks. "He was very informative. He told me they're going to replace the booths with machines."

"They're already doing it," Eugene said, mentioning the torn-down booth at the closest station.

"But who's going to service the machines?" Sylvia cried out.

"What if there's a mugging?" Eugene added.

"I don't like that at all," Sylvia said. Eugene nodded. He kidded her again about the subway guy.

"He had a great line," Eugene said.

"What was it?" I asked.

"I don't want your money, just your phone number," Eugene said and cracked up in a high-pitched, chest-wracking laugh.

Sylvia laughed with embarrassment, shaking her head, mouthing "no." Eugene admitted the man didn't say that; he was only joking. "He was the only one who stopped. The generosity—no, the caring . . ." she repeated.

Eugene also confessed that he had been concerned about getting stranded downtown one day after meeting a friend for lunch. "I worried I wouldn't be able to find a cab down there, but my friend hailed one for me and helped me get in."

As the hour grew later, Sylvia asked, "Is the other gentleman coming?" referring to Eddie. Just as he avoided using her name, she abstained from using his.

"I'm not sure," I said, glancing at the wall clock, which read 6:20 p.m. "He usually comes at 6."

"Okay, whatever, whatever," Sylvia said, uninterested in further details. She described a brief interaction the other day. "He walked by, stuck his head in, and asked, 'You seen them?' then went away. I happened to be here eating my dinner."

Moments later, Eddie appeared. Sylvia headed to the deli counter to say hello to Marco, who made her sandwiches and patted his heart whenever he saw her. While Eddie paid for his ginger ale, she returned to the table. "I said hello [to Eddie] and he didn't even say hello to me," she said.

Eugene rolled his eyes in solidarity. "You should hear what he calls me."

"I don't know how you . . ." Sylvia trailed off.

"I just let it roll off me."

"Should I say hello?" Sylvia asked. "I'm just going to say hello before I leave," she said seconds later, more to herself than to anyone else. "He's not doing too well. Look how he's bent over."

I glimpsed Eddie's stooped form; he was hunched at the register at a forty-five-degree angle. I'd grown used to his condition. Sylvia saw him less frequently. Most of the time he sat rather than stood in her presence. As Eddie approached, he shot her a sour glance, as if to say, What are you still doing here? "Hello there," she said. "I'm just leaving."

Eugene interjected, "Eddie's just had his second granddaughter."

"How beautiful," Sylvia gushed. "Congratulations."

"Thank you," Eddie said, looking downward.

"What's her name?" Sylvia asked.

"Sophia," he said, withholding additional information, such as her birth weight, that he'd supplied on other occasions.

"Alright folks, see you later," Sylvia said and left.

Eddie selected his usual seat beside the ATM. "The machine's probably out of money," Eugene said, pointing to the screen's message reading "error 33. Please call attendant." I told the guys about two occasions I'd found money left in ATMs and joked that Eddie should press "33" to see what happened.

"Should I?" he smiled, wiggling an extended index finger before pulling his hand away.

He mentioned Danny, a bakery regular who died four years before and also grew up in the neighborhood. "Danny and I used to roar in the bakery about what we'd do if we ever found any money." He described their shared fantasy about a police chase forcing crooks to dump their stolen loot, with Danny and Eddie discovering the discarded brown bag filled with cash. "As a good citizen, of course, I don't like to see litter," he joked, demonstrating how he'd hook his cane around the abandoned bag to hoist it from the street.

Eugene relayed a recent news story he'd seen. People attached dollar bills to a real tree, then secretly filmed people's behavior when they encountered this real-life money tree. "The video showed that everyone only took one to two bucks per person," Eugene said. We all laughed that we would have taken a lot more. Eddie said he'd strip the tree bare with a grabbing stick used to retrieve things from high shelves or enlist an 8-year-old to climb the tree and pull the bills off. "You got that right," Eugene agreed.

"God would never make me a millionaire. If he ever did, I'd be dead by 40. I'd be a consummate waster, spend my time drinking and carousing," Eddie said. He'd spend his time in Las Vegas, getting on a plane on a whim. If he forgot anything, he'd buy everything there.

We moved to discussing bicycles and the now not-so-new bicycle lanes installed along the nearby avenues. Bicycles served as a popular topic of heated conversation. People feared getting hit and had plenty of stories about near misses, complaining often that nobody used the bike lanes.

"I've only seen a few delivery boys use them. Everyone else is in the street or on the sidewalk," Eugene said.

We all complained about people who rode on the sidewalk. I showed the guys a recent *New York Times* article from the style section on women who dressed fashionably and rode designer bicycles. I read aloud from the article: "Ms. Page-Green, who likes to speed around on the sidewalk, has encountered hostility. 'When you're going too fast, people get mad at you,' she said. 'I've had canes waved at me in the distance.'"[1]

This last line drew the guys' ire. "Oh, I'll show her my cane," Eddie promised, picking his up and shaking it threateningly. "I threw a punch at one once, but I missed." He told us how a delivery person for a popular Chinese restaurant a block away had nearly hit him several times.

"I'd love to knock one of them off their bikes," Eugene said.

"Rob did once, I think. He got him right in the face, knocked him off," Eddie said, invoking the memory of his neighborhood buddy who died suddenly of a heart attack four years before.

Eugene and Eddie's stories about how they handled or dreamed of addressing direct challenges to their physical safety fascinated me. Eddie had a much tougher persona, having grown up in working-class New York City and worked in blue-collar construction, while Eugene presented himself as more refined, a working writer who didn't watch television and enjoyed opera. These differences primed me to expect different imagined responses to threat. It surprised me that they showed such a thirst for confrontation despite their growing physical vulnerability. The tension between their desire for confrontation and their vulnerability illuminates the challenges of old age for them in the context of gender and masculinity.

MAKING DO

Elders' slim pickings at McDonald's felt even slimmer given their competition with teenagers for space, which recalls sociologist Arlie Hochschild's insights in *The Unexpected Community* about parallels between these periods in the life course. Old age and adolescence lie furthest from early middle age, which Hochschild argues is the time in a person's life society most values for its potential to amass wealth, power, and recognition.[2] For different reasons, young and old have less involvement in institutions of work and family. While most teenagers have not yet entered full-time employment or formed their own families, retirement from paid work and retreat from child rearing push many in late life towards the work-family periphery. Elders' persistent efforts to claim their place amid McDonald's greater noise and chaos help us understand the different ways people constructed their social lives when not drawing relationships from family and work.

Tension flowed from old to young. While McDonald's teenagers appeared oblivious to the old people, mostly women, around them, elders often lambasted their noise. Sometimes I also had difficulty hearing people beside me due to adolescents' shouting. The old people expressed their frustration with more muted gestures such as eye rolling and hushed complaints among themselves like "Why do they have to be so loud?" Other times they offered sharper comments, such as, "I'd like to kick her ass." Confrontations also escalated, albeit infrequently, as when Lucy told a group of teenagers to "shut up."

One spring afternoon at McDonald's, different waves of regulars arrived and departed in quick succession. Carmen, Gladys, and Bernice began sitting around 3 p.m. Jeannette sat separately with "the lady in the hat," as former bakery regulars referred to a woman who predated them. Soon afterwards, Phyllis, Lucy, Pauline, and Theresa filed in. Gladys and Carmen headed out before George arrived at 4 p.m., moments before Diane came straight from work. Phyllis left shortly afterwards, annoyed with the teenagers' noise. Lucy yelled at kids as they departed. "Shut up. I can't hear myself." She updated us about a presentation she had attended in her building about "clutter," held in anticipation of a major, building complex–wide HVAC-replacement project commencing that fall. "I hope I never get cuckoo or batty like those hoarders they told us about. They said it's related to anxiety, and I have that but never had a clutter tendency," she said, explaining that they had to clear excess items before work began in the apartments. Lucy continued, "It's death city over there [in the co-op buildings]. And we're all going to have our turns. It depresses me."

I sat with Diane and George. Lucy, Theresa, and Bernice sat at a neighboring table. "Dottie will never make it," Lucy said about her prospects for joining the group at McDonald's that day. As she complained about noise again, I turned my attention to Diane and George.

Diane mentioned that her niece, Shanice, would be coming for Mother's Day. "My sister told me, 'She needs us to pray for her.' I told her, 'You need to talk to your daughter. She's depressed.'" With George at her side, Diane told me depression ran in her family, and she learned the other day that her cousin had planned to hang himself. His family found him in time, averting tragedy. Diane said that Shanice lived with a "friend" and their relationship of only a few months infringed on her extroverted niece's freedom "to be involved and go out with her friends." Diane continued, "I can tell she's lying when I talk to her on the phone and says everything is fine. She's putting up a front."

We talked about Diane and George's struggle to find an affordable apartment to share. George rented a single room in Brooklyn, and Diane lived in a crowded project apartment with her sister and brother-in-law, a heavy drinker with a mean temper. She avoided spending much time at home. Diane's niece told her she missed New York City. Despite the challenges of staying, Diane said she couldn't imagine living somewhere like South Carolina again. She wanted to remain in the neighborhood where she grew up. George also wanted to stay in the city. "It's the center of everything and it's part of my history too," he said and recalled fond memories hanging out in Greenwich Village "sandboxes" (i.e., parks), staying out all night, and waking up in the morning. "Nobody bothered you."

A few months later, at nearly 6 p.m., I stopped into a Dunkin' Donuts three blocks from McDonald's. Unexpectedly, I bumped into Diane and George, who called to me as I scanned the ice cream case. They were dressed up more than usual, especially George, who wore a black fedora and button-down shirt tucked into grey dress slacks instead of his everyday sneakers, t-shirt, baggy jeans, and Yankees cap. Diane wore a red flowing blouse with an intricate scrolling pattern and a long, ruffled black skirt. I assumed they had special plans this Friday night.

"What have you been up to?" George asked. I mentioned the typical school stresses.

"How about you?" I asked.

Diane leaned closer to George. "He's been going on job interviews," she said, which explained George's spiffy new attire. Diane always looked put together, in a dress or skirt and blazer. She still worked at the same AIDS nonprofit organization but expressed concern about her position, looking sideways as she chewed her lower lip. Her boss, the organization's executive director, worried about state funding cuts.

"Do you still go to McDonald's?" I asked.

"No," Diane said, with a trace of ambivalence as she drew the word into two syllables, the last rising.

"So, is this the place?" I asked.

"Yes, this is the place," she said, her mouth settling into a smile. "I come in about two o'clock, then George comes." They referred to the noise at McDonald's and friction with Theresa as having compelled their location change. Growing ties with their Harlem church community also pulled them further from the ex-bakery crowd. Despite a few false starts after the bakery's closure, they'd adapted and found their places. But compared with their older, white counterparts, they struggled harder to carve out spaces in a city that had denied them the same affordable housing opportunities that previous generations of New Yorkers had enjoyed.

ANOTHER BRICK IN THE WALL

Pete's pull-away doors remained shut one stormy evening when I doubted anyone would show due to the foreboding weather. But Sylvia and Eugene had already arrived. "Well, hello," Eugene said with a smile and hint of surprise. He wore a black raincoat over a lime-colored shirt.

Eugene explained that he had come early for dinner, gesturing to a plastic container filled with sandwich crumbs and an empty bag of Sun Chips. As I pondered what to eat, Sylvia worked on an enormous hero sandwich, made "special" for her.

"He puts everything in there—I can't eat the whole thing."

Eugene laughed, "He put spinach in there for her."

"They don't normally do this for everyone," she said. "And they gave me a slice of avocado on the side, for Eugene."

"I love avocado," he said.

I said that I might have a tuna sandwich, but Sylvia warned me off it. "I always stay away from the salads—they can hide things in there."

With a sheepish grin, Eugene said, "I just had it, the egg salad." Pointing to the crumpled chip bag, he added, "Phyllis got me hooked on them."

Sylvia nodded knowingly, as if she'd witnessed this conversion. Meal choices served as a mainstay of daily discussions. "What did you have today?" functioned as a regular conversation starter. People often gave dietary and nutrition advice, helping shape health decisions in small but concrete ways around food selections. They encouraged each other to reduce sugar, take vitamins, and swap out items in favor of healthier alternatives. Sylvia wondered aloud about the chips' sodium content. I said although they tasted salty, they contained a modest amount of sodium.

"How much sodium are you supposed to have in a day?" she asked.

"No more than 2,400 milligrams, but ideally no more than two thousand milligrams," I said. I mentioned that my then boyfriend had a genetic condition that caused heart problems and high blood pressure and thus followed a low-sodium DASH diet.³ "The whole bag has only 240 milligrams of salt," I said, while reading aloud the package's nutrition label.

"That's not bad," she said, surprised. Sylvia offered to order a sandwich on my behalf, explaining that Marco, thinking it was for her, would make a bigger sandwich.

"They should name it after you. I should order 'the Sylvia,'" I joked.

"Stacy, if you want me to order it for you, I could do it." I thanked her but declined.

Minutes later, she pushed the sandwich towards me. "Here, take it. It's too much," she said, despite my protestations that I didn't want her to be hungry. She looked over her shoulder at Marco behind the deli counter. "But don't let him see it—I don't want him to feel bad," she whispered.

Despite disliking mustard and cucumber, I ate the sandwich, while Eugene told Sylvia about restarting work on his children's story.

"You mean Igor?" she asked, referring to a character from another of Eugene's children's stories. "No," he said, recounting the current plot about a Dalmatian living at a firehouse and a mutt dog that shows up one day.

"What're their names?"

"Mutt and Dandy."

"Oh, that's cute," she said.

Eugene supplied additional plot details: Dandy is suspicious of his potential rival, but Mutt eventually wins him over. They become reluctant pals, teaching fire safety together at schools. "I'm almost finished, but I need to write a scary chapter," he said, describing how Mutt gets lost, is picked up by a dog catcher, and ends up in a pet store. "Anytime someone looks at him through the glass or looks like they want to buy him, he limps or growls at them," he said, taking pleasure in the world he had created. We talked more about his now-finished water bug story. I asked Eugene how he decided on Igor's name, changing it from Boris. "I named him after the hurricane," he said, referring to a recent storm. He told Sylvia about arriving at the story's ending. "Well, I was sick of all those cliches about women being afraid of bugs, so I took Stacy's suggestion and have a little girl come to the door selling Girl Scout cookies. She sees Igor and asks, 'Can I hold him?'"

Eddie arrived as Eugene mentioned wanting to get a patent but not knowing how. He began sharing his idea, but Sylvia interrupted him. "Eugene, you want to be careful about discussing this out in the open."

"Oh, right," he said, scanning the room and lowering his voice. He continued, "I have five ideas for patents. The one I was telling Sylvia about this morning is for metal can tops. They always break, but my idea is to have two of them [a two-pronged pull tab], so they distribute the tension."

"They always break," she said, nodding in agreement.

Eugene repeated his uncertainty about the patent process. "I sent away for a patent kit some guy advertised on the Internet."

"Be careful about what you tell him. He could steal your idea," she said. I echoed her concern.

Eddie jumped in, agreeing with Sylvia. "She's right. You send this guy all this information about your idea, and he could take it and get the patent himself."

Eugene said he'd review the information but withhold details and search independently for a patent office.

"There must be one in Manhattan," she said.

Eugene then turned to us, shielding his mouth with his hand. "Somebody's been listening the whole time," he murmured.

Sylvia craned her neck. "Who? Who?" she said loudly.

"That guy over there," he said, eyeing an older white man one table away. The portly man had long finished eating and sat with an empty juice bottle. Jowly faced and balding, with white-silver hair at the sides, he wore a checkered shirt and wool sweater knotted around his shoulders. Inky tattoos blurred from age ringed his right forearm. His clear blue-grey eyes bore into us. I had never seen this man before.

At times he leaned over the table's edge for a better listen. Eugene repeated with annoyance and incredulity, "He's been listening the whole time." Sylvia remained perplexed about the person to whom he referred, her eyes searching the store. Eugene shook his head twice, rather obviously in the man's direction, telling her, "That bozo."

Eddie looked up at the ceiling and muttered, fists clenched, "Are you kidding me? If she doesn't see . . . [the man over there]." He could barely contain his frustration with Sylvia for not catching on quick enough for his taste. He talked with Eugene and avoided engaging Sylvia, who sat across from me. As she and I chatted, I heard little of their discussion.

Sylvia routed our conversation to the familiar territory of remembrance and memorializing the dead, a popular discussion topic whenever we talked one-on-one or in a larger group of women. "Phyllis, Maria, and I are going out for Italian tomorrow, for Lorenzo's birthday," she said. He had died suddenly of a heart attack at age 79. They hatched the idea to celebrate what would have been his eightieth birthday during a shared taxi ride to his wake. Maria worked at the local pharmacy and knew Sylvia and Lorenzo but had never met Phyllis before the funeral. Sylvia mentioned that Maria wanted to go to an old Spanish restaurant in the neighborhood. "She's of Spanish descent," she explained. "I hadn't been there in about fifteen years, and Phyllis went more recently and said the food was so-so." They decided on Italian instead. "He [Lorenzo] told me when I was coming out of the bakery before it closed, 'September twenty-fifth we have an appointment. It's my eightieth birthday.'"

I asked her to repeat the running inside joke that she, Lorenzo, and Maria had at the pharmacy. A smile spread across Sylvia's face. "We had a joke. I used to ask [Maria] for birth control. And Lorenzo, he'd joke and ask for birth control for me." Of his death, Sylvia said, "It's such a shock. I never expected . . ." She revealed her surprise at hearing that Lorenzo still worked for the city's emergency management office when he died. "He said he was getting out of it. He wasn't as healthy as he looked." We discussed how he had bypassed our radar screens as the next person who might die and affirmed once more Lorenzo's generosity. I mentioned his helping Spiro, who had no family nearby, when he needed an escort after an outpatient procedure. "Yes, he went with him to the doctor, stayed there with him all day, and brought him home," she said. "And Martin," she added, referring to Lorenzo's assistance arranging Martin's funeral. "I hadn't known him for that long," she said, noting how she'd met Lorenzo at the bakery only a few years before, though they had lived in the same high-rise building for forty years.

Sylvia said good-bye to Marco at the counter before leaving. When she returned to the table, she mentioned that as she stood there, swaying to the Spanish music on the radio, he presented her with an interesting question. "He asked, 'What is the best time of your life? What age?'" She paused thoughtfully and continued. "I said, 'That's a good question.' I told him, 'I think your middle 20s. When you're no longer a teenager and starting to think about maturing and what not and settling down. Then I found out he's about 27," she said with a laugh. She added that Marco and the cashier, Ricardo, were cousins, originally from Mexico, and both had little boys.

Eugene circled back to the man who had unsettled him before. "That bozo kept listening the whole time and staring," he said, imitating the man's penetrating gaze. I asked if he'd ever seen him before. "No." His unease seemed to run deeper than believing the man wanted to steal his patent idea. It resembled his annoyance with a severely knock-kneed old woman who attempted to chat with him on occasion. Earlier, as she passed, taking painfully slow steps, he said, "She's trying to weasel in." But she refrained from trying to engage him. Such interactions revealed a darker side of Eugene, usually the last person to blow anyone off. In contrast, Eddie acted more hot tempered and closed off, but he had a different take on the staring man. After we left Pete's and split off from Eugene and Sylvia as they headed to their neighboring buildings a block away, Eddie said, "Look, he's a lonely guy, probably has nothing and just wanted to listen." His empathy stirred up the undercurrent of sadness I had also felt as I observed the man straining to hear a fairly mundane conversation. It was as if an invisible pane of glass separated him from us and he was peering in from the outside, longing for the company of strangers. Such moments of exclusion and distrust show the limits of openness and belonging and, at times, the impermeability of personal boundaries.

On a temperate, cloudless evening, Lucy stopped by Pete's with an older white woman who looked somewhat familiar, but I couldn't place her as a regular at any of the neighborhood hangout spots. She appeared in her late 60s, with wavy light brown hair and a cerulean t-shirt stretched tight around her round belly. Pete's pull-away doors remained open, and they stood on the sidewalk outside.

"Hello, folks," Lucy greeted me, Sylvia, Eugene, and Eddie in her characteristic booming voice. She seemed upbeat and held a copy of *The New York Post* with a ripped-out page crisply folded on top. "How ya doing?" she asked. We responded with the usual pleasantries, "Fine, thanks."

"Your hair looks nice. Did you do anything different to it?" Sylvia asked.

"Yeah, I just had it done today," Lucy said, brushing aside her darkened honey bangs.

"Where are you going these days?" I asked.

She gave a friendly but guarded answer. "I can't tell you all my secrets. But I know where to find you," she said, waving at the four of us. Her tight-lipped response surprised me, considering her openness on other occasions.

Lucy's impulse epitomized more common efforts to limit their friendship commitments and retain privacy about routines. She often complained about attracting "sad, broken-down women" with health problems. "Why do they want to be my friend? Mama mia!" she lamented, while telling an anecdote about how Shirley, a former bakery regular who lived in her building, had "cornered her" with her rolling walker several times.

After Lucy and her companion departed, Sylvia expressed something similar. She said that her neighbor told her, "I know where you go."

"My neighbor is a nice lady; I've known her a very long time," she said but expressed discomfort about her tracking her whereabouts. "I had another woman trailing me. She would stick her head in here, looking for me. Maybe they do it just to see if I'm still alive," she laughed. I shook my head. "No, it's true," she said and told a story about returning from a two-month trip to Arizona many years before. While leaving Johnny's bodega, she had bumped into a woman in the neighborhood she didn't know well. "She looked like she had seen a ghost and said, 'I thought you were dead.'"

Sylvia not only desired privacy about her comings and goings but also flexibility in her commitments. "I don't know if I'm going to make it tonight," she said with a tremble most mornings, limiting expectations and accountability. Still, she showed up at Pete's almost every evening.

WAITING ON A FRIEND

One late afternoon, I found Carmen alone at McDonald's. "I wonder where the young people went," she said and mentioned fewer people overall came now. "My sister says McDonald's is dirty and full of drunks, homeless, and drug addicts." Her sister lived in a house with her husband on Staten Island and had one son. Carmen had never married or had children. She contrasted her sister's propriety, middle-class aspirations, and sense of superiority with her own values. They weren't very close, and Carmen visited her infrequently. From descriptions of her sister's world, Staten Island sounded more like another planet rather than one of New York City's five boroughs. "She lives a different life."

Lucy soon arrived, followed by Phyllis and Judy. Discussion shifted to a recent suicide in the co-ops, where they all lived. The management office distributed a notice to residents, and they delved into the details. A man with a terminal illness had jumped from the roof of one of the complex's ten twenty-one-story buildings. They appreciated his efforts to minimize bystander trauma, such as shrouding himself with a blanket and selecting a building other than where he lived to spare children stumbling upon his body in the nearby playground.

Lucy revealed her "buddy system" with a friend Peggy who lived in her building. If they didn't hear from each other every day, someone called security. Judy lived alone. Her longtime boyfriend resided in the same building complex, and they saw each other several days a week. "Yes, Connie and I also check up on each other," Phyllis said of her friend and next-door neighbor. She chuckled while telling an anecdote about how Connie's medic alert necklace once went off by accident, notifying her. Building security accompanied her to check on her friend. They startled Connie in the shower. "She was so surprised, she didn't know what was going on." Lucy reminded us of Dottie's consequential connections to neighbors the day of her heart attack: "The tenant association president found her . . . See, Dottie knew everyone and that saved her. She was supposed to go down for a birthday party, and when she didn't show, they found her on the other side of the door on the floor."

Lucy reflected on the McDonald's group "falling apart" since Theresa's advanced dementia had necessitated her move to New Jersey two months before. Only half joking, she said, "She was the life of the party."

"Yeah, she slept all day," Phyllis said dryly, referring to Theresa's tendency to nod off at the table. But Lucy astutely observed how her dependable presence had drawn others. She'd stopped by in her absence but said, "It's not the same. Nobody's there." Theresa had stayed at McDonald's late into the evening, often past 8 p.m., and some nights well into the ten o'clock hour. The month before her move she spent even more time at McDonald's, looking increasingly haggard. Her ripped open shoe, held together with a dirty bit of shoelace, exposed her foot and posed a fall risk. Soon afterwards, Theresa injured her ankle, heralding an absence that became permanent as her memory problems and inability to live independently prompted family intervention.

"She spent a lot of time there," Lucy said.

"Theresa was really the glue keeping the group together," I said, affirming her observations, though there were exceptions to this sentiment, for example, in the case of George and Diane.

"She was," Lucy said.

Men face their own difficulties in old age. Eugene's world had shrunk when an avalanche of health problems struck in his mid-80s. His mobility plummeted after a second major hip surgery and heart attack that made walking a block exhausting, and one by one he dropped his activities. As men like Eddie and Eugene grew older in an expensive city, they also experienced greater financial vulnerability. Eddie always looked to save on everything from groceries to household purchases. Eugene's financial distress had mounted more incrementally over the years, and strained finances increasingly limited his access to the neighborhood and the city. The dwindling number of affordable gathering spots affected both men in great and immediate ways.

Eugene could no longer afford to eat at different establishments or enjoy a few hours of escape at the movies. Towards the later phases of my fieldwork, he ate almost exclusively at Pete's, complaining, "Pete's is a drag. About the time I am having dinner the bozo puts the chairs up and starts sweeping and stirring up dust. I can't afford to go anywhere else." While Eugene always found company with others, he also remained private and fiercely independent, often declining modest offers of help.

His financial troubles escalated as his ninetieth birthday approached, leaving him no choice but to borrow $40 from Sylvia one evening. "I didn't expect him to pay me back," she divulged when describing her offer of a "loan" he reluctantly accepted. But he refrained from revealing then that he faced a $4,000 shortfall at year's end. We found out about his subsequent hospitalization only after not seeing him for several days.

In late December, after two weeks away, I stopped into Pete's. It was four days before Eugene's birthday. My last time there, I hadn't seen him, so I called and left a voicemail. He hadn't called back during my absence, which concerned me. Sylvia also hadn't come into Pete's for a while or seen Eugene for two weeks. Last she saw him, he'd planned to cash a large check. She inquired with Ricardo at the register. He also saw him less frequently but said that "Mr. Eugene" came in a few days before. Afterwards, I spoke with the doorman in Eugene's building, a rotund Latino man in his late 20s with close cropped black hair. He said that police and EMTs had escorted Eugene out two days before. He didn't know where they took him. Eugene walked on his own but had difficulty without his cane. Fortunately, the doorman had a spare in the lobby to give him.

After our chat, he let me upstairs. I knocked on Eugene's door and rang the bell. I heard a muffled radio but no answer, which worried me. Two neighbors across the hall poked their heads out the door and walked over to ask about Eugene. They didn't know he had gone to the hospital.

When Eugene's younger sister, May, couldn't reach him by phone or email, she called me. I updated her about what I learned. May called local hospitals and the city morgue. When she had tracked down Eugene, with his permission, she disclosed that he had been admitted to an in-patient psychiatric unit and shared details about his suicide plan and the circumstances that had precipitated his hospitalization. He confirmed these details after his discharge.

Under the growing financial distress, Eugene had plunged into a major depression. After his royalty check from book earnings arrived in the amount of $30 rather than the expected $4,000, he informed an old friend and colleague from his magazine days that that he planned to kill himself.

"I was going to jump out the window," he told me matter-of-factly. "Really, I was. I had the suicide notes to my sisters all written out and ready to send."

His friend called the police, and they took him to the psychiatric emergency room for observation. He spent three weeks in the psychiatric unit at a nearby hospital. The nurses doted on him, and he became everyone's "favorite patient," but he dismissed the place as a "Mickey Mouse operation" and remained skeptical of the hospital's ability to help him or other patients.

Eugene disclosed his shaky financial situation. To his chagrin his sister had loaned him some money and had begun to send him $200 a month to tide him over. He had no choice but to accept her generosity.

"She doesn't have much money," he said. "But I didn't protest. I don't know where I'd be without May." In trying to explain how he had ended up in such dire economic straits, he said with a tinge of shame, "I once had $80,000 in the bank; I don't know what happened." As we charted his increasing cost-of-living expenses against his stagnant Social Security income, it became clear that rather than excessive spending, he had simply outlived his savings.

In old age, losing status, power, physical strength, and mobility challenges the traditional "hegemonic masculinity" that many men had enjoyed unencumbered until their later years.[4] When I first met Eugene, he seemed the least worried about money. He could afford to travel and enjoyed many international trips throughout his life. He dined out and indulged in expensive wine. But in his late 80s, financial anguish and accumulating health problems bore down on him, giving a glimpse into other older men's losses. Physical limitations had radically changed how he lived his life compared to how he had lived it in the preceding six decades. He had no reason to renew his passport since he couldn't walk more than a block without crushing fatigue. Men with blue-collar backgrounds and work histories of manual labor may experience loss of physical function even more acutely. For example, while Eddie had to retire from construction work due to back and leg pain and stiffness, Eugene continued to write. His work may have provided insufficient income, but he could draw on his writing for esteem and identity, unlike the other "old people" he avoided at the senior center.

Eugene's situation aligns with data that show higher suicide rates among older white men.[5] He faced shame and pride as "psychological cost barriers" to obtaining assistance and also reported not receiving help upon his hospital discharge.[6] For example, he had not received a caseworker to assist with SNAP (Supplemental Nutrition Assistance Program), formerly known as food stamps, and other benefits. Instead, he reluctantly relied on his sister's help and neighborhood connections. While members of racial and ethnic minorities often experience more inequality over the course of their lives,[7] Eugene's white privilege and downward mobility left him vulnerable to deprivation and need, which he was not used to and struggled to adjust to. In contrast, single women such as Lucy seemed better positioned to seek help and drew on varied connections to manage administrative processes and setbacks. A journalist once consulted me about a cautionary article she wanted to write about aging baby boomer women who never married nor had children and their grim prospects for navigating health crises without family help. I told her about some of the lifelong singletons I'd met and said that I worried least about these women lacking support as they'd spent their lifetimes cultivating a wealth of social relationships that carried them through hard times. The reporter never wrote the story.

9

THE INEVITABLE PLACE

FIFTY YEARS AGO, when anthropologist Barbara Myerhoff studied the lives of older adults, she discovered a resilient community of Eastern European Jews struggling against the tide of gentrification in Venice Beach, California. They faced poverty, displacement, scarce affordable housing, and rising rents due to urban development that ignited property values.[1] Amid such upheaval, they forged enduring connections at a local senior center. Today a new generation of poor and moderate-income elders struggles to grow old in cities like New York, Los Angeles, San Francisco, and other gentrifying areas whose residents are greying as the municipalities where they live absorb affluent arrivals. Despite escalating challenges, older adults continue to find their places, but it's proving harder.

SPIRITS IN THE MATERIAL WORLD: LOST PEOPLE, LOST PLACES, LOST WORLD

Many elders whose lives fill these pages have now departed the physical world. The dead include Eugene, Eddie, Theresa, Dottie, Lucy, Martin, Lorenzo, Maureen, Tom, and Arthur. Decades younger than the older adults she served with such care and attentiveness, Angelica also died at age 55 from a breast cancer recurrence. Given the advanced ages of most people in my study, their deaths have not shocked me in their happening, save for Angelica's. But their presence in my life continues, like friendly ghosts that say hello at the most unexpected moments, with bittersweet reminisces shaken loose, stirred, and revisited in my writing of this account.

Despite anticipating closures, the scale of place-loss continues to surprise me, especially when I tally the number of businesses now gone. In my field notes from nine months after the bakery closed, I considered the prospects of older adults' claiming spaces as their own: "I can't say we're quite here yet, but there may come the day when the only options available are subsidized spaces like the local senior centers and chains like McDonald's. Who knows . . . maybe the day will come when this place can't get its lease renewed."[2]

Something resembling that day has arrived. McDonald's and Pete's Delicatessen have now closed. At the time of this writing, the neighborhood has also lost at least eight pharmacies, including a CVS and all three Rite Aid locations that doubled as discount grocery stores for many elders. Galaxy Diner, Johnny's bodega, and a 51-year-old Puerto Rican eatery also shuttered, among other businesses, such as check cashing stores, that once catered to lower income residents. A large supermarket where Lucy ate breakfast several mornings also recently went out of business. Oversized retail spaces once containing banks and other businesses that occupied generous square footage have remained empty for years. Even before the pandemic, which accelerated the trend, vacant storefronts accumulated, leading writer Griffin Hansberry (who also uses the pen name Jeremiah Moss) to call such upscale dereliction "high-rent blight."[3]

Pete's Yelp page transformed into an online memorial, providing a digital mourning space for former customers to attest to their loss. A eulogy for Pete's written two years after the closing showed the lingering effect that small business closures have on people of all ages and how people make nondescript spaces into beloved third places:

> I dearly miss the now-closed Pete's Deli. Just before the pandemic they were forced to close due to a ceiling collapse from a broken water pipe (not their fault). They resiliently re-opened during the pandemic but were ultimately forced to close permanently due to the landlord raising rent and a decline in business from the state of the world. The space has since been completely vacant for two years, which begs the question as to what the landlord has gained from the loss these hardworking people faced. Perhaps I don't know the full story, but this is as I understand it.
>
> Marco, Ricardo, and the rest of the staff were so thoughtful and caring to people they didn't even know. New Yorkers are not always easy (an understatement?) . . . Yet the people at Pete's always treated me like a good friend, often better than my own coworkers did that day. Marco would remember about six of my different regular orders, including all of the customizations, so eager to guess what I wanted that I could barely order for myself!
>
> In the end one might say to not take a good deli for granted. But it's not about a good deli, it's good people. People who treat you with respect and kindness and take pride in what they do. These days this feels more and more rare.

Another Pete's customer of six years wrote, "This place is what makes New York great, as they're a fabulous local business who supports many who are on their own and could use a friendly face to say hello to. Being solo, I've been blessed to get the next best thing to a home cooked meal or sandwich by a business that cares about how your day went or what's going on in your life."

Practical, economic, and emotional support allows people to age safely and comfortably in their communities, but barriers persist. With growing numbers of elders living independently for as long as possible, scholars, policymakers, and ordinary people have a stake in understanding what promotes their flourishing and what administrative burdens—that is, onerous experiences of policy implementation—stymie older people from obtaining government benefits and social services, as the work of public policy professors Pamela Herd and Donald P. Moynihan powerfully demonstrates.[4]

Despite the rhetoric surrounding aging in place, both from elders who prefer to avoid retirement communities and assisted living facilities and from policymakers who see aging in place as a popular and less costly alternative to institutional options, not enough research has focused on capturing older adults' lived experiences or on understanding how places and neighborhood relationships enable them to remain at home. While large-scale survey research has provided an important window into elders' social networks, qualitative studies suggest we have much left to uncover about how neighborhoods nurture social connections. Aging in gentrifying areas further complicates older residents' ability to find places where they feel accepted economically, physically, and emotionally. Increasing numbers of elders who lack choice about where to grow old and the resources to comfortably age in place may also become "stuck in place."[5]

The La Marjolaine bakery cohort frequented establishments that promoted public interactions through their low cost and relaxed surveillance, geographic proximity to home, and inclusive physical design and layout; these findings bolster prior research and offer additional insights into what elders need to access space and secure emotional and physical comfort.[6] After their central gathering spot closed, people demonstrated tenacity and resilience in seeking out viable replacements that contained elements they had once enjoyed. But ultimately none of the new gathering spots could offer the same arrangement as the bakery. Future research should seek to uncover the features of neighborhood places that provide older people with opportunities for social support and interaction, the conditions under which such places come under threat, and the tipping point at which accessible places become impossible to replace.

Social capital and robust networks can buffer older people against isolation, depression, illness, and the loss of friends and family.[7] To date much research on late-life well-being has focused on applying findings to problems associated with old age, such as health declines. Relatively few studies have used ethnographic data. This study has addressed some of these oversights. While my research has expanded our knowledge about the life course, the social construction of age, and age segregation and stratification in society, this study has also contributed to subfields beyond aging, including gender, community, and social network research. Given sweeping demographic changes in the United States and the greying of world regions, including East Asia and Europe, this study's findings are more timely and relevant than ever.[8]

We know belonging matters for elders but less so about how, why, and what facilitates it. How do older people maintain their independence when faced with multiple vulnerabilities? What forms of social relationships exist? How do older people create or resist belonging? In what ways does belonging to a place or a group help people manage crises and everyday challenges? This final chapter synthesizes study findings from previous chapters to answer the questions investigated in the book. I then examine the policy implications of my research and elders' growing needs as the older adult population comes to include more women, minorities, and immigrants. I conclude by offering concrete suggestions to support contemporary urban aging and some final reflections on my own aging as I ponder possibilities and challenges on the horizon for us all.

TAKEAWAYS

My fieldwork suggests the following answers to the questions I pose. First, neighborhood-based social networks sustain older people straining to survive in a city increasingly inhospitable to lower-income residents. Chapter 6 explored the development of the "elastic ties" that sated their hunger for connection without sacrificing autonomy or fueling fears of dependency. This finding suggests that many ties crucial to older people's well-being are neither "strong" nor "weak" but possess elements of both; they constitute a third type of tie that corresponds to late-life conditions and to the way networks shift over the life course. Family ties and passing acquaintanceships had their place in older people's networks, but an intermediary form of elastic tie that blended closeness and distance allowed elders to reap the benefits of close ties while avoiding some the inherent risks and responsibilities of deeper connections.

Second, older residents have a unique relationship with the neighborhood. They spend more time within its confines due to retirement, less discretionary income, and onset of physical limitations. Public places, therefore, have a special role to play in facilitating social support and a sense of belonging. Chapter 5 presented data that showed how spaces close to home that didn't strain wallets or impose high levels of surveillance promoted the development of such connections. Such conditions invited elders to spend substantial time together, thus allowing them to learn information about their neighbors and develop the closeness associated with these social ties.

Freedom to make spaces their own, especially at the bakery, which had functioned as an extension of people's living rooms, helped lend these places an air of privacy and feeling of ownership despite their public nature. For example, customers brought in outside food and ordered pizza for delivery. Over years they formed a personal relationship with the evening counter person, Angelica. She performed favors for regulars, such as passing along packages and messages between customers, carrying orders to those who couldn't physically manage this task, and storing perishable groceries in the refrigerator to spare them from rushing home after shopping. The flexibility to imprint the space with their own sensibilities counterbalanced impediments in income and physical mobility, but this flexibility also corresponded to their freedom from fixed schedules. McDonald's and Pete's Delicatessen also proved open and fostered the diversity that we have traditionally cherished in our most beloved, if challenging, cities like New York. At the same time that elders found in these spaces an inclusive environment that supported their aging, they were also able to mix with different city characters, from local celebrities to an unhoused woman. A few women had become so friendly with this person that they invited her into their homes to use the shower and telephone. As Lucy observed at Pete's when a crowd of tall, slender young women in satiny evening gowns departed, they could watch "the beautiful people" and entertain themselves as spectators of this parade without feeling excluded.

Third, older people's embodied experiences not only constrain access to the neighborhood but organize an experience of gentrification that differs from the experiences of residents with greater physical mobility, as discussed in chapter 7. The body affects the experience of place, time, distance, weather, and identification with other elders in far reaching ways. The endless demands of bodily care seeped into the bulk of interactions, shaping social relations with neighbors and friends. Chapter 3 showed how discussions about others' bodies, cognitive shortcomings, or mental acuity allowed old people to measure their own deficits against their peers' and to distance themselves in order to elevate their own standing as they also succumbed to pervasive ageism. Yet despite rampant gossip and frequently avoiding each other, mutual recognition of shared age-related circumstances and limitations occurred, as I showed in chapter 4 when the bakery's loss sparked something of a social "series," however ephemeral, that encouraged age-based solidarity.

Fourth, elders often declined to seek services and benefits and encountered steep "learning costs" when attempting to secure assistance. Past negative experiences navigating the "Medicare maze," for example, also lowered trust in other systems of aid and dissuaded them from changing benefits, sometimes to their detriment. Ethnographic data revealed on-the-ground processes by which elders, often with lowered physical and cognitive reserves, confronted these barriers and their agency and resilience in persisting. Elders vulnerable to isolation cultivated a rich network of supportive neighborhood connections in public spaces that helped them respond to these administrative burdens. Among single adults who lived alone due to divorce, widowhood, or never having married, lifelong singletons and divorcees expressed more financial concern but also leveraged supportive peer networks and extended family relationships. Despite lacking spousal retirement benefits and often children to provide care, they secured the economic and social resources for aging in place.

THIS MUST BE THE PLACE: LEARNING TO MAKE A HOME IN THE WORLD AT EVERY AGE

As I came to see that elders had transformed the bakery into an alternative hub of neighborhood life—a public living room, where they developed the social ties that helped them remain in their homes—their lessons for survival and belonging enriched my life and continue to teach me how to make a home in the world wherever I go.

My ethnographic research helped me manage my own difficult life transitions while I conducted the study, as I supported my father through a lung cancer recurrence and my sister during and after a three-month psychiatric hospitalization and diagnosis of schizophrenia.[9] Elders often checked on me and asked about my family while I was providing caregiving assistance. Then, I ended my thirteen-year relationship, forcing me to navigate new grief and adjust to singlehood. Amid these upheavals, I came to San Francisco.

Older people I befriended in the Bay Area soon brought me into their web of care and served as important guides, just as elders in New York City had for years. My San Francisco roommate, a retired taxi driver in his late 70s from Dublin, Ireland, played the piano every morning, listened to my romantic ups and downs, and included me in his friendship group of older men, who took me to lunch at the United Irish Cultural Center of San Francisco. Another older friend in the Castro showed me baby owls in Golden Gate Park and drew me into his motley social circle of people he'd met serendipitously in the City. These San Francisco elders faced their own challenges aging in place, including a shortage of affordable housing and residences on steep hills with stairs not designed for mobility problems. To cope, they also sought places for connection where they felt comfortable and supported. Even with pandemic stay-at-home orders and indoor dining bans, I observed elders gather in public, such as the older Latino men in the Mission District who regularly congregated outside a McDonald's at the busy intersection of 24th Street and Mission. The group of six numbered too many to share a single bench, and some lounged in folding camping chairs they'd brought. A little white poodle kept them company.

In cities like San Francisco and New York, with a rich "public realm"—which the sociologist Lyn Lofland characterizes as spaces where strangers interact and form relationships—I've implemented strategies that I learned from older people to foster a sense of belonging.[10] After my breakup, like many elders I met, I struggled to fill my weekend time. Becoming a regular at different places helped me assuage loneliness as I created new routines—spending my Saturdays in North Beach, rotating with other regulars among Caffe Trieste, Caffe Greco, Specs', and Vesuvio Cafe.

When Eugene turned 90, I asked him how quickly his life had passed thus far. With a grin he snapped his fingers, giving me a startling reminder not to waste time and to slow down. Elders have imparted wisdom that has helped me thrive in my later years. I'm now planning for a home where I can grow old and accommodate increasing disability, securing a pension and building retirement savings, accessing preventative health care, and advocating for myself in health-care settings. I strive for a purposeful life filled with connection as I cultivate different sources of social support, which includes a steadfast partner who takes care of me with the same generosity I have tried to show others in my caretaking over the years.

At 43, I'm firmly ensconced in the "old age of youth."[11] I try not to lament every new grey hair, wrinkle, and dark spot. I'm grateful to elders for helping me to embrace the pleasures of growing older, feel more comfortable in my skin, and accept my mistakes as I learn to approach late life with less fear, judgment, and dread.

OUR INEVITABLE PLACE

A century before my fieldwork, on the other side of the country, acclaimed poet of the American West Robinson Jeffers wrote of his unexpected detour to coastal Carmel, California: "When the stage-coach topped the hill from Monterey, and we looked down through pines and sea-fogs on Carmel Bay, it was evident that we had come without knowing it to our inevitable place."[12] For Jeffers and his wife, Una, the central California coastline provided respite from their tumultuous relationship, which began as a seven-year affair, the death of their newborn daughter, and the start of World War I, which had derailed plans to live abroad. They would spend the rest of their lives, nearly half a century, in this "inevitable place."[13] With failing eyesight, Jeffers continued to write and live there for twelve more years following Una's death, dying in his sleep at age 75.[14]

Jeffers's personal epiphany about stumbling upon the rugged terrain that would become a lifelong home mirrors the sometimes serendipitous discoveries and turns the elders I spent time with made while finding their own inevitable places. Like the poet's process of aging in place, older adults in my study embarked on a neither wholly deliberate nor accidental journey of becoming rooted in the physical, cognitive, and temporal places that sustained them in later years. Rarely settled, these places served as sites of negotiation and adaptation, alternating cycles of stability and unpredictability, providing space for experimentation and transformation.

Drawing inspiration from Big Sur's isolation, over decades Jeffers constructed a home and a life from materials available in the surrounding wilderness. At "the world's end," as Jeffers described California's shores,[15] he built "Tor House" and the forty-foot Hawk Tower overlooking the Pacific Ocean with massive granite stones he pulled from the beach below.[16] Such images later found their way into his poetry. According to Vince Huth, former president of the foundation dedicated to preserving the poet's legacy, "Not only did Jeffers build the tower, but the tower built Jeffers . . . without plans or designs."[17] Despite periods of idyll, he also struggled with depression, attempted suicide, and self-loathing.[18] Of the untamed geography, steep cliffs and remote canyons, Jeffers observed, "It is not possible to be quite sane here."[19] We could say something similar about living in New York City, famously known as the "city that never sleeps." George Gershwin's iconic musical composition "Rhapsody in Blue" captures the city's frenetic energy, or "our metropolitan madness," as the composer described to his biographer.[20] Among New York City's extreme landscape of soaring skyscrapers and dramatic skylines, elders built their lives and homes, balancing on the edge of different precipice, above late life's choppy waters. When confronted with new obstacles, some anticipated and others unexpected, they fought to hang onto their homes, independence, cognitive and physical functioning, and way of life.

Rather than follow a rigid life map or plan, they improvised responses to setbacks and adapted to changing conditions. Most had weathered personal catastrophes, losses that required them to work within their constraints, alternately pressing on with determination or, when necessary, retreating during life's storms to survive. In some cases, they had rebuilt life from the wreckage of homes destroyed during large-scale urban redevelopment that decimated entire neighborhoods. They also possessed varying material resources with which to secure a strong foundation for late life, whether a pension, retirement savings, or the arrangement of their final affairs to give themselves peace of mind and spare family the trouble.

Amid the city noise, crowds, and grime, they orchestrated seeming chaos into days with a rhythm and a sense of order and predictability. Their apartments provided a modest base, which they augmented with neighborhood "home territories," places that ringed their residences and helped fulfill their needs for attachment and comfort.[21] From these fertile surroundings, connections that fortified them in old age added another layer of protective insulation. In carving out personal spheres of belonging from nearby public spaces, they participated in collective placemaking and created a powerful model for tending to community ties outside traditional institutions of work and family.[22]

As the organization of workplaces and the physical spaces where we spend time continues to shift, elders' lessons for fashioning a mosaic of social ties can help us acclimate to changing tides and challenges. By distributing the weight of social and emotional needs across multiple sites and people, they demonstrate how to avoid overstressing any single tie. Their skillful maintenance of motley formal and informal relationships offers an important contrast to the potential isolation and withdrawal from extended family and community ties in contemporary marriage, which sociologists Lewis A. Coser and Rose Laub Coser described as a "greedy institution."[23] Despite long held beliefs that marriage confers protective benefits such as increased wealth and health, sociologists Naomi Gerstel and Natalia Sarkisian argue that "greedy marriages" also compete with and even undermine community ties, diminishing connections to extended family, neighbors, and friends. Cultural expectations of intense emotional involvement, commitment, time, and energy demanded of modern "soul mate" marriages may lead to disinvestment in other relationships. In their research, Gerstel and Sarkisian found that married people have less contact with relatives such as parents and siblings, socialize less with friends and neighbors, and provide less emotional support and practical support to extended family, friends, and neighbors.[24] Elders' community ties offer an important counternarrative to popular accounts of disengagement, social decline, and increasing isolation in old age.[25] Their example should encourage people of all ages to hone their improvisational skills and flexibility in cultivating relationships beyond the confines of work and family and to expand our imaginations about the range of inevitable places where we may find solace, belonging, and connection.

SOCIAL EVICTION: WE MAY NEVER PASS THIS WAY (AGAIN)

Though older people managed to gather elsewhere after losing their central gathering place, they never recreated the same arrangement the bakery offered. They shared concerns that their newfound hangout spots would also close and joked about being "evicted" one day. Their dark humor betrayed genuine fears and anxieties. Though few faced formal eviction threats, even those with stable, affordable housing expressed chronic insecurity about retaining their apartments. They suffered what I view as a kind of "social eviction"—that is, exile in the form of growing alienation—as they became displaced from the public spaces that had once catered to them and thus had allowed them to claim symbolic control. The bakery closing heralded a loss of important "elder territory." Deprived of power to secure conditions in alternative spaces and forced to contend with noise, disruption, and discomfort, they encountered limited possibilities for staking out new elder territory. Dwindling options not only had long-term consequences for socializing but also undermined people's psyches and esteem; and feeling threatened and unwanted subjected them to a nomadic existence. "I'm the last of the Mohicans," Sylvia said to illustrate her solitariness.

A situation that arose towards the end of my fieldwork demonstrated the potential repercussions for elders who gained "too much" symbolic control over semipublic spaces. At a different McDonald's in Flushing, Queens, a New York City neighborhood with a large Asian population, a group of Korean-American older adults faced loitering accusations. Frustrated management claimed that they spent all day at the establishment, while purchasing little and taking space away from paying customers. On multiple occasions, they called police and 911 to remove them from the premises. The dispute gained national and international media attention, with news outlets referring to the conflict as a "stand-off" or "war" between McDonald's and its elder patrons and to these customers as "defiant" and "a gang of gossiping Korean pensioners."[26] Accounts investigated why they eschewed senior centers in favor of the fast-food restaurant. The elder McDonald's enthusiasts identified the drawbacks of the institutional alternative; the senior center had limited hours, was located a mile and a half away, and was housed in a church basement. One McDonald's regular, Kun Pae Yim, 86, told a reporter, "There's a van that will take us there. We're grateful for the offer. But we are not schoolchildren or government workers. We want to see our friends when we choose."[27] My own commentary in The New York Times opinion pages identified elders' desire for the intergenerational contact unavailable in age-segregated settings such as senior centers.[28]

The New York Times covered the saga in multiple installments, and a slew of unsympathetic reader comments cast the older customers as pests that warranted removal.[29] One reader commented, "It is only in the inner city that McDonald's and Starbucks are the gathering places for the unwashed, elderly, incompetent and infirm. I suppose this is the price for being a city dweller. These people ruin everything!" Others proposed to "solve" the problem by making the seating uncomfortable or eliminating it altogether, suing the elder customers, or blaring rap music to drive them away. Ultimately, a local assembly member, Ron Kim, helped broker a compromise. The older patrons could linger, provided they vacated during the lunchtime rush, and the owner agreed to work with the assembly member's office instead of calling police.

Despite potential benefits for urban residents who remain amid gentrification, including reductions in crime, increased property values, and proximity to new businesses and green space, neighborhood change can also negatively affect health. The displacement, isolation, financial burden, disruption of social networks, increased psychological and physiological stress, and differential access to resources that often accompany these changes have prompted researchers to investigate gentrification as a public health problem or emergency.[30] The Centers for Disease Control identifies populations especially at risk of gentrification's negative health consequences, including women, children, older adults, the poor, and members of racial and ethnic minorities.[31] Research that analyzes gentrification's health implications remains in its infancy. Early findings suggest deepening urban inequality and health disparities for groups such as low-income and Black Americans, but scholars engaged in this work call for future studies to help us understand how gentrification may harm health and worsen inequities so that we can more carefully and powerfully shape policy.[32]

As someone who studies aging and neighborhoods, I often consider how a lack of public transportation, safe sidewalks and traffic intersections, nearby medical services, and essential businesses such as pharmacies and grocery stores can make life unnecessarily difficult for elders with disabilities aging in place.[33] The organization of our communities, workplaces, schools, and health care facilities often deny people with disabilities, which include many older adults, full personhood. The social model of disability posits that structural barriers like these make people with disabilities sicker and more isolated over time, while a medical model locates disability in individuals.[34] Limitations arise not due to a person's functional abilities or other individual deficits but due to escalating external demands.

Gentrification can exacerbate disabilities in subtle ways and contribute to structural conditions that deprive people of opportunities to strengthen their health and physical functioning. As mobility issues mount and affordable places to socialize diminish, elders' need to walk further heightens gentrification's negative effects on their bodily experience of place and further ages them. The bakery provided unrestricted access to a central gathering spot, and this convenient location mitigated the social consequences of physical limitations. A few blocks away, across from another set of housing projects and a city-run senior center, a similar turnover of retail spaces occurred. When a large building containing six retail spaces sold, three-quarters of the businesses on the block closed within a few months. For years afterwards, with the exception of a bank that occupied two corner retail spaces, most of those storefronts sat empty. Long "superblocks" devoid of retail space surrounded the housing projects with buildings erected in a tower-in-the-park style. Depending on where a resident lives in this sprawling, multi-building complex, they might have to walk more than three blocks before reaching a deli and even further to reach a pharmacy.

Heightened physical demands to accomplish tasks essential for independent living can leave older people feeling frail, and thus excluded, over time. The cratering of lower-cost retail infrastructure affected elders' mental and physical health. Diminishing affordable establishments transformed elders into wanderers as they searched for new places. Already anticipating future closures, they prematurely prepared themselves to move on. Reduced options left those with greater physical difficulties, such as Dottie, stranded at home. Many experienced increased stress and felt unmoored due to the loss of neigh-borhood anchors, which contributed to feelings of depression, loneli-ness, and anxiety. These findings have implications for health equity and healthy aging. Facilitating strong networks and places for support-ive discussion can help older adults avoid social isolation and loneli-ness-related conditions, including depression, heart disease, cognitive decline, and weakened immune systems.[35] With the loss of such spaces, elders such as Dottie also missed opportunities for physical movement, as already strenuous outings stretched into impossible journeys. She died five months after the bakery closed.

A few weeks following McDonald's closure, eight years after the study's conclusion, a glimpse at a sleek coffee shop nearby confirmed this reconfigured reality for elders. The shop's interior, with long work-ing tables and mostly backless stools with hard metallic seats, hardly promised to accommodate older bodies. The younger customer base appeared in their early 20s to late 40s, with many hunched over laptops, suggesting a mix of students and remote workers. The packed store revealed how much younger people also need third places, reminding me of my father's observation fifteen years ago at a Starbucks on Man-hattan's Upper East Side. While we waited for his doctor's appoint-ment, perplexed that customers who likely paid high rents in this well-heeled area preferred spending hours there instead of at home, he asked, "Why are these people living here?"

At the cafe near the shuttered McDonald's, an old man with a full head of powdery white hair sat alone at a corner table, a rolling walker by his side, contentedly reading a newspaper. I saw no groups or tables filled with elders there or at other businesses in the surrounding blocks, making the scenes I observed only a few years ago seem part of a bygone era. Older people were still accessing public space and neigh-borhood establishments but, as the man's solitary presence demon-strated, not with the same degree of symbolic control they had during my study. Recent social trends have also reduced elders' claims to public space. The pandemic understandably complicated older adults' ability to spend time outside of their homes and limited opportunities for social contact, depending on their risk tolerance, vaccination status, and underlying medical conditions—all of which can leave people vulnerable to severe illness and death from Covid-19.[36] Public safety has also risen as a concern for people of many ages,[37] with high profile street crimes targeting elders and racially motivated attacks on Asian people contributing to fear, isolation, and reduced feelings of security and belonging among older adults.[38] And gentrification continues to keep rents high, limiting the businesses that can pay the monthly sums and the customers for new establishments—either because they cannot afford them or travel to them or feel otherwise unwelcome. By allowing these converging problems to fester, we shirk our collective responsibility to safeguard the right of people with vulnerabilities to safely, freely, and confidently access public space, which forces them to stay home more than they prefer to and to languish in a social eviction not of their choosing.

POLICY IMPLICATIONS

Gimme Shelter: Late Life Economic and Housing Precarity

While elder poverty rates have dropped over the past half century, older adults remain insecure economically, especially as they move further away from the traditional retirement age. As they move into deep old age, they must also cobble together financial support from dwindling savings, if they have savings at all, and fixed incomes that increasingly lack employer-sponsored defined pension benefits. Poor older adults—increasingly women, racial and ethnic minorities, and immigrants—require more consideration of their significant needs, which poses additional challenges for urban areas with a higher percentage of vulnerable residents. Elders living alone may also experience precariousness due to their difficulty accessing necessary resources and bewilderment in navigating complex social services.[39] Even those who had enjoyed comfortable middle-class incomes in their younger years have suffered the fallout of economic shocks, such as the Great Recession and pandemic-related inflation.[40]

While overall poverty rates for older adults have declined from 35 percent in 1959 to 10.9 percent in 2022, they have climbed for two consecutive years, up from 8.9 percent in 2020.[41] The economic picture worsens when using alternate poverty measures such the Census Bureau's Supplemental Poverty Measure (SPM), which factors in regional cost-of-living differences and medical expenses.[42] Using the Senior Financial Stability Index (SFSI), the Institute on Assets and Social Policy at Brandeis University found that more than a third of older adults were economically insecure and in danger of outliving their financial resources.[43] And, using the "Elder Index," UCLA's Center for Health Policy Research has found that a half million California elders living alone lacked sufficient income to pay for basic expenses such as housing, food, transportation, and health care.[44]

Women continue to shoulder significant economic disadvantages in late life.[45] In 2021, the most recent year for which United States Census Bureau poverty data are available, the poverty rate for women over 65 hit 11.6 percent compared to 8.8 percent for men.[46] My analysis of Census Bureau data has also found that the proportion of older women in poverty increases as they age.[47] Women of color have even higher poverty rates, and analysis from sociologist Deborah Carr has found the highest among older Hispanic women (40.5 percent) and older Black women (37.5 percent) who lived alone.[48] The greater vulnerability of women, minority, and immigrant elders reflects the long shadow of gender and racial discrimination in the labor market, the wage gap, singlehood, and in more limited educational and employment opportunities as sociologist Katherine Newman shows in her study of Black and Latino elders in New York City.[49]

Securing affordable housing poses a steep hurdle for people on fixed incomes and is a growing concern even for older adults with more resources, who in another era, likely would have experienced greater housing support. Since 2004, the number of elder households that spent more than 30 percent of their income on housing has increased. Brandeis's Institute on Assets and Social Policy cited growing housing costs as a "significant policy concern" given the desire to age in place,[50] and proposals to cut Social Security and Medicare benefits only exacerbate potential problems. Housing costs in expensive urban areas take an even greater bite out of elders' household budgets. For example, in Los Angeles, rent accounts for more than half the expenses of an older person living alone, and 70 percent of these older California renters struggle to make ends meet.[51] More recently, homeless shelters have reported an increase in people over 60 without a place to live, due to soaring rents; nursing home closures; and insufficient Social Security, Medicaid, and Medicare benefits.[52]

Urban areas are ideal for people to grow old in because they are more walkable and have public transportation, shopping nearby, and denser social service infrastructure. The advantages that make them attractive for older adults often draw younger, more affluent professionals who can afford higher rents and desire upscale amenities and businesses. With "revitalization," elders in these formerly poor or otherwise undesirable stretches now must shoulder the added threat of gentrification, squeezed with housing costs that show no signs of easing. At worst, they face the risk of eviction and the danger of ending up on the street. At best, they may feel estranged from their neighborhoods as once familiar streets grow less recognizable and hospitable with the influx of wealth.

The city should invest in helping older New Yorkers who have lived here for decades remain in their communities and homes independently and safely for as long as possible; these elders deserve it. The elder housing crisis will only escalate with the aging of the city and the state's population. Mirroring national demographic trends, New York State's older adult population has surged over the last decade. Residents aged 65 and older comprised 16.2 percent of New York City's population in 2021, up from 12.3 percent in 2011, and projected to increase 20 percent by 2040.[53] Future generations will also grow more diverse and vulnerable as the population of immigrant and minority elders increases.[54] These elders tend to have poorer health and higher poverty rates, combined with lower levels of English language fluency, which leaves them at risk of cultural and linguistic isolation. Many older immigrants receive fewer or no Social Security and Medicare benefits due to years of working "off the books."[55] Although many live with family, a shortage of affordable housing for people of all ages can lead to overcrowding and strained household relationships, according to a report on immigrant aging from the Center for an Urban Future.[56]

While shorter-term sprucing up of historically working-class and low-income districts, like downtown Los Angeles's Skid Row, for high-income newcomers may seem like good economic sense, preserving affordable housing is more cost-effective and humane in the long run.[57] Along with a substantial investment in new affordable housing that integrates supportive services, which is far less expensive than building nursing homes,[58] New York City and other municipalities can take some modest measures to preserve the affordable housing where elders already live. I recommend strengthening eviction prevention services and legal assistance for those who wind up in housing court and providing in-court referrals to nonprofit organizations that serve older adults, such as the Jewish Association Serving the Aging (JASA), which connects clients to comprehensive services including benefits screening for Medicaid and SNAP (Supplemental Nutrition Assistance Program). We should also require landlords to include applications for SCRIE (Senior Citizen Rent Increase Exemption), a program that helps people 62 and older with annual incomes below $50,000 to avoid rent increases, with all lease renewals to ensure elder tenants know about the program.[59] Finally, we can provide supplemental financial assistance to older people struggling to pay rent. California has already set an example for the rest of the country by signing into law the "Elder Index," which gives social service agencies a more accurate measurement to assess elder poverty.[60] Gaining a fuller picture of material deprivation among older adults would help address their unmet needs and increase budgets for these interventions.

In many ways, New York City is an excellent place for people to grow old, with its plentiful public transportation and stores that people can walk to. After his heart attack, Eugene's access to the neighborhood diminished as he grew exhausted walking more than a block or two from home. But when confronted with the prospect of losing his apartment, despite the stress and humiliation of housing court, he preferred to stay and fight rather than live in Dallas with his younger sister, who extended this offer throughout the years. Eugene's building management had also suggested he relocate to his sister's during their eviction proceedings. But moving to a suburb would have guaranteed losing autonomy, since he didn't drive and would depend on others for rides. Whenever I see mostly young white women on Manhattan's streets toting canvas bags emblazoned with the slogan "New York or Nowhere," I recall Eugene's plight. Older people have little choice but to stay, given the infeasibility of transporting their 80- or 90-year-old lives elsewhere. And moving older New Yorkers to cheaper parts of the country to live with family doesn't solve the affordable housing crisis and shortfall in long-term-care support. In reimagining urban downtowns across the country, we must address the looming challenges that all municipalities will encounter as their residents age.

Bringing It All Back Home: Strengthening Our Aging in Place Ecology

The changing demographics of older adults, who have higher rates of divorce, singlehood, and childlessness and often live far from family, necessitate new strategies to promote health and well-being. Access to high-quality social and medical services is crucial for elders' ability to age in their communities. While medical settings are not age separated by design, they serve a disproportionate number of older people who use health-care services more frequently. Often, they find that these organized settings are permeated with ageism, reducing their willingness to participate.

This study presented empirical insights into how older people drew on neighborhood-based support in conjunction with settings where they received services. External and internalized ageism emerged as an important reason for their preference for "third places" over institutional spaces such as senior centers and health-care settings. They used public spaces for health-related support and information when their interactions in other formal contexts disappointed or confused them, and neighborhood places offered important physical venues to process negative or rushed exchanges in physicians' offices.

Emphasis on organized spaces obscures the importance of informal venues for aging in place. Baby boomers have evolving service needs and preferences for maintaining community connections. Despite urban areas' many advantages, challenges remain for older adults to access care. Even when eligible for different programs, studies have found that older people do not always take advantage of them. For example, participation in the Supplemental Nutrition Assistance Program (SNAP) is much lower among older adults due to confusion about eligibility, difficulty enrolling, and stigma, with an estimated three out of five eligible elders, or five million people, missing out on food assistance.[61] The National Council on Aging (NCOA) estimates $30 billion in aid goes unclaimed each year by people who qualify for public and private benefit programs but have not enrolled.[62] The advocacy organization offers a free, online screening tool, BenefitsCheckUp, to connect elders and people with disabilities to nearly two thousand programs to help pay for food, medicine, utilities, and other daily expenses.[63]

How can we improve care for elders who eschew the institutional spaces that may assist them? Understanding these dynamics can lead to new measures to improve outcomes for care recipients and for their caregivers. Reducing age bias is a paramount concern, along with improving exchanges between health-care providers and older patients so that they feel recognized and respected. Following social psychologist Todd D. Nelson's suggestions to mitigate age bias in the medical system, I also recommend encouraging medical professionals to become more aware of their ageist beliefs, instituting anti-ageism training early in medical education, and expanding geriatrics programs in hospitals and mental health offices.[64]

The Creating Age-Friendly Health Systems Initiative offers a promising model of care for older adults. It emphasizes four high-level, evidenced-based interventions, known as the 4 Ms, to foster a broader shift by health systems to prioritize the needs of older adults and reduce clinical harm, cost, and patient dissatisfaction.[65] The 4 Ms are: (what) *matters* (for patients' health outcome goals and care preferences); *medication* (only medication if necessary and aligned with patients' needs); *mobility* (safe movement to maintain function); and *mentation* (screening, treatment, and management of dementia, depression, and delirium).[66] Developing attractive and appealing intergenerational spaces and dispatching caseworkers to public spaces where elders congregate, whether on a park bench or at a coffee shop or fast-food joint, can also help increase the usage of essential services. This study's findings may translate to implementable improvements in the delivery of medical and social services to older adults who live alone and avoid institutional settings and prefer public neighborhood spaces where they can socialize across the age spectrum.

Despite their shortcomings, I recognize the value of elder-serving institutions such as senior centers and suggest improving these spaces so that they might be more attractive and inviting to elders but caution against rebranding them in ways that alienate or abandon their core constituency—for example, by no longer providing free or low cost nutritious meals.[67] Given the stigma attached to such organized spaces, many scholars and practitioners have proposed modifying senior centers to align with older adults' spontaneous and voluntary uses of public spaces. For example, based on a survey of baby boomers in the Midwest, Jan Walker and colleagues suggest that service providers re-envision them as multipurpose age-integrated centers instead of spaces targeted towards elders.[68] Aging advocate Sandy Markwood recommends creating "ageless" activities and services for everyone in addition to programs for older adults. This proposal also moves services outside of traditional senior centers and suggests that health-education classes could occur in local hospitals, computer and technology training classes in community colleges, fitness classes at recreational centers, lifelong learning classes at libraries, and financial planning courses at shopping malls. By branding these elder-serving spaces "intergenerational community centers," researchers expect them to directly benefit more older adults.[69]

Among the new generation of programming, Mather's More Than a Café model (MMC) has gained a lot of positive attention, and more than forty organizations across the United States have adopted it.[70] The nonprofit cafe provides a bottomless coffee cup for 95¢ and opportunities for all ages to socialize. They host dozens of classes for adults over 50, including painting, cooking, flower arranging, strength training, and iPhone basics.[71] They also implemented a "telephone topics" program in which older adults can call toll-free and participate in activities such as guided chair yoga or meditation sessions, sports and movie discussions, vocal performances, and storytelling sessions.[72] Evaluation studies of the MMC programs suggest that participation provides mental relief from fatigue, loneliness, and difficult life events such as death, divorce, retirement, and illness.[73] The retirement community New-Bridge on the Charles has also received acclaim for its multigenerational programs.[74] By bringing together residents and elementary to college-level students, programs disrupt barriers between old and young, offering companionship and helping students understand elders' experiences and needs.[75]

Other than designing age-integrated and intergenerational programs, we can also create more age-friendly public spaces for elders who seek care in informal settings such as parks, diners, and shopping malls. Local governments can improve the quality of urban spaces by incorporating "green space" and "blue space," such as gardens and courtyard fountains.[76] I also recommend installing comfortable street furniture (chairs, chess tables, etc.), mending potholes, maintaining free-of-obstruction pavement, and providing clean public toilets to make streets more accessible.[77] Businesses can also help cultivate spontaneous and supportive relationships among customers by installing accessible seating and allowing customers to linger.[78]

As my research discovered, many older people avoided institutional spaces like senior centers, which help identify elders at risk of poverty and social isolation and which connect them with supportive services such as home meal-delivery services. Given this tendency, I propose that social service agencies dispatch teams of social workers to conduct on-the-spot benefits screening and case management to elders at neighborhood gathering spots. Meeting people "where they are" rather than requiring them to travel to an age-separated space would reduce delays to accessing preventive services and would help people avoid unnecessary hassle, cost, and emotional drain involved in crisis management after prolonged neglect.

Community-based organizations can also host affordable or free events in neighborhood businesses or other public spaces, thus helping service providers reach underserved older adults. Indeed, health professionals have already recognized the importance of third places in elders' lives. The ElderSmile program at Columbia University College of Dental Medicine, for example, has delivered preventative oral health care in such locations. Elders who had received services later helped recruit additional participants for other activities, including dental, diabetes, and hypertension screenings.[79] Interventions to provide health information and medication management in Black-owned barbershops have also effectively reduced high blood pressure in Black men, who have the highest rates of hypertension-related death, less interaction with physicians, and lower rates of blood pressure treatment and control.[80] Similar outreach efforts to improve cardiovascular health have taken place in Black churches, another long trusted community space.[81]

As this study used ethnographic data collected from a group of mostly ethnic-white and Puerto Rican, poor to middle-income elders who identified as heterosexual, future studies should consider variations in experiences of aging in place among racial- and ethnic-minority, immigrant, and LGBTQ+ elders.[82] For example, compared with whites, African American elders have greater mistrust of the health-care system due to persistent discrimination, while Chinese American elders report more language difficulties.[83] Older racial and ethnic minorities also often use alternative treatments to Western medicine, such as herbalists or music for self-care.[84] For example, elders living in Mexico and Mexican migrants to the United States may turn to traditional healers, or *curanderas*, and participate in treatments such as *limpias* (spiritual cleansings) to address physical and mental health symptoms.[85] How do diverse elders perceive the health-care system? Are they underserved in these settings? Where do they socialize and find connection and social support? What beneficial health practices do they use? Lastly, how shall we design public spaces to meet their needs so that future generations may receive innovative care in the community?

The Stanford Center on Longevity's "New Map of Life" initiative urges us to increase investment in core social domains (early childhood, education, work, financial security, built environment, climate, health and technology, lifestyle and fitness, and intergenerational relationships) to support longer, perhaps even 100-year lives.[86] The Village Movement offers a promising model to help fulfill the goal of creating "longevity-ready" communities by connecting local network members to comprehensive services and social activities that enable them to age in place. Founded as a grassroots, member-led, volunteer-run organization in Boston's Beacon Hill neighborhood in 2002, the model has since expanded to include at least 268 Villages with more than seventy-thousand members.[87] While many Villages offer subsidized memberships to encourage the participation of people with lower incomes, members remain largely white, middle-class and upper-income, and highly educated, suggesting much work remains to expand the model beyond a "boutique option" for a privileged few.[88]

Through our spending priorities and choice of elected representatives, we can fortify the places that make a community a home and protect people of all ages from the vagaries of fortune. We must continue striving for social inclusivity and to retain community diversity across the dimensions of race and ethnicity, gender, class, sexuality, ability, and age no matter how distant this dream or goal seems. I advocate an approach to collective care that draws inspiration from philosopher John Rawls's "veil of ignorance," a classic thought experiment that requires us to consider how we would design public policy and a political and economic system if we had no knowledge of our social position.[89] Imagine the progress we could make towards ensuring everyone a safety net if we adopted the veil of ignorance as guiding principle for developing a social contract for late life.[90] Putting aside our personal circumstances and predictions about where we might end up in old age when determining policy would promote equal opportunity for everyone to thrive and thereby safeguard the interests of the least advantaged.

If we are lucky and privileged enough, we will grow old one day. Given the extensive needs of an increasingly diverse older adult population, how well elders age rests in part on how well cities like New York prioritize supporting its poorest and oldest residents so that they can remain here with dignity and contribute to city life.

YESTERDAY ONCE MORE

On my way to a cozy cafe in the West Village where I finish drafting this book's conclusion, I reflect on my own aging in place. Down the same streets I walked as a little girl growing up in the city, I feel my own 43-year-old body changing. Wounds take longer to heal, aches linger, fatigue accumulates. Intermittent pain now flares in my knees, forcing me to stretch daily to keep it at bay. My right leg throbs from a varicose vein that still plagues me after a procedure I had hoped would provide more relief. With age, new routine health screenings, such as colonoscopies and mammograms, populate my calendar. I don't take my long walks for granted. One day, I will have more difficulty, perhaps losing my ability to walk altogether.

Growing older has also helped me see the arc of my life and appreciate my tiny corner of this vast social world. As the novelist William Faulkner observed, "I discovered that my own little postage stamp of native soil was worth writing about and that I would never live long enough to exhaust it."[91] Living so long amid the city's "here today, gone tomorrow" impermanence has challenged me to balance attachment to beloved places, people, and things with discerning detachment. All things must pass. I think about how much being a New Yorker has prepared me for and toughened me against loss. As the title of a favorite Amy Winehouse song goes, "Love Is a Losing Game." Despite my resistance, I've had to get more comfortable with letting go. Strengthening this skill isn't easy. My time with older adults has helped me better accept this transience, to focus on the present and appreciate people, places, and things while I have them. But I can't help getting attached, reminding me of the late life wisdom of Roger Angell, essayist and longtime fiction editor at *The New Yorker*, who wrote, "Getting old is the second-biggest surprise of my life, but the first, by a mile, is our unceasing need for deep attachment and intimate love."[92]

Despite losing many places and people I've loved, I'm still here. With loss comes learning to live with a persistent phantom ache. Some people remain in physical form. Others live on in spirit and memory; their voices and images reside in my head. When I consider this landscape, I think about how much older people like Sylvia, now 94, have taught me about carrying on with emotional and physical pain. "Dear, I just have to live with it," she tells me on the phone before putting me on hold so she can slowly ease into a more comfortable position. Her arthritic knee makes her scream in agony if she doesn't turn in just the right way. "Please, take your time," I say.

Gentrification has accelerated the process of saying goodbye, making me feel prematurely old. Walking in a city where I have lived most of my life, it often feels as though I have memories on every street corner—alternately comforting and overwhelming. Images of places that once were overlay the montage of storefronts I pass daily. Skylines and sight lines change; new construction interrupts some favorite views of the Empire State Building, and the absence of the Twin Towers still feels like a missing anchor for the lower Manhattan I remember from my first twenty-one years. More recently, the pandemic's desolation imprinted memories of empty streets and vacant businesses. The break from shoulder-to-shoulder crowds bestowed upon me surprise solitude and extra breathing room. Shuttered retail spaces remain, but the throngs have since returned, compelling me to mask outdoors, even though most have abandoned face coverings.

The cafe on Hudson Street where I head now sits in a low-rise tenement, next door to a three-story brick building where urbanist and activist Jane Jacobs lived when writing *The Life and Death of American Cities*; it is a few blocks from my old elementary school. I never knew the building's rich history until I saw its gilded plaque last year. Stumbling upon this landmark hiding in plain sight reminds my jaded eyes that if I look harder, there's always room for discovery in this city.

There's no plaque for the places recorded in this book.

I still find myself drawn to old places and old people. Older men and women join the weekday afternoon crowd that shuffles into the cafe when I come in. They're longtime New Yorkers like me. The clientele is mixed age-wise and mostly white, with younger people more self-contained and focused on laptops and smartphones here than the places where elders held court in my study. Fewer older customers have control over space here, but they do find a place nonetheless. The cubbyhole cafe somehow accommodates everyone, including elders' rolling walkers and canes, without feeling suffocated. New Yorkers accustomed to living cheek by jowl, packed into subways and shoe box–sized apartments, make room for each other. A bearded man in late middle age walks by daily with his trio of dogs and beckons another older regular outside to feed handfuls of treats to a pit bull with a vanilla and caramel fur; a pointy-eared, yellow dog; and a Siberian Husky barking exuberantly. My mind's eye conjures the memory of Eugene, giving belly rubs to Ollie the dog on warm summer days when Pete's accordion doors opened to the sidewalk.

The murmur of conversation transports me back to the places and people I've loved and lost. In the knowing laughter and observing eyes of the elders here, I recall the older people who shared their lives with me a decade ago. Admission costs a little more now. For $3.62, I buy a small coffee and a place to linger for a few hours, allowing me to hang out in something of a time warp. A fair deal. Nobody bothers me. Tall, recessed windows frame the entrance, each holding a window seat nook with comfy cushions. Chalk board menus list coffee drinks and panini sandwiches. Immigrant men from Mexico operate the register and prepare food at the front counter and in the back kitchen, behind swinging saloon doors as weathered as the wooden floorboards. They call regulars by their first names and know their usual orders.

The workers remind me of my father, who came to the United States from Chile in 1975, at a time when it was still possible for a working-class immigrant like him to secure affordable housing and a union job.

He retired as a doorman with a lifelong pension. What "retirement" can his counterparts look forward to these days? I wonder. Will they find themselves collecting cans to redeem for cash in their old age, like the elders I see scouring trashcans for empties? I passed one such figure earlier, an older, brown-skinned man neatly outfitted in trousers, a tan jacket, wool Yankees hat, and Velcro-strapped orthopedic shoes. He used a metallic grabbing rod to fish cans and bottles from deep-welled trashcans, loaded them into his plastic-lined pushcart, and moved methodically to the next receptacle. Pondering the future of a restless old age for those with no choice but to keep working into their last years, many juggling chronic illnesses, I see more ghosts and think of Angelica. At the end of her life, she worked as a Whole Foods cashier, unable to obtain paid sick leave while cancer spread throughout her body. Months later she died in Barcelona, after returning for respite, family care, and access to Spain's universal health coverage.[93]

All of us who come here need a break from something. For me, the coffee shop provides a welcome interlude from working at home. Due to my autoimmune disease and heightened risks of Covid infection complications, the pandemic has limited my options for accessing public space.[94] I sit at a solo table behind the register, near the restroom, and mask. Despite the additional precautions I must make, I'm grateful there's a place here for me too. Though I don't interact much with anyone, sharing space with others, alone together, keeps me from sinking low and getting depressed. These past few years have taken their toll on me in terms of loss and isolation, and leaving the house helps combat loneliness and lifts my spirits. I always feel better after going outside, and though I never wear make-up, I recall Sylvia's mantra, "You've got to get out of bed and put your lipstick on."

New York has always been a city of change and reinvention, testing residents' tenacity in the face of upheaval and ruin, renewal and rebirth. Its older denizens have survived multiple booms and busts. They persevere and find their places. But their resilience shouldn't be abused or subjected to unnecessary trials. Growing older may be inevitable, but we shouldn't accept chronic instability in late life or a grinding elder-hood for the too many who lack a social and economic safety net. I hope third places remain for me in my old age. I've learned many of the conditions necessary for a good life, but no one can create a social contract that supports us in our later years alone. We must work to build communities that give all of us the opportunity to find our inevitable places—sites of support and connection, not desolation and insecurity—now and in the future. Together.

Notes

1. ANOTHER NEW YORK STORY

Joan Didion epigraph: Guardian Books (2021).

Robinson Jeffers epigraph: Literary America (2020).

1. For confidentiality reasons, I have changed the names of most sites and people.

2. Aging scholars debate how to define age categories (for more discussion, see Neugarten and Neugarten 2002) but have reached some consensus that in Western societies, old age begins somewhere between ages 60 and 65, when adults become eligible for public social benefits. I use the terms *elder* and *older adult* to describe people over the age of 60.

3. Dixon and Henderson (1926).

4. FDNY stands for New York City Fire Department.

5. Guardian Books (2021).

6. A co-op is a residence where a buyer purchases a share in the corporation that owns the building where they live and has the right to occupy a specified unit and a vote in the corporation.

Low equity co-ops limit the resale of shares, helping to preserve affordable housing (National Association of Housing Cooperatives 2012).

7. Strickland (2010).

8. Niesz (2007); New York City Department for the Aging (n.d.).

9. New York State Office for the Aging (n.d.).

10. Centers for Disease Control and Prevention (2009b); National Institute on Aging (n.d.).

11. According to 2015 American Community Survey five-year estimates, 14 percent of this neighborhood's population are 65 years and older, with 75 percent of those women and 25 percent men. About 52 percent of these households have older adults living alone; men make up 40 percent of these solo dwellers and women 60 percent. Forty-nine percent of renters and 26 percent of homeowners over age 65 have lived there for more than thirty-six years; only 9 percent of renters and 7 percent of homeowners over 65 have less than five years of residence (U.S. Census Bureau 2015).

12. For additional examples of activities of daily living (ADLs), see Edemekong et al. (2022).

13. On these stereotypes, see Pampel (1998).

14. On the *familiar stranger*, see Milgram (1977).

15. The term *research participants* feels an awkward fit to describe these relationships. I much prefer to think of them as *research companions*, as sociologist Teresa Gowan (2010, p. 10) calls the unhoused people with whom she conducted ethnographic fieldwork over several years in San Francisco. For me, Gowan's term better captures the complexity of relationships developed with people over a long period of embeddedness.

16. Tannen (n.d.).

17. On flares, see Carteron (2022). On the disease, "Sjogren's Syndrome" (2022).

18. I received approval from my university's Institutional Review Board to conduct participant observations and interviews. To potential participants I explained that I wanted to learn more about how older people age in place by spending time with and interviewing residents over age 60. Many expressed interest in wanting to help me with my schoolwork. Participants permitted me to record observations of their interactions and a subset participated in a digitally recorded interview. I explained my efforts to protect confidentiality, including changing the names of participants and most locations. Many people

were intensely private and guarded about personal information, in some cases refusing to reveal even their age. Gaining trust took time and patience. My decision to mask identifying information and use pseudonyms for people and locations reassured them of my efforts to protect their confidentiality, though I explained that no researcher can guarantee anonymity. Other participants such as Eugene continually voiced their permission for me to disclose their identities. On these occasions, I expressed my appreciation for their openness but explained that disclosing one person's identity might compromise others' confidentiality. I ensured participants understood that participation was voluntary and that they could choose to participate in some parts of the study and not others (e.g., they could take part in the ethnography or in interviews or both) and withdraw any time.

19. Gerhardt (2020); "Silent Generation" (2023).

20. I put quotation marks around speech that I wrote down in my notebook as people were speaking or shortly thereafter and around transcribed dialogue from tape recordings made in the field or during an interview. Speech in quotations should be taken only as a close approximation. After writing detailed notes of the day's observations and conversations, I added brief analytic notes and memos, which helped later to uncover patterns, spark or prompt additional questions, and connect my data to prior scholarship. My analysis consisted of manually reviewing field notes and interview transcripts and coding for relevant concepts and categories generated from the literature and my data in order to uncover related themes and emerging patterns.

21. Aronson (2019, p. 269). For more information on age-inclusive language, see Van Vleck (2022); Trucil, Lundebjerg, and Busso (2021).

22. Hochschild (1973, p. xiv).

23. World Health Organization (2022).

24. Sethumadhavan and Saunders (2021); Bloom and Zucker (2022).

25. Garver (2007).

26. Bennett (2021).

27. Sample (2022).

28. Zola (1991, p. 8).

29. Torres (2019b).

30. On the rise of ageism during the pandemic, see United Nations (2020); on the social media trend, see Whalen (2020); Sood (2020).

31. Calasanti and Slevin (2006).

32. For more information on eligibility requirements for federal benefits such as Social Security, Medicare, and Medicaid and special challenges for older immigrants, see Burke and Kean (2019); Sevak and Schmidt (2014); National Immigration Forum (2022).

33. Laz (1998); West and Zimmerman (1987); Torres (2016a).

34. Centers for Disease Control and Prevention (2022a).

35. Noah (2019); "Red, White, and Gray: How America's Gerontocracy is Threatening Weakening Democracy" (2022); "Gerontocracy" (2023).

36. Hochschild (1973).

37. Bowling and Dieppe (2005).

38. Oldenburg ([1989] 1999); see also Ben Noon and Ayalon (2017) for a more recent discussion of older adults gathering in public spaces such as parks.

39. Binette and Vasold (2018).

40. Administration on Aging (2022).

41. Vespa and Schondelmyer (2015).

42. Klinenberg (2012); Gratton and Haber (1993).

43. Scharlach and Lehning (2016).

44. Medicare covers custodial care (i.e., nonmedical homemaker services) only for limited periods during home health aide visits to provide services such as skilled nursing care and physical therapy, occupational therapy, or speech therapy. Providing custodial care cannot serve as the main purpose of the visit (Medicare Interactive 2023c). Under Medicare's hospice benefit, dying patients obtain coverage for personal care, such as help with bathing, dressing, and toileting, and homemaker services, including light cleaning and laundry (Medicare Interactive 2023b; Torres 2021b). People certified as "homebound" and in need of intermittent skilled nursing or therapy care qualify for home health services, but due to complex and at times inconsistent eligibility requirements and a dearth of home-based primary care services, access to and coverage of these services remains limited (Medicare Interactive 2023a; Klein, Hostetter, and McCarthy 2017; Ornstein et al. 2015; Bao, Eggman, Richardson, and Bruce 2014).

45. Carr (2019); Pugh (2023).

46. As the age of family caregivers trends downward, the "sandwich generation" balancing care for parents and children is also getting younger (Lee 2023; Torres 2021a).

47. Villa (2019).

48. Portacolone (2013); Herd and Moynihan (2018).

49. Torres-Gil and Hofland (2012).

50. For some recent ethnographic studies of older adults, see Plasencia (2023); Abramson (2015); Rúa (2017); Sun (2021); Kavedžija (2019).

51. For a timely example of ethnographic fieldwork conducted with elders in Japan, see Kavedžija (2019). On the greying of low- and middle-income countries, see World Health Organization (2022).

52. See Mair (2019) for an excellent discussion of "kinlessness" among increasing numbers of older adults who may not have children or partners but who report higher numbers of friends in their social networks, challenging assumptions that people without family are "alone."

53. Torres (2014a); Crowley (2018).

54. "New York City" (2023).

55. Harvard T. H. Chan School of Public Health (2023); Berg (2023); Centers for Disease Control and Prevention (2022c).

56. Seitz (2023); Office of the U.S. Surgeon General (2023).

57. Klinenberg (2018, p. 5). See also King (2023).

58. Gerstel and Sarkisian (2006).

59. Weil (2014).

60. See Wellman (1979); but see Sampson (2012); Small (2009); Brown-Saracino (2011).

61. Fischer (1982, p. 184).

62. Harrington Meyer (2014).

63. Torres (2019c).

64. Literary America (2020).

65. Smith, Lehning, and Kim (2018).

66. Desmond (2016).

67. Weil (2014).

68. Ferraro (2018, pp. 34–35).

69. Torres and Lacy (2021); Plasencia (2023); Carr (2019).

70. "12 Inspiring African Proverbs" (2017).

71. See Torres (2018) for a detailed review of earlier ethnographic studies of aging in place, including Hochschild (1973); Myerhoff (1978); Kugelmass ([1986] 1996); Duneier (1992); Newman (2003); Loe (2011); and Abramson (2015).

72. For more on transnational aging and dispersed networks among older immigrants, see Cao (2021); Sun (2021).

73. National Social Life, Health, and Aging Project (2011); Survey of Health, Ageing and Retirement in Europe (2015); Longitudinal Aging Study Amsterdam (2017).

74. For some classic and contemporary ethnographic studies of older adults, see Hochschild (1973); Gubrium (1975); Myerhoff (1978); Kugelmass ([1986] 1996); Diamond (1992); Duneier (1992); Furman (1997); Newman (2003); Loe (2011); Abramson (2015). See Abramson (2021) for more on why integration of participant observation and ethnography is both useful and necessary for advancing social scientific research on aging and the life course.

75. Thompson (2019).

76. Barmann (2021).

77. Thompson (2019).

78. Torres (2016b); Torres (2020a); Fagan (2019); Bolton (2022).

79. Grawert and Kim (2022).

2. THE PUBLIC LIVING ROOM

1. Oldenburg ([1989] 1999).

2. Oldenburg and Brissett (1982).

3. Granovetter (1973, p. 1,361).

4. McClear (2010).

5. "Rheumatoid Arthritis" (2023).

6. For more on "familiarized locales," including paths, rounds, and ranges, see Lofland (1998).

7. See Small (2009); Small (2017).

8. Zerubavel (1991, pp. 25–27).

9. Hochschild (1973) has an interesting discussion about the creation of "social sibling" bonds among older adults she encountered during her fieldwork (p. 65), which developed in part due to conditions of social similarity and reciprocity. Social similarity could prompt comparison and rivalry. Hochschild points to adolescence as another fertile time in the life course for forming sibling bonds.

10. Rodgers (2020).

11. See Plickert, Côté, and Wellman (2007) for more discussion of network reciprocity.

12. City of New York (2016).

13. Durkheim ([1897] 1951); Simmel ([1908] 1971; [1910] 1971).

14. Bellah et al. ([1985] 1996); Putnam (2000).

15. McPherson, Smith-Lovin, and Brashears (2006); Paik and Sanchagrin (2013); Rainie and Wellman (2012).

16. Office of the U.S. Surgeon General (2023).

17. Centers for Disease Control and Prevention (2023).

18. Loe (2011); Small (2009).

19. Putnam (2000).

20. Cornwell, Laumann, and Schumm (2008); Kharicha et al. (2007).

21. Courtin and Knapp (2017); Kharicha et al. (2007).

22. Klinenberg (2002); Klinenberg (2012); Townsend (1957).

23. Gusmano and Rodwin (2006).

24. York Cornwell and Waite (2009).

25. Thoits (2011); Uchino, Cacioppo, and Kiecolt-Glaser (1996).

26. Hawkley and Cacioppo (2010).

27. Krueger et al. (2009); Zunzunegui, Alvarado, Del Ser, and Otero (2003); Perry et al. (2022a).

28. Cornwell et al. (2008).

29. Carstensen (1992); Schnittker (2007).

30. Carstensen (1992); Cornwell et al. (2008); Hooyman and Kiyak (2008); Schnittker (2007); York Cornwell and Waite (2009).

31. Ben Noon and Ayalon (2018); Cagney et al. (2013); Hochschild (1973).

32. Fischer (1982, p. 184).

33. Abramson (2015).

34. Freedman, Martin, and Schoeni (2002).

35. U.S. Department of Health and Human Services et al. (2016).

36. Ben Noon and Ayalon (2018); Cagney et al. (2013); Kugelmass ([1986] 1996); Myerhoff (1978); Oldenburg ([1989] 1999).

37. Fischer (1982).

38. Hochschild (1973). See also Duneier (1992); Furman (1997); Victor, Scambler, and Bond (2009).

39. Gieryn (2000); Lofland (1998); Oldenburg ([1989] 1999).

40. Gieryn (2000).

41. Milligan (1998).

42. Jacobs (1961); Oldenburg ([1989] 1999).

43. See Duneier (1992).

44. Oldenburg ([1989] 1999, p. 38).

45. Gardner (2011).

46. Northridge et al. (2016); Oldenburg ([1989] 1999).

47. Oldenburg ([1989] 1999).

48. Cheang (2002); Graham, Graham, and MacLean (1991); Rosenbaum, Sweeney, and Windhorst (2009).

49. Pardasani and Berkman (2021); MaloneBeach and Langeland (2011); Gillespie (2019).

50. Walker et al. (2004).

51. Zaslow (2003).

52. Hostetler (2011); Gillespie (2019).

53. Finlay et al. (2015). See Klinenberg (2018) for more on how investment in social infrastructure, such as libraries, parks, and mixed-age residential communities, can improve health and longevity and increase social interaction in public spaces for older adults.

54. Wexler, Mark, and Oberlander (2017).

55. White, Toohey, and Asquith (2015).

56. Graham, Graham, and MacLean (1991). For a fascinating cultural history of shopping malls, as both consumer and community hubs, see Lange (2022).

57. Cheang (2002).

58. Tsai (2011).

59. Ben Noon and Ayalon (2018).

3. AGING ALONE, GOSSIPING TOGETHER

1. Foster (2004).

2. This study offers insights into the motivations and processes of gossip for elders but shares the limitations of many small qualitative studies that draw on nonrandom samples and cannot generalize to the population. Due to the sensitivity of the subject and the focus of interviews on the bakery closure, like

Degnen (2007), I did not ask participants directly about their own social standing or involvement in gossip and cannot speak to participants' assessments of the costs and benefits of gossip for themselves. Despite these limitations, this study adds to a small number of gossip studies and qualitative sociological studies of older adults, with most drawing their samples from organized institutional settings, such as senior centers; senior housing; and religious organizations, such as churches and synagogues. For examples, see Abramson (2015); Loe (2011); McAuley (1998); Portacolone (2013); Weil (2014).

3. Goffman (1959).

4. Schnittker (2007).

5. For more discussion of dementia symptoms, see Hooyman and Kiyak (2008).

6. Gluckman (1963).

7. Blumberg (1972); Watson (2012).

8. Foster (2004).

9. Foster (2004).

10. Fine and Rosnow (1978); Stirling (1956); Suls (1977); Sánchez-Jankowski (2008); Watson (2012).

11. Gluckman (1963).

12. Percival (2000).

13. Degnen (2007).

14. Gluckman (1963).

15. Foster (2004).

16. Hannerz (1967). See Sánchez-Jankowski (2008) for an excellent discussion of how gossip functions and flourishes in neighborhood institutions such as mom-and-pop grocery stores.

17. For more discussion, see Torres (2020b).

18. Scharlach and Lehning (2016); Torres-Gil and Hofland (2012).

19. Blau and Fingerman (2009, p. 3).

20. Small (2017).

21. Offer and Fischer (2018).

22. Courtin and Knapp (2017); Thoits (2011).

23. For prior studies, see Cheang (2002); Murphy (2017); Richman (1995).

24. Degnen (2007).

4. THE BAKERY CLUB

1. Myerhoff (1978).

2. For more discussion of the development of stigmatized and old age subcultures, see Goffman (1963b); Hochschild (1973); Fischer (1982).

3. Degnen (2007); Torres (2019a).

4. See Goffman (1963b, p. 81) for an excellent discussion of how stigma and social identity shape a person's daily and weekly rounds and divides their world spatially into places that offer different degrees of acceptance, such as "forbidden or out-of-bounds places," "civil places," and "back places." "Sympathetic others" who share a particular stigma can offer support, acceptance, and "the comfort of feeling at home" (Goffman 1963b, p. 20).

5. For more information on some less commonly known mid-twentieth-century New York gangs, see "New York Gangs, and Clubs from New York" (n.d.).

6. Nunez (2018, p. 211).

7. "The East Side's Long-Gone Gas House District" (2011); "Building Stuyvesant Town in the 1940s" (2010); Smyth (2018).

8. "A History of Stuytown and Peter Cooper Village" (2019).

9. "Our History" (n.d.); "Stuy Town Slum Clearance, 1946" (2019).

10. "Stuyvesant Town–Peter Cooper Village" (2023).

11. Cooper (1945).

12. Rúa (2017).

13. On "cumulative disadvantage," see Dannefer (2003); Carr (2019).

14. Aronson (2019). For critiques of successful aging and the biomedical approach, see Bowling and Dieppe (2005). Liang and Luo (2012) criticize successful aging based on their analysis of its inherent ageism, cultural neglect, quantification, and scant attention to capitalism and consumerism ideologies. Among the many theoretical advancements of their approach, they propose a shift to "harmonious aging" inspired by Eastern philosophy to broaden the exploration and understanding of challenges and opportunities in old age and to capture cross-cultural diversity in global aging.

15. See *Encylopedia Britannica* (2020) for more on WAC.

16. Cruikshank (2009). For more on the associations between internalized ageism and negative health outcomes, including lower life expectancy, high blood pressure, and reduced self-esteem, see Gendron, Welleford, Inker, and White (2016).

17. Greve, Leipold, and Kappes (2018); Köber, Oberwittler, and Wickes (2022).

18. Francis (2003); Levitt (2004).

19. Sisak and Price (2022).

20. O'Toole (2018).

21. Goffman (1963b); Wallhagen (2010).

22. Goffman (1963b).

23. Goffman (1963b, p. 3).

24. Goffman (1963b, p. 19).

25. Neugarten and Neugarten (2002); Laz (1998).

26. Neugarten and Neugarten (2002); Achenbaum (2006).

27. Vierck and Hodges (2003, p. 2).

28. Neugarten and Neugarten (2002, p. 33).

29. Intersectionality is one of feminist scholarship's greatest contributions to our understanding of how interlocking oppressions shape human experience. But early gender theorists erred in claiming to speak for "women" as a group and from a marginalized position while, in fact, articulating women's concerns from a white, middle-class perspective. In presuming to speak for all oppressed women, feminists managed to leave out and thus alienate poor and working-class women and women of color. Intersectional approaches helped remedy these shortcomings, advancing the feminist project by including difference. But gender theorists continue to wrestle with preserving a way to group women in some collective sense while also accommodating intersectionality's complexities.

30. Reinharz (2002).

31. Calasanti and Slevin (2006, p. 1); King (2006); Cruikshank (2009); Hearn (2011); but see Utrata (2011); Laz (1998).

32. Laz (1998).

33. Blumer ([1969] 1986).

34. West and Zimmerman (1987).

35. Calasanti and Slevin (2006). For an excellent discussion of the Gray Panthers' founding and social justice activist Maggie Kuhn, see Douglas (2020); "Maggie Kuhn" (2023); "Gray Panthers" (2023).

36. On age privilege, see Utrata (2011).

37. Calasanti and Slevin (2006).

38. Young's (1994, p. 724) project also involves trying to preserve a means of grouping women in some fashion without stepping on the land mines of ascribing common attributes or identity. She defends the necessity of grouping people in some collective sense and argues that the alternative, abandoning groups altogether and viewing people only at the level of the individual, masks oppression: "Without conceptualizing women as a group in some sense, it is not possible to conceptualize oppression as a systematic, structured institutional process."

39. Young (1994, p. 724).

40. Young (1994, p. 735).

41. See Young's note (1994, p. 724) about Sartre's distinctions between different groups and their varying levels of organization: the group in fusion, the statutory group, the organization, and the institution. "Each is less spontaneous, more organized and rule bound, and more materialized than the last."

42. Cruikshank (2009, p. 159).

43. Torres and Lacy (2021).

44. PBS NewsHour (2021).

45. Nawaz, Fritz, and Jackson (2021).

46. On these proposals, see Torres (2010).

47. Stop AAPI Hate (2023).

48. Kopecki, Higgins-Dunn, and Miller (2020); Cohen (2020).

49. Saturday Night Live (2021).

50. United Nations (2020).

51. Whalen (2020); Sood (2020).

52. Samuel (2020); Knodel (2020); United Nations (2020).

53. Picon (2021).

54. Douglas (2020).

5. REBUILDING THE WORLD OF YESTERDAY

1. Smith, Lehning, and Kim (2018).

2. Desmond (2016); Eviction Lab (2018).

3. Newman (2003); Burns, Lavoie, and Rose (2012).

4. For an interesting discussion about how people connect with animals as a way to interact with their pet owners and how dogs can help promote

"engagements among the unacquainted," see Goffman (1963a). Moreover, Goffman (1963a, pp. 125–126) notes that people with less social status, such as older adults and children, face higher levels of engagement in public and writes, "Furthermore, there are broad statuses in our society, such as that of old persons or the very young, that sometimes seem to be considered so meager in sacred value that it may be thought their members have nothing to lose through face engagement, and hence can be engaged at will. None of these persons, it may be noted, has the kind of uniform that can be taken off; none can be off duty during part of the day. Here, then, persons are exposed, not merely incumbents; they are 'open persons.'" Tissot (2011, p. 277) offers a contemporary example of how dog owners value their connections forged at the dog park as "personal" and "involving friendship."

5. O'Dell (n.d.).
6. Fischer (1982).
7. Milligan (1998, p. 3).
8. Fried ([1963] 1966).
9. Humphreys ([1970] 1975); Suttles (1968).
10. Anderson (1990); Jacobs (1961); Rieder (1985); Suttles (1968).
11. Whyte ([1980] 2001).
12. Glass ([1964] 2010, p. 22–23).
13. Davidson (2008).
14. Marcuse (1986); Davidson (2008).
15. Davidson (2008).
16. Hyra (2015).
17. Tissot (2011).
18. Centner (2008).
19. Davidson and Lees (2010).
20. Tuan (1977, p. 3).
21. Davidson and Lees (2010); Rúa (2017).
22. Hyra (2015).
23. Smith, Lehning, and Kim (2018); Rúa (2017); García and Rúa (2018).
24. Smith, Lehning, and Kim (2018).
25. Torres (2018); Torres (2020b); Rúa (2017); García and Rúa (2018).
26. Davidson and Lees (2010, p. 407).
27. Oldenburg ([1989] 1999).

28. Morrill and Snow (2005).

29. This study has offered insights into dimensions of places that emerged as important to people in late life but shares the limitations of many small qualitative studies that draw on nonrandom samples and cannot generalize to the population. I also did not ask my research companions to assess and compare the places they frequented, which could have provided additional data to help explain people's choices about where to spend their time in the neighborhood. Future qualitative research that collects these data systematically would provide additional depth for our understanding of how to promote and preserve spaces that facilitate support and interaction for people with fewer material, cultural, and physical resources in the midst of gentrification pressures.

30. Lofland (1998, p. 70).

6. THE STRENGTH OF ELASTIC TIES

1. Portnoy and Hart Angelo (1982).

2. Granovetter (1973). See Huxhold et al. (2020) and Perry et al. (2022b) for more on the importance of weak ties for older adults' well-being.

3. The General Social Science Survey (GSS) social network module, introduced in 1985, provides crucial data on how Americans structure their discussion networks (Bearman and Parigi 2004). The central question reads: "From time to time, most people discuss important matters with other people. Looking back over the last six months—who are the people with whom you discussed matters important to you? Just tell me their first names or initials" (Fischer 2009).

4. Granovetter (1973).

5. See Feld (1981).

6. See Stueve and Gerson (1977).

7. Desmond (2012).

8. Gratton and Haber (1993, p. 192) find that compared with the diminished power of older women living in three-generation, rural households, older women living separately from their families in urban areas often felt closer to relatives. Social Security benefits helped enable their financial independence, and they preferred "intimacy at a distance" with relatives. Kavedžija (2019,

p. 120–121) draws on this concept to argue elders' close relationships need not always include their families, especially adult children.

9. See Fine (1979).

10. Wellman (1979).

11. Abramson (2015); Portacolone (2013); Victor et al. (2009).

12. Cornwell et al. (2008).

13. Fischer (1982); Hochschild (1973).

14. Taylor et al. (2009); Victor et al. (2009).

15. Cruikshank (2009).

16. Bearman and Parigi (2004).

17. McPherson et al. (2006).

18. See McPherson et al. (2006) for more on how the "important matters" question sparked new discussion in the longstanding debate over isolation. For critiques and further investigations of these findings, see Fischer's discussion (2009, p. 657) of the possibility that interviewee fatigue from the detailed preceding questions or difficulty interpreting the question influenced these results. Additional critiques have attributed the 2004 GSS isolation findings to measurement error at the interviewer level. Paik and Sanchagrin (2013) further argue that the substantial interviewer bias they detected in the 2004 GSS exists in all egocentric name generator questions that ask respondents to list their social network members, rendering estimates of social connectivity based on this data collection method inaccurate. This, then, raises more general questions about the validity of using survey methods to measure social networks and isolation. Fischer (2009, p. 657) claims that such a dramatic social change without explanation was an artifact, perhaps the result of interviewee fatigue or difficulty interpreting the question.

19. Bailey and Marsden (1999).

20. Bearman and Parigi (2004); Marsden (1987); Marsden (1993); but see Small (2013).

21. Cagney et al. (2013); Suanet, van Tilburg, and van Groenou (2013).

22. McPherson, Smith-Lovin, and Cook (2001).

23. Offer and Fischer (2022); UC Berkeley Social Networks Study (UCNets) (2020).

24. For example, although the Survey of Health, Ageing and Retirement in Europe (SHARE) (2015, p. 16) offers twenty-seven categories from which

respondents can list network members with whom they discussed important things, follow-up questions stress people who are "important to you" as the key characteristic of the relationship. The National Social Life, Health, and Aging Project (NSHAP) (2011, p. 6) uses a similar important-things question, with a list of relationship options, followed by probes about frequency and method of contact between network members and family and friend support. Meanwhile, the Longitudinal Aging Study Amsterdam (LASA) (2017) uses repeated probes that stress contacts with whom the respondent is "in touch regularly" and finds "important," potentially missing anyone outside a recognizable relationship significant to the interviewee.

25. NSHAP and SHARE broadly define the neighborhood as the area within a twenty-minute walk, or a kilometer to a mile, around the home. All three surveys gauge respondents' agreement with statements about neighborhood safety and cleanliness, feelings of belonging, availability of help, and perceptions that the area is close knit or people can be trusted.

26. Goldman and York Cornwell (2023).

27. I replicated the "important matters" question from York Cornwell and Waite (2009).

28. Katz (1997).

29. See Desmond (2012); Goffman (2009); Jerolmack and Khan (2014); Khan and Jerolmack (2013); LaPiere (1934); Liebow (1967).

30. Paik and Sanchagrin (2013).

31. Victor et al. (2009).

32. Simmel ([1908] 1971, p. 143).

33. Simmel ([1908] 1971, p. 144).

34. Desmond (2012).

35. Liebow (1967).

36. Liebow (1967, p. 117).

37. Desmond (2012).

38. Small (2017, p. 6).

39. Granovetter (1973).

40. Desmond (2012).

41. Wireman (1984, p. 10).

42. Lofland (1998).

43. Small (2009).

44. Greer (1962).

45. Greer (1962); see also Guest et al. (2006); Wellman and Leighton (1979).

46. On retaining demanding network members, see Offer and Fischer (2018).

47. Rainie and Wellman (2012, p. 125).

48. Scharlach and Lehning (2016); Torres-Gil and Hofland (2012).

49. See Weil (2014) for more discussion of senior centers.

50. Victor et al. (2009).

51. Small (2009).

52. *Merriam-Webster* (2017).

53. For an excellent discussion about why people may avoid confiding in close relations, see Small (2017).

54. Stuart (2016).

55. For more on the advantages of focusing on contexts that provide people with opportunities to form social ties, see Offer and Fischer (2018); Small (2017).

56. Simmel ([1908] 1971); Jacobs (1961).

7. I SING THE BODY ELECTRIC

Epigraph: Whitman ([1855] 2023).

1. Victor, Scambler, and Bond (2009).

2. Wacker and Roberto (2013).

3. Granovetter (1973).

4. According to the United States Census, only 5.8 percent of all women 55 and older had never married in 2009 (Kreider and Ellis 2011).

5. Scheffer et al. (2008).

6. Kuhne (2014).

7. Manhattan's streets and sidewalks generally receive greater attention in terms of snow removal and the salting of surfaces from the city, business own-ers, and building workers than those in the outer boroughs (G. Smith 2011; McQuillan 2010). The pavement surrounding the co-op buildings where many older people lived received prompt and thorough snow removal. Only a mas-sive storm of historic proportions would shut down Manhattan, and even then normal operations recover rather quickly. Compare this upkeep to the snowy corners I observed in Queens that winter, where people often had a narrow

passageway the width of a shovel carved through many snow mounds. Sometimes this shoddy passage only formed after people had trampled unshoveled snow piles. See also Torres (2017).

8. Bernstein (2014); Jin and Christakis (2009); Livingston (2014).

9. For more on social comparison, physical health, and embodied age, see Laz (2003).

10. Adams et al. (2006); Hochschild (1973).

11. Hurd Clarke and Korotchenko (2016); Torres and Cao (2019).

12. Chrisler, Barney, and Palatino (2016).

13. Aronson (2015).

14. Nelson (2005).

15. Band-Winterstein (2015).

16. Kane and Kane (2005).

17. Nelson (2016).

18. Hatch (2005).

19. Kane and Kane (2005); Adams et al. (2006); Ouchida and Lachs (2015).

20. Centers for Disease Control and Prevention (2022b).

21. Nelson (2005).

22. Kane and Kane (2005); Pan et al. (2014); Walker et al. (2004).

23. This study shares the limitations of many small qualitative studies that draw on nonrandom samples and cannot generalize to the population. I also do not have observations of elders' stressful interactions at medical offices. Future qualitative research that includes these data would provide additional depth. Despite these limitations, this work expands prior scholarship on elders' socializing in public spaces and adds to a small but growing number of qualitative studies on lived experiences of aging in place. For some recent examples, see Abramson (2015); Kavedžija (2019); Loe (2011); Plasencia (2023); Portacolone (2013); Rúa (2017); Weil (2014).

8. AT HOME IN THE CITY

1. La Ferla (2010).

2. Hochschild (1973, p. 17).

3. DASH stands for "Dietary Approaches to Stop Hypertension." "DASH Eating Plan" (2023).

4. Connell (1987).

5. Carr (2019).

6. Herd and Moynihan (2018).

7. Abramson (2015); Carr (2019).

9. THE INEVITABLE PLACE

1. Myerhoff (1978).

2. Fieldnotes recorded in November 2010.

3. Moss (2017).

4. Herd and Moynihan (2018).

5. Torres-Gil and Hofland (2012).

6. Ben Noon and Ayalon (2018); Cheang (2002); Rosenbaum, Sweeney, and Windhorst (2009); Rúa (2017).

7. Putnam (2000); Klinenberg (2002); Small (2009); Loe (2011); Klinenberg (2012).

8. On East Asia, see U.S. Census Bureau (2022). On Europe, Vallese (2022).

9. I grappled with loss, grief, and illness throughout the research process, from conceiving the study to writing up results. I never anticipated the toll absorbing the losses, health crises, and other hardships elders experienced during my study would take on me. No matter how much distance I imagined I had from my study participants, their deaths inflicted varying amounts of psychic pain, depending on how involved I was with them. Few road maps exist for navigating this form of scholarly emotional labor. The pandemic's upheaval deepened personal and scholarly reflections on loss as I worked on this material while caring for my father, who was in his mid-70s, and my 37-year-old sister. My sister's severe isolation and two hospitalizations led to her nursing home admission in 2020. Six months later, my father died from a lung cancer recurrence.

These accumulated griefs affected me directly as I worked steadily on my book, although I was not entirely conscious of it; my slow progress frustrated me, and severe depression left me emotionally and physically exhausted. I cried every day. Studies highlight that scholars often don't anticipate how research may affect their emotions. Research further suggests that topics such as violence, death, loss, and terminal or chronic illnesses can contribute to researcher distress and highlights the importance of self-care techniques, talking with others, and seeking professional help when needed. As an important first step, we might encourage discussions with colleagues, mentors, and advisors about encountering difficult topics and sharing resources and lessons learned. Along with intentional planning around encountering difficult stories and considering how to provide support for research participants who share their experiences, we might encourage researchers to prioritize their own well-being and consider self-care strategies, such as reflective writing. See Torres and Pond (2023).

10. Lofland (1998).

11. "A Quote by Victor Hugo" (n.d.).

12. Literary America (2020).

13. Gioia and Koss (n.d.); Karman (n.d.); "Robinson Jeffers" (2023); "Robinson & Una Jeffers—'Our Inevitable Place'" (2019).

14. Gioia and Koss (n.d.).

15. Monroe (1926, p. 163).

16. *Tor* means "rocky hill" in Gaelic. Ruchowitz-Roberts (n.d.).

17. Walsh (2012).

18. Walsh (2012).

19. Karman (n.d.).

20. "Rhapsody in Blue" (2023).

21. Lofland (1998).

22. "Placemaking" (2023).

23. Gerstel and Sarkisian (2006).

24. Gerstel and Sarkisian (2006).

25. See Torres (2018) for more discussion about how earlier qualitative work helped to form an important wave of critique against "disengagement theory," which posited that old people chose to withdraw from the social fabric and their social ties, sensing death on the near horizon.

26. Colletti (2014); Boyle (2014).

27. Kimmelman (2014).

28. Torres (2014b).

29. Nir and Ham (2014); Kimmelman (2014).

30. Smith et al. (2020); Hayes (2022).

31. Versey (2018); Centers for Disease Control and Prevention (2009a).

32. Smith et al. (2020); Hayes (2022).

33. Torres (2019d).

34. "Social Model of Disability" (n.d.).

35. Hawkley and Cacioppo (2010); Krendl and Perry (2021).

36. For more on pandemic-related fear of public places, see Newberry (2022).

37. Elassar (2022).

38. Jeung et al. (2022); Moses (2022); Eyewitness News ABC7 (2022); Yakas (2023).

39. Portacolone (2013).

40. Cavallo and Kryvtsov (2021).

41. Torres (2014a); Benson (2023); The National Council on Aging (2022a).

42. Li and Dalaker (2022).

43. Meschede at al. (2015).

44. Wallace and Smith (2009).

45. Torres (2014a); Roig and Maruichi (2022).

46. U.S. Department of Labor (2023).

47. Torres (2014a).

48. Carr (2010).

49. Newman (2003).

50. Meschede et al. (2015).

51. Wallace and Smith (2009).

52. Bolton (2022).

53. "What Older New Yorkers Deserve" (2024); New York City Council (2024).

54. Bowles, Dvorkin, and Shaviro (2023).

55. Plasencia (2023).

56. González-Rivera (2013).

57. "History of Skid Row and the Trust" (n.d.); Marshall (2015); Gudis (with Skid Row Now & 2040 Coalition) (2022).

58. See Diamond (1992) for more on the commodification of long-term care.

59. "A Guide for Tenants-Senior Citizens (62 and over) and People with Disabilities" (2015); "SCRIE/DRIE" (n.d.).

60. S. Smith (2011).

61. Fuller-Thomson and Redmond (2008); McGovern (2021).

62. Alwin and Bauer (2023).

63. The National Council on Aging (2022b).

64. Nelson (2005).

65. Mate et al. (2018).

66. Institute for Healthcare Improvement (2024).

67. Weil (2014).

68. Walker et al. (2004).

69. Markwood (2013).

70. Gustke (2016); Café Plus Model (2014).

71. More at Mather's (n.d.).

72. Telephone Topics (n.d.).

73. Rosenbaum et al. (2009); Rosenbaum et al. (2007).

74. Gawande (2014).

75. Intergenerational Programming, Hebrew SeniorLife (n.d.).

76. Finlay et al. (2015).

77. Noon and Ayalon (2018); World Health Organization (2007).

78. Rosenbaum et al. (2007).

79. Northridge et al. (2016).

80. Victor et al. (2018).

81. Chatlani (2023).

82. See Yeh (2022) for an example of recent qualitative research with a diverse sample of older adults that sought to understand their lived experiences and personal understandings of "age-friendly" environments as they aged in place.

83. Pan et al. (2014).

84. Hansen, Hodgson, and Gitlin (2016).

85. López Sánchez and Nance (2020); Morgan-Consoli and Unzueta (2018); González-Vázquez, Pelcastre-Villafuerte, and Taboada (2016).

86. Stanford Center on Longevity (2022).

87. Graham (2022); Beacon Hill Village (2024).

88. Graham (2022); Graham and Guzman (2022); Nicholson, Scharlach, and Graham (2017).

89. "Veil of Ignorance" (2023); Wenar (2021).

90. On ensuring a safety net for all, see Boteach (2022). See also Estes, DiCarlo, and Yeh (2023) for how precarity and inequity across the life course and aging has accelerated via the COVID-19 pandemic. They suggest that

emancipatory sciences can offer a hopeful path towards shaping practice, research, policy, and legislation that seek alleviation of health and social intergenerational inequities by addressing injustices and opportunities for social change.

91. Gourevitch (2006, p. 57).
92. Angell (2014).
93. OECD/European Observatory on Health Systems and Policies (2021).
94. Torres (2022).

References

Abramson, Corey M. 2015. *The End Game: How Inequality Shapes Our Final Years*. Cambridge, MA: Harvard University Press.

Abramson, Corey M. 2021. "Ethnographic Methods for Research on Aging: Making Use of a Fundamental Toolkit for Understanding Everyday Life." Pp. 15–31 in *Handbook of Aging and the Social Sciences*, 9th ed., edited by Kenneth F. Ferraro and Deborah Carr. New York: Elsevier. doi: https://doi.org/10.1016/B978-0-12-815970-5.00002-4.

Achenbaum, W. Andrew. 2006. "Historical Gerontology: It Is a Matter of Time." Pp. 203–224 in *Enduring Questions in Gerontology*, edited by Debra J. Sheets, Dana Burr Bradley, and Jon Hendricks. New York: Springer Publishing.

Adams, Ann, Christopher D. Buckingham, Sara Arber, John B. McKinlay, Lisa Marceau, and Carol Link. 2006. "The Influence of Patient's Age on Clinical Decision-making About Coronary Heart Disease in the USA and the UK." *Ageing and Society* 26:303–321. doi:10.1017/S0144686X05004265.

Administration on Aging. 2022. *2021 Profile of Older Americans*. Washington, DC: U.S. Department of Health and Human Services, Administration for Community Living. https://acl.gov/sites/default/files/Profile%20of %20OA/2021%20Profile%20of%20OA/2021ProfileOlderAmericans_508 .pdf.

Alwin, Ramsey, and Brandy Bauer. 2023. "$30 Billion Left on the Table: Connecting More Older Adults With Money-Saving Public Benefits." The National Council on Aging. Retrieved December 31, 2023 (https://www .ncoa.org/article/30-billion-left-on-the-table-connecting-more-older-adults-with-money-saving-public-benefits).

Anderson, Elijah. 1990. *Streetwise: Race, Class, and Change in an Urban Community*. Chicago: University of Chicago Press.

Angell, Roger. 2014. "This Old Man." *The New Yorker*, February, 17 & 24. Retrieved March 9, 2023 (https://www.newyorker.com/magazine/2014/02 /17/old-man-3).

Aronson, Louise. 2015. "The Human Lifecycle's Neglected Stepchild." *Lancet* 385: 500–501. doi:10.1016/ s0140-6736(14)61819-5.

Aronson, Louise. 2019. *Elderhood: Redefining Aging, Transforming Medicine, Reimagining Life*. New York: Bloomsbury Publishing.

Bailey, Stephanie, and Peter Marsden. 1999. "Interpretation and Interview Context: Examining the General Social Survey Name Generator Using Cognitive Methods." *Social Networks* 21(3):287–309. https://doi.org/10.1016/S0378–8733(99)00013–1.

Band-Winterstein, Tova. 2015. "Health Care Provision for Older Persons: The Interplay Between Ageism and Elder Neglect." *Journal of Applied Gerontology* 34:NP113–NP127. doi:10.1177/0733464812475308.

Bao, Yuhua, Ashley A. Eggman, Joshua E. Richardson, and Martha L. Bruce. 2014. "Misalignment between Medicare Policies and Depression Care in Home Health Care: Home Health Provider Perspectives." *Psychiatric Services* 65(7):905–910. doi:10.1176/appi.ps.201300158.

Barmann, Jay. 2021. "San Francisco Only Got More Childless in the Last Decade." *SFist*. Retrieved February 23, 2023 (https://sfist.com/2021/08/13 /san-francisco-only-got-more-childless-in-the-last-decade/).

Beacon Hill Village. 2024. "Home." Retrieved January 1, 2024 (https://www .beaconhillvillage.org/content.aspx?page_id=0&club_id=332658).

Bearman, Peter, and Paolo Parigi. 2004. "Cloning Headless Frogs and Other Important Matters: Conversation Topics and Network Structure." *Social Forces* 83(2):535–557. https://doi.org/10.1353/sof.2005.0001.

Bellah, Robert, Richard Madsen, William M. Sullivan, Ann Swidler, and Steven M. Tipton. [1985] 1996. *Habits of the Heart: Individualism and Commitment in American Life*. Berkeley: University of California Press.

Bennett, Beth. 2021. *Defy Aging: A Beginner's Guide to the New Science of Longer Life and Better Health*. New York: Rowman & Littlefield.

Ben Noon, Rinat, and Liat Ayalon. 2018. "Older Adults in Open Public Spaces: Age and Gender Segregation." *The Gerontologist* 58(1):149–158. https://doi.org/10.1093/geront/gnx047.

Benson, Craig. 2023. "Child Poverty Rate Still Higher than for Older Populations but Declining." United States Census Bureau. Retrieved December 31, 2023 (https://www.census.gov/library/stories/2023/12/poverty-rate-varies-by-age-groups.html).

Berg, Sara. 2023. "What Doctors Wish Patients Knew about Falling U.S. Life Expectancy." American Medical Association. Retrieved January 3, 2024 (https://www.ama-assn.org/delivering-care/public-health/what-doctors-wish-patients-knew-about-falling-us-life-expectancy).

Bernstein, Elizabeth. 2014. "After the Loss of a Spouse, There Is No Right Amount of Time before Moving On: Why Men Are More Likely to Seek Out a New Relationship than Women." *The Wall Street Journal*, November 14. Retrieved August 5, 2015 (http://www.wsj.com/articles/after-the-loss-of-a-spouse-there-is-no-right-amount-of-time-before-moving-on-416251499).

Binette, Joanne, and Kerri Vasold. 2018. *2018 Home and Community Preferences: A National Survey of Adults Age 18-Plus*. Washington, DC: AARP Research. https://doi.org/10.26419/res.00231.001

Blau, Melinda, and Karen L. Fingerman. 2009. *Consequential Strangers: Turning Everyday Encounters Into Life-Changing Moments*. New York, NY: W. W. Norton.

Bloom, David E., and Leo M. Zucker. 2022. "Aging Is the Real Population Bomb." International Monetary Fund. Retrieved February 24, 2023 (https://www.imf.org/en/Publications/fandd/issues/Series/Analytical-Series/aging-is-the-real-population-bomb-bloom-zucker).

Blumberg, Herbert H. 1972. "Communication of Interpersonal Evaluation." *Journal of Personality and Social Psychology* 23(2):157–162. doi:10.1037/h0033027.

Blumer, Herbert. [1969] 1986. *Symbolic Interactionism: Perspective and Method.* Berkeley, CA: University of California Press.

Bolton, Aaron. 2022. "Homeless Shelters Are Seeing More Senior Citizens with No Place to Live." NPR. Retrieved February 23, 2023 (https://www.npr.org/2022/11/17/1137334895/homeless-shelters-are-seeing-more-senior-citizens-with-no-place-to-live).

Boteach, Melissa. 2022. "Reimagining Our Social Contract: The Safety Net Is Social Insurance for All Americans." Center for American Progress. Retrieved March 11, 2023 (https://www.americanprogress.org/article/reimagining-our-social-contract-the-safety-net-is-social-insurance-for-all-americans/).

Bowles, Jonathan, Eli Dvorkin, and Charles Shaviro. 2023. "Keeping Pace With an Aging New York State." Center for an Urban Future. Retrieved February 29, 2024 (https://nycfuture.org/research/keeping-pace-with-an-aging-new-york-state).

Bowling, Ann, and Paul Dieppe. 2005. "What is Successful Ageing and Who Should Define It?" *British Medical Journal* 331(7531):1548–1551. doi: 10.1136/bmj.331.7531.1548.

Boyle, Louise. 2014. "McDonald's at War with a Group of Elderly Koreans for Hogging Booths." *Daily Mail Online.* Retrieved March 7, 2023 (https://www.dailymail.co.uk/news/article-2539892/McDonalds-war-group-gossiping-elderly-men-spend-entire-days-hogging-booths.html).

Brown-Saracino, Japonica. 2011. "From the Lesbian Ghetto to the Ambient Community: The Perceived Costs and Benefits of Integration for Community." *Social Problems* 58(3):361–388. doi:10.1525/sp.2011.58.3.361.

"Building Stuyvesant Town in the 1940s." 2010. *Ephemeral New York.* Retrieved March 1, 2023 (https://ephemeralnewyork.wordpress.com/2010/06/02/building-stuyvesant-town-in-the-1940s/).

Burke, Georgia, and Natalie Kean. 2019. "Issue Brief: Older Immigrants and Medicare." Justice in Aging. Retrieved February 24, 2023 (https://www.justiceinaging.org/wp-content/uploads/2019/04/FINAL_Older-Immigrants-and-Medicare.pdf).

Burns, Victoria F., Jean-Pierre Lavoie, and Damaris Rose. 2012. "Revisiting the Role of Neighbourhood Change in Social Exclusion and Inclusion of Older People." *Journal of Aging Research*, Article ID 148287. doi: 10.1155/2012/148287.

Café Plus Model. 2014. Retrieved May 16, 2024 (https://www.mather.com/wp-content/uploads/2013/02/CafePlusWorkshops_June14_FNL_1.pdf).

Cagney, Kathleen A., Christopher R. Browning, Aubrey L. Jackson, and Brian Stoller. 2013. "Networks, Neighborhoods, and Institutions: An Integrated 'Activity Space' Approach for Research on Aging." Pp. 150–74 in *New Directions on the Sociology of Aging*, edited by L.J. Waite and T.J. Plewes. Washington, DC: National Academies Press. (https://www.ncbi.nlm.nih.gov/books/NBK184369/).

Calasanti, Toni M., and Kathleen F. Slevin. 2006. "Introduction: Age Matters." Pp. 1–14 in *Age Matters: Realigning Feminist Thinking*, edited by Toni M. Calasanti and Kathleen F. Slevin. New York: Routledge.

Cao, Xuemei. 2021. "Intergenerational Relations of Older Immigrants in the United States." *Sociology Compass* 15(10):1–13. doi: 10.1111/soc4.12908.

Carr, Deborah. 2010. "Golden Years? Poverty Among Older Americans." *Contexts* 9(1): 62–63. https://doi.org/10.1525/ctx.2010.9.1.62.

Carr, Deborah. 2019. *Golden Years? Social Inequality in Late Life*. New York: Russell Sage Foundation.

Carstensen, Laura L. 1992. "Social and Emotional Patterns in Adulthood: Support for Socioemotional Selectivity Theory." *Psychology and Aging* 7(3):331–338. http://dx.doi.org/10.1037/0882-7974.7.3.331.

Carteron, Nancy. 2022. "Ask the Expert: What Is a Sjögren's Flare?" Sjögren's Foundation. Retrieved February 23, 2023 (https://www.sjogrens.org/blog/2022/ask-the-expert-what-is-a-sjogrens-flare).

Cavallo, Alberto, and Oleksiy Kryvtsov. 2021. "How the Pandemic Has Affected the Economy, from Empty Shelves to Higher Prices." PBS. Retrieved March 7, 2023 (https://www.pbs.org/newshour/economy/how-the-pandemic-has-affected-the-economy-from-empty-shelves-to-higher-prices).

Centers for Disease Control and Prevention. 2009a. "Health Effects of Gentrification." Retrieved March 7, 2023 (https://www.cdc.gov/healthyplaces/healthtopics/gentrification.htm).

Centers for Disease Control and Prevention. 2009b. "Healthy Places Terminology." Retrieved February 23, 2023 (https://www.cdc.gov/healthyplaces/terminology.htm).

Centers for Disease Control and Prevention. 2022a. "Birth Cohort." National Center for Health Statistics. Retrieved February 23, 2023 (https://www.cdc.gov/nchs/hus/sources-definitions/birth-cohort.htm).

Centers for Disease Control and Prevention. 2022b. "Depression is Not a Normal Part of Growing Older." Retrieved March 6, 2023 (https://www.cdc.gov/aging/depression/index.html).

Centers for Disease Control and Prevention. 2022c. "New Report Confirms U.S. Life Expectancy Has Declined to Lowest Level since 1996." Retrieved January 3, 2024 (https://www.cdc.gov/nchs/pressroom/nchs_press_releases/2022/20221222.htm).

Centers for Disease Control and Prevention. 2023. "U.S. Teen Girls Experiencing Increased Sadness and Violence." Retrieved January 1, 2024 (https://www.cdc.gov/nchhstp/newsroom/2023/increased-sadness-and-violence-press-release.html).

Centner, Ryan. 2008. "Places of Privileged Consumption Practices: Spatial Capital, the Dot-Com Habitus, and San Francisco's Internet Boom." *City and Community* 7(3):193–223. https://doi.org/10.1111/j.1540–6040.2008.00258.x.

Chatlani, Shalina. 2023. "A Black Church in Louisiana Aims to Educate People on How to Be Healthy." WBUR. Retrieved March 7, 2023 (https://www.wbur.org/npr/1155014863/a-black-church-in-louisiana-aims-to-educate-people-on-how-to-be-healthy).

Cheang, Michael. 2002. "Older Adults' Frequent Visits to a Fast-Food Restaurant: Nonobligatory Social Interaction and the Significance of Play in a 'Third Place.'" *Journal of Aging Studies* 16:303–321. doi:10.1016/S0890–4065(02)00052-X.

Chrisler, Joan C., Angela Barney, and Brigida Palatino. 2016. "Ageism Can Be Hazardous to Women's Health: Ageism, Sexism, and Stereotypes of Older Women in the Healthcare System." *The Journal of Social Issues* 72:86–104. doi:10.1111/josi.12157.

City of New York. 2016. "Senior Citizen Rent Increase Exemption (SCRIE)." The Official Website of the City of New York. Retrieved September 26, 2017 (http://www1.nyc.gov/nyc-resources/service/2424/senior-citizen-rent-increase-exemption-scrie).

Cohen, Elizabeth. 2020. "New CDC Guidance Says Older Adults Should 'Stay at Home as Much as Possible' Due to Coronavirus." CNN. Retrieved March 2, 2023 (https://www.cnn.com/2020/03/06/health/coronavirus-older-people-social-distancing/index.html).

Colletti, Roseanne. 2014. "'Lovin' It' Too Much: McDonald's in Standoff with Elderly Who Stay for Hours." NBC New York. Retrieved March 7, 2023 (https://www.nbcnewyork.com/news/local/mcdonalds-elderly-senior-citizens-wont-leave-standoff-flushing-queens/1473445/).

"Collyer Brothers." 2023. Wikipedia. Retrieved February 27, 2023 (https://en.wikipedia.org/wiki/Collyer_brothers).

Connell, Raewyn. 1987. *Gender and Power: Society, the Person, and Sexual Politics.* Stanford, CA: Stanford University Press.

Cooper, Lee E. 1945. "Uprooted Thousands Starting Trek From Site for Stuyvesant Town." *The New York Times*, March 3. Retrieved March 1, 2023 (https://www.nytimes.com/1945/03/03/archives/uprooted-thousands-starting-trek-from-site-for-stuyvesant-town-vans.html).

Cornwell, Benjamin, Edward O. Laumann, and Philip L. Schumm. 2008. "The Social Connectedness of Older Adults: A National Profile." *American Sociological Review* 73:185–203. https://doi.org/10.1177/000312240807300201.

Courtin, Emilie, and Martin Knapp. 2017. "Social Isolation, Loneliness and Health in Old Age: A Scoping Review." *Health & Social Care in the Community* 25:799–812. doi:10.1111/hsc.12311.

Crowley, Jocelyn Elise. 2018. *Gray Divorce: What We Gain and Lose from Mid-Life Splits.* Oakland, CA: University of California Press.

Cruikshank, Margaret. 2009. *Learning to Be Old: Gender, Culture, & Aging.* New York: Rowman & Littlefield Publishers.

Dannefer, Dale. 2003. "Cumulative Advantage/Disadvantage and the Life Course: Cross-fertilizing Age and Social Science Theory." *Journal of Gerontology: Social Sciences* 58B(6):S327–S337. https://doi.org/10.1093/geronb/58.6.S327.

"DASH Eating Plan." 2023. National Heart, Lung, and Blood Institute. Retrieved December 30, 2023 (https://www.nhlbi.nih.gov/education/dash-eating-plan).

Davidson, Mark. 2008. "Spoiled Mixture: Where Does State-Led 'Positive' Gentrification End?" *Urban Studies* 45(12):2385–2405. https://doi.org/10.1177/0042098008097105.

Davidson, Mark, and Loretta Lees. 2010. "New-Build Gentrification: Its Histories, Trajectories, and Critical Geographies." *Population, Space, and Place* 16:395–411. doi:10.1002/psp.584.

Degnen, Cathrine. 2007. "Minding the Gap: The Construction of Old Age and Oldness amongst Peers." *Journal of Aging Studies* 21(1):69–80. doi:10.1016/j.jaging.2006.02.001.

Desmond, Matthew. 2012. "Disposable Ties and the Urban Poor." *American Journal of Sociology* 117(5):1295–1335. doi:10.1086/663574

Desmond, Matthew. 2016. *Evicted: Poverty and Profit in the American City.* New York: Crown.

Diamond, Timothy. 1992. *Making Gray Gold: Narratives of Nursing Home Care.* Chicago: University of Chicago Press.

Dixon, Mort, and Ray Henderson. 1926. "Bye Bye Blackbird." Historic Sheet Music Collection. 1825. Retrieved February 22, 2023 (https://digitalcommons.conncoll.edu/sheetmusic/1825).

Douglas, Susan J. 2020. *In Our Prime: How Older Women Are Reinventing the Road Ahead.* New York: W. W. Norton.

Duneier, Mitchell. 1992. *Slim's Table: Race, Respectability, and Masculinity.* Chicago: University of Chicago Press.

Durkheim, Emile. [1897] 1951. *Suicide: A Study in Sociology*, translated by John A. Spaulding and George Simpson. New York: Free Press.

"The East Side's Long-Gone Gas House District." 2011. *Ephemeral New York.* Retrieved March 1, 2023 (https://ephemeralnewyork.wordpress.com/2011/06/20/the-east-sides-long-gone-gas-house-district/).

Edemekong, Peter F., Deb L. Bomgaars, Sukesh Sukumaran, and Caroline Schoo. 2022. "Activities of Daily Living." Treasure Island, FL: StatPearls Publishing. Retrieved February 23, 2023 (https://www.ncbi.nlm.nih.gov/books/NBK470404/).

Elassar, Alaa. 2022. "New Yorkers Don't Feel Safe at Home Anymore." CNN. Retrieved March 7, 2023 (https://www.cnn.com/2022/04/30/us/new-york-crime-safety-fears/index.html).

Encyclopedia Britannica. 2020. "Women's Army Corps." Retrieved March 2, 2023 (https://www.britannica.com/topic/Womens-Army-Corps).

Estes, Carroll L., Nicholas B. DiCarlo, and Jarmin C. Yeh. 2023. "Building Back Better: Going Big with Emancipatory Sciences." *Journal of Aging & Social Policy*:1–16. doi:10.1080/08959420.2023.2182998.

Eviction Lab. 2018. "Home." Retrieved January 3, 2024 (https://evictionlab.org/).

Eyewitness News ABC7. 2022. "Trial Set in October for Alleged Suspect in 87-Year-Old Grandmother's Shove Death." ABC7 New York. Retrieved March 9, 2023 (https://abc7ny.com/nyc-woman-pushed-barbara-maier-gustern-chelsea-87-year-old-elderly/12132970/).

Fagan, Kevin. 2019. "Aging onto the Street." *The San Francisco Chronicle.* Retrieved February 23, 2023 (https://www.sfchronicle.com/bayarea/article/Aging-onto-the-street-Nearly-half-of-older-13668900.php).

Feld, Scott L. 1981. "The Focused Organization of Social Ties." *American Journal of Sociology* 86(5):1015–1035. https://doi.org/10.1086/227352.

Ferraro, Kenneth F. 2018. *The Gerontological Imagination: An Integrative Paradigm of Aging.* New York: Oxford University Press.

Fine, Gary Alan, and Ralph L. Rosnow. 1978. "Gossip, Gossipers and Gossiping." *Personality and Social Psychology Bulletin* 4:161–168. doi:10.1177/014616727800400135.

Fine, Gary Alan. 1979. "Small Groups and Culture Creation: The Idioculture of Little League Baseball Teams." *American Sociological Review* 44:733–745. doi:10.2307/2094525.

Finlay, Jessica, Thea Franke, Heather McKay, and Joanie Sims-Gould. 2015. "Therapeutic Landscapes and Wellbeing in Later Life: Impacts of Blue and Green Spaces for Older Adults." *Health & Place* 34:97–106. doi:10.1016/j.healthplace.2015.05.001.

Fischer, Claude S. 1982. *To Dwell Among Friends: Personal Networks in Town and City.* Chicago: University of Chicago Press.

Fischer, Claude S. 2009. "The 2004 GSS Finding of Shrunken Social Networks: An Artifact?" *American Sociological Review* 74(4):657–669. https://doi.org/10.1177/000312240907400408.

Foster, Eric K. 2004. "Research on Gossip: Taxonomy, Methods, and Future Directions." *Review of General Psychology* 8(2):78–99. doi:10.1037/1089-2680.8.2.78.

Francis, David R. 2003. "What Reduced Crime in New York City?" *The NBER Digest,* January 2003. https://www.nber.org/sites/default/files/2019-08/jan03.PDF.

Freedman, Vicki A., Linda G. Martin, and Robert F. Schoeni. 2002. "Recent Trends in Disability and Functioning Among Older Adults in the United States: A Systematic Review." *JAMA* (288):3137–3146. doi:10.1001/jama.288.24.3137.

Fried, Marc. [1963] 1966. "Grieving for a Lost Home: Psychological Costs of Relocation. Pp. 359–379 in *The Urban Renewal: The Record and the Controversy*, edited by James Q. Wilson. Cambridge, MA: The MIT Press.

Fuller-Thomson, Esme, and Melissa Redmond. 2008. "Falling Through the Social Safety Net: Food Stamp Use and Nonuse Among Older Impoverished Americans." *The Gerontologist* 48:235–244.doi:10.1093/geront/48.2.235.

Furman, Frida Kerner. 1997. *Facing the Mirror: Older Women and Beauty Shop Culture*. New York: Routledge.

García, Ivis, and Mérida M. Rúa. 2018. "Our Interests Matter: Puerto Rican Older Adults in the Age of Gentrification." *Urban Studies* 55(14): 3168–3184. https://doi.org/10.1177/0042098017736251

Gardner, Paula J. 2011. "Natural Neighborhood Networks—Important Social Networks in the Lives of Older Adults Aging in Place." *Journal of Aging Studies* 25:263–271. doi:10.1016/j.jaging.2011.03.007.

Garver, Lloyd. 2007. "Is 60 the New 40 or is 40 the New 60?" CBS News. Retrieved February 24, 2023 (https://www.cbsnews.com/news/is-60-the-new-40-or-is-40-the-new-60–02–05–2007/).

Gawande, Atul. 2014. *Being Mortal: Medicine and What Matters in the End*. New York: Metropolitan Books.

Gendron, Tracey L., E. Ayn Welleford, Jennifer Inker, and John T. White. 2016. "The Language of Ageism: Why We Need to Use Words Carefully." *The Gerontologist* 56(6):997–1006. doi:10.1093/geront/gnv066.

Gerhardt, Megan. 2020. "Covid Means Silent Generation Is Getting Worst of History, Again. They Deserve to Be Heard." NBC News. Retrieved February 23, 2023 (https://www.nbcnews.com/think/opinion/covid-means-silent-generation-getting-worst-history-again-they-deserve-ncna1248859).

"Gerontocracy." 2023. Wikipedia. Retrieved February 24, 2023 (https://en.wikipedia.org/wiki/ Gerontocracy).

Gerstel, Naomi, and Natalia Sarkisian. 2006. "Marriage: The Good, the Bad, and the Greedy." *Contexts* 5(4):16–21. https://doi.org/10.1525/ctx.2006.5.4.16.

Gieryn, Thomas F. 2000. "A Space for Place in Sociology." *Annual Review of Sociology* 26:463–96. https://doi.org/10.1146/annurev.soc.26.1.463.

Gillespie, Lisa. 2019. "As Boomers Age, Senior Centers Face Lower Attendance amid Social Isolation." Louisville Public Media. Retrieved February 27, 2023 (https://www.lpm.org/news/2019–05–31/as-boomers-age-senior-centers-face-lower-attendance-amid-social-isolation).

Gioia, Dana, and Erika Koss. n.d. "The Poetry of Robinson Jeffers." *National Endowment for the Arts Reader Resources.* Retrieved March 7, 2023 (https://www.arts.gov/sites/default/files/Readers-Resources-RobinsonJeffers.pdf).

Glass, Ruth. [1964] 2010. "Aspects of Change." Pp. 19–30 in *The Gentrification Debates,* edited by Japonica Brown-Saracino. New York: Routledge.

Gluckman, Max. 1963. "Papers in Honor of Melville J. Herskovits: Gossip and Scandal." *Current Anthropology* 4:307–316. doi:10.1086/200378.

Goffman, Alice. 2009. "On the Run: Men Wanted in a Philadelphia Ghetto." *American Sociological Review* 74:339–357. https://doi.org/10.1177/000312240907400301

Goffman, Erving. 1959. *The Presentation of Self in Everyday Life.* Garden City, New York: Doubleday Anchor Books.

Goffman, Erving. 1963a. *Behavior in Public Places: Notes on the Social Organization of Gatherings.* New York: Free Press.

Goffman, Erving. 1963b. *Stigma: Notes on the Management of Spoiled Identity.* Englewood Cliffs, NJ: Prentice-Hall.

Goldman, Alyssa W., and Erin York Cornwell. 2023. "Stand by Me: Social Ties and Health in Real Time." *Socius* 9. https://doi.org/10.1177/23780231231171112

González-Rivera, Christian. 2013. "The New Face of New York's Seniors." Center for an Urban Future. Retrieved March 11, 2023 (https://nycfuture.org/pdf/The-New-Face-of-New-Yorks-Seniors.pdf).

González-Vázquez, Tonatiuh, Blanca Estela Pelcastre-Villafuerte, and Arianna Taboada. 2016. "Surviving the Distance: The Transnational Utilization of Traditional Medicine Among Oaxacan Migrants in the US." *Journal of Immigrant and Minority Health* 18(5):1190–1198. doi:10.1007/s10903-015-0245-6. PMID: 26159886.

Gourevitch, Philip, ed. 2006. *The Paris Review, Interviews Vol. II.* New York: Picador.

Gowan, Teresa. 2010. *Hobos, Hustlers, and Backsliders: Homeless in San Francisco.* Minneapolis, Minnesota: University of Minnesota Press.

Graham, Carrie, and Shannon Guzman. 2022. "The Village Model: Current Trends, Challenges, and Opportunities." AARP Public Policy Institute. Retrieved January 3, 2024 (https://www.aarp.org/pri/topics/livable-communities/housing/the-village-model-current-trends-challenges-opportunities.html).

Graham, Dawn Fowler, Ian Graham, and Michael J. MacLean. 1991. "Going to the Mall: A Leisure Activity of Urban Elderly People." *Canadian Journal on Aging* 10(4):345–358. doi:10.1017/S0714980800011375.

Graham, Judith. 2022. "Despite Seniors' Strong Desire to Age in Place, the Village Model Remains a Boutique Option." KFF Health News. Retrieved January 1, 2024 (https://kffhealthnews.org/news/article/seniors-aging-in-place-village-movement-boutique-option/).

Granovetter, Mark. 1973. "The Strength of Weak Ties." *American Journal of Sociology* 78:1360–80. https://doi.org/10.1086/225469.

Gratton, Brian, and Carol Haber. 1993. "In Search of 'Intimacy at a Distance': Family History from the Perspective of Elderly Women." *Journal of Aging Studies* 7(2):183–194. https://doi.org/10.1016/0890-4065(93)90033-G.

Grawert, Ames, and Noah Kim. 2022. "Myths and Realities: Understanding Recent Trends in Violent Crime." Brennan Center for Justice. Retrieved February 23, 2023 (https://www.brennancenter.org/our-work/research-reports/myths-and-realities-understanding-recent-trends-violent-crime).

"Gray Panthers." 2023. Gray Panthers NYC. Retrieved March 2, 2023 (https://www.graypanthersnyc.org/).

Greer, Scott. 1962. *The Emerging City: Myth and Reality.* New York: Free Press.

Greve, Werner, Bernhard Leipold, and Cathleen Kappes. 2018. "Fear of Crime in Old Age: A Sample Case of Resilience?" *Journals of Gerontology: Psychological Sciences* 7(7):1224–1232. doi:10.1093/geronb/gbw16.

Guardian Books. 2021. "Joan Didion, in Her Own Words: 23 of the Best Quotes." *The Guardian.* Retrieved March 9, 2023 (https://www.theguardian.com/books/2021/dec/23/joan-didion-in-her-own-words-23-of-the-best-quotes).

Gubrium, Jaber F. 1975. *Living and Dying at Murray Manor.* New York: Palgrave Macmillan.

Gudis, Catherine (with Skid Row Now & 2040 Coalition). 2022. *Containment and Community: The History of Skid Row and Its Role in the Downtown Community Plan.* Los Angeles Poverty Department. Retrieved March 8, 2023 (https://www.lapovertydept.org/skid-row-now-and-2040/).

Guest, Avery M., Jane K. Cover, Ross L. Matsueda, and Charis E. Kubrin. 2006. "Neighborhood Context and Neighboring Ties." *City & Community* 5:363–385. https://doi.org/10.1111/j.1540–6040.2006.00189.x.

"A Guide for Tenants-Senior Citizens (62 and over) and People with Disabilities." 2015. New York City Department of Finance. Retrieved August 5, 2015 (http://www1.nyc.gov/assets/finance/downloads/pdf/brochures/scriedriebrochure.pdf).

Gusmano, Michael K., and Victor G. Rodwin. 2006. "The Elderly and Social Isolation." Testimony to Committee on Aging, NYC Council, February 13, 2006. Retrieved March 21, 2010 (http://www.nr9.org/releif.org/media/pdfs/ElderlyandSocialIsolation.pdf).

Gustke, Constance. 2016. "Bingo? Pass. Bring on Senior Speed-Dating and Wine-Tasting." *The New York Times*, November 11. Retrieved January 27, 2019 (https://www.nytimes.com/2016/11/12/your-money/new-senior-centers-offer-baby-boomers-speeddating-wine-tasting.html).

Hannerz, Ulf. 1967. "Gossip, Networks and Culture in a Black American Ghetto." *Ethnos* 32:35–60. doi:10.1080/00141844.1 967.9980988.

Hansen, Brian R., Nancy A. Hodgson, and Laura N. Gitlin. 2016. "It's a Matter of Trust: Older African Americans Speak about Their Health Care Encounters." *Journal of Applied Gerontology* 35:1058–1076. doi:10.1177/0733464815570662.

Harrington Meyer, Madonna. 2014. *Grandmothers at Work: Juggling Families and Jobs*. New York: New York University Press.

Harvard T. H. Chan School of Public Health. 2023. "What's Behind 'Shocking' U.S. Life Expectancy Decline—And What to Do About It." Retrieved January 3, 2024 (https://www.hsph.harvard.edu/news/hsph-in-the-news/whats-behind-shocking-u-s-life-expectancy-decline-and-what-to-do-about-it/).

Hatch, Laurie Russell. 2005. "Gender and Ageism." *Generations* 29(3):19–24.

Hawkley, Louise C., and John T. Cacioppo. 2010. "Loneliness Matters: A Theoretical and Empirical Review of Consequences and Mechanisms." *Annals of Behavioral Medicine: A Publication of the Society of Behavioral Medicine* 40(2):218–27. doi:10.1007/s12160–010–9210–8.

Hayes, Theresa. 2022. "Modern Day Colonization: Gentrification as a Public Health Emergency and its Impact on Health, Safety, and Wellbeing." MA Thesis, Public Health, University of San Francisco. 1443. Retrieved March 8,

2023 (https://repository.usfca.edu/cgi/viewcontent.cgi?article=2777&context=capstone).

Hearn, Jeff. 2011. "Neglected Intersectionalities in Studying Men: Age (ing), Virtually, Transnationality." Pp. 89–104 in *Framing Intersectionality: Debates on a Multi-Faceted Concept in Gender Studies*, edited by Helma Lutz, Maria Theresa, Herrera Vivar, and Lind Supik. Burlington, VT: Ashgate.

Herd, Pamela, and Donald P. Moynihan. 2018. *Administrative Burden: Policymaking by Other Means*. New York: Russell Sage Foundation.

"History of Skid Row and the Trust." n.d. Skid Row Housing Trust. Retrieved March 8, 2023 (https://skidrow.org/about/history/).

"A History of Stuytown and Peter Cooper Village." 2019. StuyTown. Retrieved March 1, 2023 (https://www.stuytown.com/guides/stuytown/history).

"Our History." n.d. Stuyvesant Town–Peter Cooper Village Tenants Association. Retrieved March 1, 2023 (https://www.stpcvta.org/history).

Hochschild, Arlie Russell. 1973. *The Unexpected Community: Portrait of an Old Age Subculture*. Englewood Cliffs, NJ: Prentice-Hall.

Hooyman, Nancy R., and Asuman H. Kiyak. 2008. *Social Gerontology: A Multidisciplinary Perspective*. 8th ed. New York: Pearson.

Hostetler, Andrew J. 2011. "Senior Centers in the Era of the 'Third Age:' Country Clubs, Community Centers, or Something Else?" *Journal of Aging Studies* 25(2):166–176. doi:10.1016/j.jaging.2010.08.021.

Humphreys, Laud. [1970] 1975. *Tearoom Trade: Impersonal Sex in Public Places*. New York: Aldine De Gruyter.

Hurd Clarke, Laura and Alexandra Korotchenko. 2016. "'I Know It Exists . . . But I Haven't Experienced It Personally': Older Canadian Men's Perceptions of Ageism as a Distant Social Problem." *Ageing and Society* 36:1757–1773. doi:10.1017/S0144686X15000689.

Huxhold, Oliver, Katherine L. Fiori, Noah J. Webster, and Toni C. Antonucci. 2020. "The Strength of Weaker Ties: An Underexplored Resource for Maintaining Emotional Well-Being in Later Life." *The Journals of Gerontology: Series B: Psychological Sciences and Social Sciences* 75(7):1433–1442. https://doi.org/10.1093/geronb/gbaa019.

Hyra, Derek. 2015. "The Back-to-the-City Movement: Neighbourhood Redevelopment and Processes of Political and Cultural Displacement." *Urban Studies* 52(10):1753–1773. https://doi.org/10.1177/0042098014539403.

"12 Inspiring African Proverbs to Start a Great Week." 2017. BizWatch Nigeria. Retrieved February 23, 2023 (https://bizwatchnigeria.ng/12-african-proverbs-start-week/).

Institute for Healthcare Improvement. 2024. "Age-Friendly Health Systems." Retrieved February 27, 2024 (https://www.ihi.org/initiatives/age-friendly-health-systems).

Intergenerational Programming—Hebrew SeniorLife, for All Seniors of All Backgrounds. n.d. Retrieved January 30, 2019 (https://www.hebrewseniorlife.org/multigen).

Jacobs, Jane. 1961. *The Death and Life of Great American Cities.* New York: Modern Library.

Jerolmack, Colin, and Shamus Khan. 2014. "Talk is Cheap: Ethnography and the Attitudinal Fallacy." *Sociological Research Methods* 43(2):178–209. https://doi.org/10.1177/0049124114523396.

Jeung, Russell, Aggie J. Yellow Horse, Theresa Chen, Anne Saw, Boaz Tang, Alison Lo, Mika Ro, Layla Schweng, Samiksha Krishnamurthy, Winnie Chan, Matthew Chu, and Candice Cho. 2022. *Anti-Asian Hate, Social Isolation, and Mental Health among Asian American Elders During COVID-19.* Stop AAPI Hate/AARP. Retrieved March 8, 2023 (https://stopaapihate.org/wp-content/uploads/2022/05/SAH-Elder-Report-526.pdf).

Jin, Lei, and Nicholas A. Christakis. 2009. "Investigating the Mechanism of Marital Mortality Reduction: The Transition to Widowhood and Quality of Health Care." *Demography* 46(3):605–625. doi:10.1353/dem.0.0066.

Kane, Robert L., and Rosalie A. Kane. 2005. "Ageism in Healthcare and Long-Term Care." *Generations* 29(3):49–54.

Karman, James. n.d. "Jeffers and California." *National Endowment for the Arts Reader Resources.* Retrieved March 7, 2023 (https://www.arts.gov/sites/default/files/Readers-Resources-RobinsonJeffers.pdf).

Katz, Jack. 1997. "Ethnography's Warrants." *Sociological Methods and Research* 25(4):391–423. https://doi.org/10.1177/0049124197025004002.

Kavedžija, Iza. 2019. *Making Meaningful Lives: Tales From an Aging Japan.* Philadelphia, PA: University of Pennsylvania Press.

Khan, Shamus, and Colin Jerolmack. 2013. "Saying Meritocracy and Doing Privilege." *The Sociological Quarterly* 54:9–19. https://doi.org/10.1111/tsq.12008.

Kharicha, Kalpa, Steve Iliffe, Danielle Harari, Cameron Swift, Gerhard Gill-mann, and Andreas E. Stuck. 2007. "Health Risk Appraisal in Older People 1: Are Older People Living Alone an 'At-Risk' Group?" *British Journal of General Practice* 57(537):271–276. Retrieved July 8, 2018 (https://www.ncbi.nlm.nih .gov/pubmed/17394729).

Kimmelman, Michael. 2014. "The Urban Home Away From Home." *The New York Times*. Retrieved March 7, 2023 (https://www.nytimes.com/2014/01/29 /arts/design/lessons-from-mcdonalds-clash-with-older-koreans.html).

King, Colby. 2023. "Public Libraries as Social Infrastructure." *Everyday Sociology Blog*, April 3. Retrieved January 1, 2024 (https://www.everydaysociologyblog .com/2023/04/public-libraries-as-social-infrastructure.html).

King, Neal. 2006. "The Lengthening List of Oppressions: Age Relations and the Feminist Study of Inequality." Pp. 47–74 in *Age Matters: Realigning Femi-nist Thinking*, edited by Toni M. Calasanti and Kathleen F. Slevin. New York: Routledge.

Klein, Sarah, Martha Hostetter, and Douglas McCarthy. 2017. "An Overview of Home-Based Primary Care: Learning from the Field." *Issue Brief (Commonwealth Fund)* 15:1–20. Retrieved February 27, 2023 (https://www .commonwealthfund.org/publications/issue-briefs/2017/jun/overview-home-based-primary-care-learning-field).

Klinenberg, Eric. 2002. *Heat Wave: A Social Autopsy of Disaster in Chicago*. Chi-cago: University of Chicago of Press.

Klinenberg, Eric. 2012. *Going Solo: The Extraordinary Rise and Surprising Appeal of Living Alone*. New York: Penguin Press.

Klinenberg, Eric. 2018. *Palaces for the People: How Social Infrastructure Can Help Fight Inequality, Polarization, and the Decline of Civic Life*. New York: Crown.

Knodel, Jamie. 2020. "Texas Lt. Gov. Dan Patrick Suggests He, Other Seniors Willing to Die to Get Economy Going Again." *NBC News*. Retrieved March 2, 2023 (https://www.nbcnews.com/news/us-news/texas-lt-gov-dan-patrick-suggests-he-other-seniors-willing-n1167341).

Köber, Göran, Dietrich Oberwittler, and Rebecca Wickes. 2022. "Old Age and Fear of Crime: Cross-national Evidence for a Decreased Impact of Neigh-bourhood Disadvantage in Older Age." *Ageing & Society* 42(7):1629–1658. doi:10.1017/S0144686X20001683.

Kopecki, Dawn, Noah Higgins-Dunn, and Hannah Miller. 2020. "CDC Tells People over 60 or Who Have Chronic Illnesses like Diabetes to Stock up on Goods and Buckle Down for a Lengthy Stay at Home." CNBC. Retrieved March 2, 2023 (https://www.cnbc.com/2020/03/09/many-americans-will -be-exposed-to-coronavirus-through-2021-cdc-says.html).

Kreider, Rose M., and Renee Ellis. 2011. "Number, Timing, and Duration of Marriages and Divorces: 2009." *Current Population Reports*, P70–125, U.S. Census Bureau. Retrieved March 6, 2023 (https://www.census.gov/library /publications/2011/demo/p70–125.html).

Krendl, Anne C., and Brea L. Perry. 2021. "The Impact of Sheltering in Place During the COVID-19 Pandemic on Older Adults' Social and Mental Well-Being." *The Journals of Gerontology: Series B* 76(2):e53–e58. doi:10.1093 /geronb/gbaa11.

Krueger, Kristin R., Robert S. Wilson, Julia M. Kamenetsky, Lisa L. Barnes, Julia L. Bienias, and David A. Bennett. 2009. "Social Engagement and Cognitive Function in Old Age." *Experimental Aging Research* (35):45–60. doi:10.1080/03610730802545028.

Kugelmass, Jack. [1986] 1996. *Miracle of Intervale Avenue: The Story of a Jewish Congregation in the South Bronx*. New York: Columbia University Press.

Kuhne, Michael. 2014. "One of the Coldest Winters in 20 Years Shatters Snow Records." AccuWeather.com. Retrieved August 18, 2015 (http:// www.accuweather.com/en/weather-news/record-breaking-cold-winter-we /24831365).

Lange, Alexandra. 2022. *Meet Me by the Fountain: An Inside History of the Mall*. New York: Bloomsbury Publishing.

La Ferla, Ruth. 2010. "Bicycle Chic Gains Speed." *The New York Times*, September 30, E1. Retrieved March 6, 2023 (https://www.nytimes.com/2010/09/30 /fashion/30BICYCLE.html).

LaPiere, Richard T. 1934. "Attitudes vs. Actions." *Social Forces* 13(1):230–237. https://doi.org/10.2307/2570339.

Laz, Cheryl. 1998. "Act Your Age." *Sociological Forum* 13:85–113. doi: https://doi .org/10.1023/A:1022160015408.

Laz, Cheryl. 2003. "Age Embodied." *Journal of Aging Studies* 17(4):503–519. doi: https://doi.org/10.1016/S0890–4065(03)00066–5.

Lee, Jaeah. 2023. "The Agony of Putting Your Life on Hold to Care for Your Parents." *The New York Times Magazine*, April 2, 40. Retrieved January 3, 2024 (https://www.nytimes.com/2023/03/28/magazine/elder-child-care-millennials.html).

Levitt, Steven D. 2004. "Understanding Why Crime Fell in the 1990s: Four Factors that Explain the Decline and Six that Do Not." *Journal of Economic Perspectives* 18(1):163–190. doi:10.1257/089533004773563485.

Li, Zhe, and Joseph Dalaker. 2022. *Poverty Among the Population Aged 65 and Older*. Congressional Research Service. R45791. Retrieved January 1, 2024 (https://crsreports.congress.gov/product/pdf/R/R45791).

Liang, Jiayin, and Baozhen Luo. 2012. "Toward a Discourse Shift in Social Gerontology: From Successful Aging to Harmonious Aging." *Journal of Aging Studies* 26(3):327–334. doi:10.1016/j.jaging.2012.03.001.

Liebow, Elliot. 1967. *Tally's Corner: A Study of Negro Streetcorner Men*. Boston: Little, Brown.

Literary America. 2020. "Robinson Jeffers." Retrieved March 11, 2024 (https://literaryamerica.net/robinson-jeffers/).

Livingston, Gretchen. 2014. "Four-in-Ten Couples are Saying 'I Do,' Again." Washington, DC: Pew Research Center, November. Retrieved August 5, 2015 (http://www.pewsocialtrends.org/files/2014/11/2014-11-14_remarriage-final.pdf).

Loe, Meika. 2011. *Aging Our Way: Lessons for Living from 85 and Beyond*. New York: Oxford University Press.

Lofland, Lyn H. 1973. *A World of Strangers: Order and Action in Urban Public Space*. New York: Basic Books.

Lofland, Lyn H. 1998. *The Public Realm: Exploring the City's Quintessential Social Territory*. New York: Aldine de Gruyter.

Longitudinal Aging Study Amsterdam. 2017. Vrije Universiteit Amsterdam. Retrieved July 14, 2017 (http://www.lasa-vu.nl/index.htm).

López Sánchez, Oliva, and Douglas C. Nance. 2020. "'Something Born of the Heart': Culturally Affiliated Illnesses of Older Adults in Oaxaca." *Issues in Mental Health Nursing* 41(3):235–242. doi:10.1080/01612840.2019.1650854

"Maggie Kuhn." 2023. National Women's Hall of Fame. Retrieved March 2, 2023 (https://www.womenofthehall.org/inductee/maggie-kuhn/).

Mair, Christine A. 2019. "Alternatives to Aging Alone?: 'Kinlessness' and the Importance of Friends Across European Contexts." *Journals of Gerontology: Social Sciences* 74(8):1416–1428. doi:10.1093/geronb/gbz029.

MaloneBeach, Elieen E., and Karen L. Langeland. 2011. "Boomers' Prospective Needs for Senior Centers and Related Services: A Survey of Persons 50–59." *Journal of Gerontological Social Work* 54(1):116–130. doi:10.1080/01634372.2010.524283.

Marcuse, Peter. 1986. "Abandonment, Gentrification and Displacement: The Linkages in New York City." Pp. 153–177 in *Gentrification of the City*, edited by Neil Smith and Peter Williams. London: Unwin Hyman.

Markwood, Sandy. 2013. "Is the Senior Center Here to Stay?" *Generations* 37:75–76. https://www.jstor.org/stable/e26555999.

Marsden, Peter V. 1987. "Core Discussion Networks of Americans." *American Sociological Review* 52(1):122–131. doi:10.2307/2095397.

Marsden, Peter V. 1993. "The Reliability of Network Density and Composition Measures." *Social Networks* 15:399–421. https://doi.org/10.1016/0378–8733(93)90014-C.

Marshall, Colin. 2015. "The Gentrification of Skid Row—A Story That Will Decide the Future of Los Angeles." *The Guardian*. Retrieved March 8, 2023 (https://www.theguardian.com/cities/2015/mar/05/gentrification-skid-row-los-angeles-homeless).

Mate, Kedar S., Amy Berman, Mara Laderman, Andrea Kabcenell, and Terry Fulmer. 2018. "Creating Age-Friendly Health Systems—A Vision for Better Care of Older Adults." *Healthcare* 6:4–6. https://doi.org/10.1016/j.hjdsi.2017.05.005.

McAuley, William J. 1998. "History, Race, and Attachment to Place Among Elders in the Rural All-Black Towns of Oklahoma." *The Journals of Gerontology, Series B: Psychological Sciences and Social Sciences* 53:S35–S45. doi:10.1093/geronb/53B.1.S35.

McClear, Sheila. 2010. "Why the Classic Noo Yawk Accent Is Fading Away." *New York Post*. Retrieved February 27, 2023 (https://nypost.com/2010/02/06/why-the-classic-noo-yawk-accent-is-fading-away/).

McGovern, Erin Kee. 2021. "7 Facts About Older Adults and SNAP." The National Council on Aging. Retrieved December 31, 2023 (https://www.ncoa.org/article/7-facts-about-older-adults-and-snap).

McQuillan, Alice. 2010. "Mayor Mike Admits City Response Fell Short." NBC New York. Retrieved March 6, 2023 (https://www.nbcnewyork.com/news/local/the-great-blizzard-dig-out-of-2010/1877355/).

McPherson, Miller, Lynn Smith-Lovin, and James M. Cook. 2001. "Birds of a Feather: Homophily in Social Networks." *Annual Review of Sociology* 27: 415–444. https://doi.org/10.1146/annurev.soc.27.1.415.

McPherson, Miller, Lynn Smith-Lovin, and Matthew E. Brashears. 2006. "Social Isolation in America: Changes in Core Discussion Networks over Two Decades." *American Sociological Review* 71(3):353–375. https://doi.org/10.1177/000312240607100301.

Medicare Interactive. 2023a. "Home Health Basics." Retrieved February 27, 2023 (https://www.medicareinteractive.org/get-answers/medicare-covered-services/home health-services/home-health-basics).

Medicare Interactive. 2023b. "Hospice Costs and Coverage." Retrieved February 27, 2023 (https://www.medicareinteractive.org/get-answers/medicare-covered-services/hospice/hospice-costs-and-coverage).

Medicare Interactive. 2023c. "Services Excluded from Home Health Coverage." Retrieved February 27, 2023 (https://www.medicareinteractive.org/get-answers/medicare-covered-services/home-health-services/services-excluded-from-home-health-coverage).

Merriam-Webster. 2017. "Collegiality." Retrieved October 7, 2017 (https://www.merriam-webster.com/dictionary/collegiality).

Meschede, Tatjana, Lauren Bercaw, Laura Sullivan, and Martha Cronin. 2015. "Living Longer on Less: Post-Recession Senior In-Security Remains High." Institute on Assets and Social Policy, Heller School for Social Policy and Management, Brandeis University, Waltham, MA. Retrieved May 19, 2015 (http://iasp.brandeis.edu/pdfs/2015/LLOL7.pdf).

Milgram, Stanley. 1992. "The Familiar Stranger: An Aspect of Urban Anonymity." Pp. 68–71 in *The Individual in a Social World: Essays and Experiments*, McGraw-Hill Series in Social Psychology, edited by John Sabini and Maury Silver. New York: McGraw-Hill.

Milligan, Melinda J. 1998. "Interactional Past and Potential: The Social Construction of Place Attachment." *Symbolic Interaction* 21(1):1–33.

Monroe, Harriet. 1926. "Review: Power and Pomp." *Poetry* 28(3): 160–164. Retrieved May 15, 2024 (https://www.jstor.org/stable/20575562).

More at Mather's: April| May| June 2019. n.d. Retrieved April 16, 2019 (https://s17480.pcdn.co/wp-content/uploads/2019/03/MNPHiggins_AprilMayJune19_5FNL.pdf).

Morgan-Consoli, Melissa L., and Emily Unzueta. 2018. "Female Mexican Immigrants in the United States: Cultural Knowledge and Healing." *Women & Therapy* 41(1–2):165–179. doi:10.1080/02703149.2017.1323473.

Morrill, Calvin, and David A. Snow. 2005. "The Study of Personal Relationships in Public Places." Pp. 1–22 in *Together Alone: Personal Relationships in Public Places*, edited by Calvin Morrill, David A. Snow, and Cindy White. Berkeley, CA: University of California Press.

Moses, Dean. 2022. "Asian Seniors Terrified to Leave Homes amidst Hate Crime Spate, Study Finds." AM New York. Retrieved March 8, 2023 (https://www.amny.com/news/asian-seniors-terrified-to-leave-homes-amidst-hate-crime-spate-study-finds/).

Moss, Jeremiah. 2017. "Dressing up High-rent Blight." *Jeremiah's Vanishing New York*. April 10, 2017. Retrieved March 7, 2023 (https://vanishingnewyork.blogspot.com/2017/04/dressing-up-high-rent-blight.html).

Murphy, Scott Patrick. 2017. "Humor Orgies as Ritual Insult: Putdowns and Solidarity Maintenance in a Corner Donut Shop." *Journal of Contemporary Ethnography* 46:108–132. doi:10.1177/0891241615605218.

Myerhoff, Barbara. 1978. *Number Our Days*. New York: Simon & Schuster.

National Association of Housing Cooperatives. 2012. "Housing Cooperatives Comparisons and Definitions." Retrieved August 13, 2012 (http://www.coophousing.org/DisplayPage.aspx?Id=122).

The National Council on Aging. 2022a. "Latest Census Bureau Data Shows Americans 65+ Only Group to Experience Increase in Poverty." Retrieved December 31, 2023 (https://www.ncoa.org/article/latest-census-bureau-data-shows-americans-65-only-group-to-experience-increase-in-poverty).

The National Council on Aging. 2022b. "NCOA's Newly Redesigned Benefits-CheckUp Makes it Easier for Older Adults to Worry Less, Age Better." Retrieved December 31, 2023 (https://www.ncoa.org/article/ncoas-newly-redesigned-benefitscheckup-makes-it-easier-for-older-adults-to-worry-less-age-better).

National Immigration Forum. 2022. "Fact Sheet: Undocumented Immigrants and Federal Health Care Benefits." Retrieved February 24, 2023 (https://

immigrationforum.org/wp-content/uploads/2022/09/Fact-Sheet-Undocuemnted-Immigrants-and-Health-Care.pdf).

National Institute on Aging. n.d. "Aging in Place: Growing Older at Home." Retrieved February 23, 2023 (https://www.nia.nih.gov/health/aging-place-growing-older-home).

National Social Life, Health, and Aging Project. 2011. "National Social Life, Health, and Aging Project." NORC at the University of Chicago. Retrieved July 14, 2017 (http://www.norc.org/Research/Projects/Pages/national-social-life-health-and-aging-project.aspx).

Nawaz, Amna, Mike Fritz, and Lena I. Jackson. 2021. "America's Prison Population Is Aging, but Care Options for Older Parolees Remain Limited." PBS. Retrieved March 2, 2023 (https://www.pbs.org/newshour/show/americas-prison-population-is-aging-but-care-options-for-older-parolees-remain-limited).

Nelson, Todd D. 2005. "Ageism: Prejudice Against Our Feared Future Self." *The Journal of Social Issues* 61:207–221. doi:10.1111/j.1540-4560.2005.00402.x.

Nelson, Todd D. 2016. "The Age of Ageism." *The Journal of Social Issues* 72:191–198. doi:10.1111/josi.1216.

Neugarten, Bernice L., and Dail A. Neugarten. 2002. "Age in the Aging Society." Pp. 281–99 in *Disciplinary Approaches to Aging*, vol. 3, *Sociology of Aging*, edited by Donna Lind Infeld. New York: Routledge.

Newberry, Laura. 2022. "The Fear of Public Places in the Age of Covid: Is It Agoraphobia or Something Else?" *Los Angeles Times*. Retrieved March 7, 2023 (https://www.latimes.com/california/newsletter/2022-09-20/group-therapy-agoraphobia-group-therapy).

Newman, Katherine. 2003. *A Different Shade of Gray: Midlife and Beyond in the Inner City*. New York: New Press.

"New York City." 2023. Wikipedia. Retrieved February 23, 2023 (https://en.wikipedia.org/wiki/New_York_City).

New York City Council. 2024. "New York City Council Passes Legislation to Improve Health and Extend Life Expectancy for All New Yorkers." Retrieved February 29, 2024 (https://council.nyc.gov/press/2024/02/08/2558/).

New York City Department for the Aging. n.d. "Naturally Occurring Retirement Communities." Retrieved February 23, 2023 (https://www.nyc.gov/site/dfta/services/naturally-occurring-retirement-communities.page).

"New York Gangs, and Clubs from New York." n.d. *Stone Grease.* Retrieved March 1, 2023 (https://www.stonegreasers.com/greaser/new_york_gangs .html).

New York State Office for the Aging. n.d. "Naturally Occurring Retirement Community (NORC)." Retrieved February 23, 2023 (https://aging.ny.gov /naturally-occurring-retirement-community-norc).

Nicholson, Roscoe F., Andew E. Scharlach, and Carrie L. Graham. 2017. "Removing Financial Barriers to Membership within the Village Movement." *Innovation in Aging* 1(Suppl 1): 1086. https://doi.org/10.1093/geroni /igx004.3984.

Niesz, Helga. 2007. *Naturally Occurring Retirement Communities.* Office of Legislative Research: Research Report. Hartford, CT: Connecticut General Assembly. Retrieved December 21, 2009 (http://www.cga.ct.gov/2007/rpt /2007-R-0148.htm).

Nir, Sarah Maslin, and Jiha Ham. 2014. "Fighting a McDonald's in Queens for the Right to Sit. and Sit. and Sit." *The New York Times.* Retrieved March 7, 2023 (https://www.nytimes.com/2014/01/15/nyregion/fighting-a-mcdonalds-for-the-right-to-sit-and-sit-and-sit.html).

Noah, Timothy. 2019. "America, the Gerontocracy." *POLITICO Magazine.* Retrieved February 24, 2023 (https://www.politico.com/magazine/story/2019 /09/03/america-gerontocracy-problem-politics-old-politicians-trump-biden-sanders-227986/).

Northridge, Mary E., Susan S. Kum, Bibhas Chakraborty, Ariel Port Greenblatt, Stephen E. Marshall, Hua Wang, Carol Kunzel, and Sara S. Metcalf. 2016. "Third Places for Health Promotion with Older Adults: Using the Consolidated Framework for Implementation Research to Enhance Program Implementation and Evaluation." *Journal of Urban Health: Bulletin of the New York Academy of Medicine* 93:851–870. doi:10.1007/s11524-016-0070-9.

Nunez, Sigrid. 2018. *The Friend: A Novel.* New York: Riverhead Books.

O'Dell, Cary. n.d. "Fiorello Laguardia Reading the Comics (July 8, 1945)." Library of Congress. Retrieved March 3, 2023 (https://www.loc.gov/static /programs/national-recording-preservation-board/documents/LaGuardia Comics.pdf).

OECD/European Observatory on Health Systems and Policies. 2021. *Spain: Country Health Profile 2021, State of Health in the EU.* Brussels: European

Observatory on Health Systems and Policies; Paris: OECD Publishing. Retrieved January 1, 2024 (https://health.ec.europa.eu/system/files/2021 –12/2021_chp_es_english.pdf).

Offer, Shira, and Claude S. Fischer. 2018. "Difficult People: Who Is Perceived to Be Demanding in Personal Networks and Why Are They There?" *American Sociological Review* 83(1):111–142. https://doi.org/10.1177/0003122417737951.

Offer, Shira, and Claude S. Fischer. 2022. "How New Is 'New'? Who Gets Added in a Panel Study of Personal Networks?" *Social Networks* 70:284–294. https://doi.org/10.1016/j.socnet.2022.02.011. PMCID: PMC9116615.

Office of the U.S. Surgeon General. 2023. *Our Epidemic of Loneliness and Isolation: The U.S. Surgeon General's Advisory on the Healing Effects of Social Connection and Community.* Retrieved January 1, 2024 (https://www.hhs.gov/sites /default/files/surgeon-general-social-connection-advisory.pdf).

Oldenburg, Ray. [1989] 1999. *The Great Good Place: Cafes, Coffee Shops, Bookstores, Bars, Hair Salons and Other Hangouts at the Heart of a Community.* New York: Marlowe & Company.

Oldenburg, Ramon, and Dennis Brissett. 1982. "The Third Place." *Qualitative Sociology* 5(4):265–284. doi:10.1007/BF00986754.

Ornstein, Katherine A., Bruce Leff, Kenneth E. Covinsky, Christine S. Ritchie, Alex D. Federman, Laken Roberts, Amy S. Kelley, Albert L. Siu, and Sarah L. Szanton. 2015. "Epidemiology of the Homebound Population in the United States." *JAMA Internal Medicine* 175(7): 1180–1186. doi:10.1001/jamainternmed .2015.1849.

O'Toole, Garson. 2018. "I Don't Want to Belong to Any Club That Will Accept Me as a Member." Quote Investigator. Retrieved March 11, 2023 (https:// quoteinvestigator.com/2011/04/18/groucho-resigns/).

Ouchida, Karen M., and Mark S. Lachs. 2015. "Not For Doctors Only: Ageism in Healthcare." *Generations* 39(3):46–57.

Paik, Anthony, and Kenneth Sanchagrin. 2013. "Social Isolation in America: An Artifact." *American Sociological Review* 78(3):339–360. https://doi.org/10.1177 /0003122413482919.

Pampel, Fred C. 1998. *Aging, Inequality, and Social Policy.* Thousand Oaks, CA: Sage.

Pan, Sarah, Julie Stutzbach, Suzanne Reichwein, Brian K. Lee, and Nabila Dahodwala. 2014. "Knowledge and Attitudes about Parkinson's Disease among a Diverse Group of Older Adults." *Journal of Cross-Cultural Gerontology* 29:339–352. doi:10.1007/s10823–014–9233-x.

Pardasani, Manoj, and Cathy Berkman. 2021. "New York City Senior Centers: Who Participates and Why?" *Journal of Applied Gerontology* 40(9):985–996. https://doi.org/10.1177/0733464820917304.

PBS NewsHour. 2021. "LGBTQ Seniors Fear Discrimination When Searching for Housing." PBS, October 10. Retrieved March 2, 2023 (https://www.pbs .org/video/lgbtq-seniors-fear-discrimination-when-searching-for-housing-1633893768/).

Percival, John. 2000. "Gossip in Sheltered Housing: Its Cultural Importance and Social Implications." *Ageing and Society* 20(3):303–325. doi:10.1017/ S0144686X0000773X.

Perry, Brea L., Will R. McConnell, Max E. Coleman, Adam R. Roth, Siyun Peng, and Liana G. Apostolova. 2022a. "Why the Cognitive 'Fountain of Youth' May Be Upstream: Pathways to Dementia Risk and Resilience Through Social Connectedness." *Alzheimer's & Dementia* 18:934–941. https://doi .org/10.1002/alz.12443.

Perry Brea L., William R. McConnell, Siyun Peng, Adam R. Roth, Max Coleman, Mohit Manchella, Meghann Roessler, Heather Francis, Hope Sheean, and Liana A. Apostolova. 2022b. "Social Networks and Cognitive Function: An Evaluation of Social Bridging and Bonding Mechanisms." *The Gerontologist* 62(6): 865–875. doi:10.1093/geront/gnab112. PMID: 34338287; PMCID: PMC9290895.

Picon, Andres. 2021. "Senior, Disabled Protesters Occupy S.F. AT&T Store Demanding Wi-Fi Access." *San Francisco Chronicle*. Retrieved March 2, 2023 (https://www.sfchronicle.com/bayarea/article/Senior-disabled-protesters-occupy-S-F-AT-T-16543718.php).

"Placemaking." 2023. Wikipedia. Retrieved March 7, 2023 (https://en.wikipedia .org/wiki/Placemaking#See_also).

Plasencia, Melanie Z. 2023. "'I Don't Have Much Money, but I Have a Lot of Friends': How Poor Older Latinxs Find Social Support in Peer Friendship Networks." *Social Problems* 70(3):755–772. https://doi.org/10.1093/socpro /spab081.

Plickert, Gabriele, Rochelle R. Côté, and Barry Wellman. 2007. "It's Not Who You Know, It's How You Know Them: Who Exchanges What With Whom?" *Social Networks* 29: 405–429. https://doi.org/10.1016/j.socnet.2007.01.007

Portacolone, Elena. 2013. "The Notion of Precariousness among Older Adults Living Alone in the U.S." *Journal of Aging Studies* 27(2):166–174. https://doi.org/10.1016/j.jaging.2013.01.001.

Portnoy, Gary, and Judy Hart Angelo. 1982. "Where Everybody Knows Your Name (The Theme from Cheers)." Recorded by Gary Portnoy. *Keeper* [CD]. Portland, Oregon: CD Baby. (January 2, 2007).

Pugh, Tony. 2023. "Home Health Agencies Gird for Battle over Medicare Payment Cuts." Bloomberg Law. Retrieved December 30, 2023 (https://news.bloomberglaw.com/health-law-and-business/home-health-agencies-gird-for-battle-over-medicare-payment-cuts).

Putnam, Robert D. 2000. *Bowling Alone: The Collapse and Revival of American Community.* New York: Simon & Schuster.

"A Quote by Victor Hugo." n.d. Goodreads. Retrieved March 6, 2023 (https://www.goodreads.com/quotes/292083-forty-is-the-old-age-of-youth-fifty-is-the).

Rainie, Lee, and Barry Wellman. 2012. *Networked: The New Social Operating System.* Cambridge, MA: The MIT Press.

"Red, White, and Gray: How America's Gerontocracy is Threatening Weakening Democracy." 2022. *Business Insider.* Retrieved February 24, 2023 (https://www.businessinsider.com/gerontocracy-united-states-government-red-white-gray-2022–9).

Reinharz, Shulamit. 2002. "Friends or Foes: Gerontological and Feminist Theory." Pp. 179–200 in *Disciplinary Approaches to Aging*, vol. 3, *Sociology of Aging*, edited by Donna Lind Infeld. New York: Routledge.

"Rhapsody in Blue." 2023. Wikipedia. Retrieved March 7, 2023 (https://en.wikipedia.org/wiki/Rhapsody_in_Blue).

"Rheumatoid Arthritis." 2023. Mayo Clinic. Retrieved February 27, 2023 (https://www.mayoclinic.org/diseases-conditions/rheumatoid-arthritis/symptoms-causes/syc-20353648).

Richman, Joseph. 1995. "The Lifesaving Function of Humor with the Depressed and Suicidal Elderly." *The Gerontologist* 35:271–273. doi:10.1093/geront/35.2.271.

Rieder, Jonathan. 1985. *Canarsie: The Jews and Italians of Brooklyn against Liberalism.* Cambridge, MA: Harvard University Press.

"Robinson Jeffers." n.d. Poetry Foundation. Retrieved March 7, 2023 (https://www.poetryfoundation.org/poets/robinson-jeffers).

"Robinson & Una Jeffers—'Our Inevitable Place.'" 2019. Carmel Public Library. Retrieved March 7, 2023 (https://ci.carmel.ca.us/library-event/robinson-una-jeffers-our-inevitable-place).

Rodgers, Kara. 2020. "1968 Flu Pandemic." *Encyclopædia Britannica*. Retrieved February 27, 2023 (https://www.britannica.com/event/1968-flu-pandemic).

Roig, Marta, and Daisuke Maruichi. 2022. "Old-Age Poverty Has a Woman's Face." Global Dialogue for Social Development Branch, Division for Inclusive Social Development, UN-DESA. Retrieved December 31, 2023 (https://www.un.org/development/desa/dspd/2022/11/old-age-poverty/).

Rosenbaum, Mark S., Jillian C. Sweeney, and Carla Windhorst. 2009. "The Restorative Qualities of an Activity Based, Third Place Café for Seniors: Restoration, Social Support, and Place Attachment at Mather's–More Than a Café." *Seniors Housing & Care Journal* 17(1):39–54. https://www.mather.com/wp-content/uploads/2012/05/SHCJ09_RestorativeQualities.pdf.

Rosenbaum, Mark S., James Ward, Beth A. Walker, and Amy Ostrom. 2007. "A Cup of Coffee With a Dash of Love: An Investigation of Commercial Social Support and Third-Place Attachment." *Journal of Service Research* 10:43–59. doi:10.1177/1094670507303011.

Rúa, Mérida M. 2017. "Aging in Displacement: Urban Revitalization and Puerto Rican Elderhood in Chicago." *Anthropology & Aging* 38(1):44–59.

Ruchowitz-Roberts, Elliot. n.d. "Tor House and Hawk Tower." *National Endowment for the Arts Reader Resources*. Retrieved March 7, 2023 (https://www.arts.gov/sites/default/files/Readers-Resources-RobinsonJeffers.pdf).

Sample, Ian. 2022. "If They Could Turn Back Time: How Tech Billionaires Are Trying to Reverse the Ageing Process." *The Guardian*. Retrieved February 24, 2024 (https://www.theguardian.com/science/2022/feb/17/if-they-could-turn-back-time-how-tech-billionaires-are-trying-to-reverse-the-ageing-process).

Sampson, Robert J. 2012. *Great American City: Chicago and the Enduring Neighborhood Effect*. Chicago: University of Chicago Press.

Samuel, Sigal. 2020. "Older and Immunocompromised People Don't Deserve to Be Second-Class Citizens." *Vox*. Retrieved March 2, 2023 (https://www.vox.com/future-perfect/2020/5/28/21259238/coronavirus-elderly-immunocompromised-stay-at-home).

Sánchez-Jankowski, Martín. 2008. *Cracks in the Pavement: Social Change and Resilience in Poor Neighborhoods*. Oakland, CA: University of California Press.

Saturday Night Live. 2021. "Boomers Got the VAX—SNL." YouTube, March 27. Video. Retrieved March 2, 2023 (https://www.youtube.com/watch?v= 2hekDuCBxCc).

Scharlach, Andrew. E., and Amanda J. Lehning. 2016. *Creating Aging-Friendly Communities*. New York: Oxford University Press.

Scheffer, Alice C., Marieke J. Schuurmans, Nynke van Dijk, Truus van der Hooft, and Sophia E. de Rooij. 2008. "Fear of Falling: Measurement Strategy, Prevalence, Risk Factors and Consequences Among Older Persons." *Age and Ageing* 37(1): 19–24. doi:10.1093/ageing/afm169

Schnittker, Jason. 2007. "Look (Closely) at All the Lonely People: Age and the Social Psychology of Social Support." *Journal of Aging and Health* 19(4):659–682. https://doi.org/10.1177/0898264307301178.

"SCRIE/DRIE." n.d. NYC Housing Preservation & Development. Retrieved March 7, 2023 (https://www.nyc.gov/site/hpd/services-and-information /scrie.page).

Seitz, Amanda. 2023. "Loneliness Poses Health Risks as Deadly as Smoking, U.S. Surgeon General Says." PBS. Retrieved December 30, 2023 (https:// www.pbs.org/newshour/health/loneliness-poses-health-risks-as-deadly-as-smoking-u-s-surgeon-general-says).

Sethumadhavan, Arathi, and Megan Saunders. 2021. "Ageing: Looming Crisis or Booming Opportunity?" World Economic Forum. Retrieved February 24,2023(https://www.weforum.org/agenda/2021/03/ageing-looming-crisis-or-booming-opportunity/).

Sevak, Purvi, and Lucie Schmidt. 2014. "Immigrants and Retirement Resources." *Social Security Bulletin* 74(1):27–45. Retrieved February 24, 2023 (https://www.ssa.gov/policy/docs/ssb/v74n1/v74n1p27.pdf).

"Silent Generation." 2023. Wikipedia. Retrieved February 23, 2023 (https:// en.wikipedia.org/wiki/Silent_Generation).

Simmel, Georg. [1908] 1971. "The Stranger." Pp. 143–149 in *On Individuality and Social Forms*, edited by Donald N. Levine. Chicago: University of Chicago Press.

Simmel, Georg. [1910] 1971. "Sociability." Pp. 127–140 in *On Individuality and Social Forms*, edited by Donald N. Levine. Chicago: University of Chicago Press.

Sisak, Michael R., and Michelle L. Price. 2022. "Is NYC Safe? Violence, Perception and a Complicated Reality." NBC New York. Retrieved March 2, 2023 (https://www.nbcnewyork.com/news/local/crime-and-courts/is-nyc-safe-violence-perception-and-a-complicated-reality/3528912/).

"Sjogren's Syndrome." 2022. Mayo Clinic. Retrieved February 23, 2023 (https://www.mayoclinic.org/diseases-conditions/sjogrens-syndrome/symptoms-causes/syc-20353216).

Small, Mario Luis. 2009. *Unanticipated Gains: Origins of Network Inequality in Everyday Life.* New York: Oxford University Press.

Small, Mario Luis. 2013. "Weak Ties and the Core Discussion Network: Why People Regularly Discuss Important Matters with Unimportant Alters." *Social Networks* 235:470–483. doi:10.1016/j.socnet.2013.05.004.

Small, Mario Luis. 2017. *Someone to Talk To.* New York: Oxford University Press.

Smith, Genee S., Hannah Breakstone, Lorraine T. Dean, and Roland J. Thorpe Jr. 2020. "Impacts of Gentrification on Health in the US: A Systematic Review of the Literature." *Journal of Urban Health* 97(6):845–856. doi:10.1007/s11524–020–00448–4.

Smith, Greg B. 2011. "Despite Bloomberg's Stance, Facts Show City Dropped the Ball on Snow Removal." *New York Daily News.* Retrieved March 6, 2023 (https://www.nydailynews.com/new-york/bloomberg-stance-facts-show-city-dropped-ball-snow-removal-article-1.152877).

Smith, Susan E. 2011. "New Cal Law Could Be Game Changer on Elder Poverty." New American Media. Retrieved May 19, 2015 (http://newamericamedia.org/2011/10/new-cal-law-could-be-game-changer-on-elder-poverty.php).

Smith, Richard J., Amanda J. Lehning, and Kyeongmo Kim. 2018. "Aging in Place in Gentrifying Neighborhoods: Implications for Physical and Mental Health." *The Gerontologist* 58(1):26–35. https://doi.org/10.1093/geront/gnx105.

Smyth, Ted. 2018. "New York's Gas House District." *Resurrecting the Ethnic Village: A Digital History Resource from New York University's Glucksman Ireland House.* Retrieved March 1, 2023 (https://ethnic-village.org/the-gas-house-district/).

"Social Model of Disability." n.d. Scope. Retrieved March 7, 2023 (https://www.scope.org.uk/about-us/social-model-of-disability/).

Sood, Samira. 2020. "Covid-19 a 'Boomer Remover'—Why Millennials Are Angry and Done with Older Generation." *ThePrint.* Retrieved February 23, 2023 (https://theprint.in/opinion/pov/covid-19-a-boomer-remover-why-millennials-are-angry-and-done-with-older-generation/381223/).

Stanford Center on Longevity. 2022. *The New Map of Life: 100 Years to Thrive.* Retrieved January 3, 2024 (https://longevity.stanford.edu/the-new-map-of-life-report/).

Stirling, Rebecca Birch. 1956. "Some Psychological Mechanism Operative of Gossip." *Social Forces* 34(3):262–267. doi:10.2307/2574050.

Stop AAPI Hate. 2023. Retrieved March 2, 2023 (https://stopaapihate.org/).

Strickland, Roy. 2010. "Reimagining Towers-in-the-Park." Urban Omnibus/ The Architectural League of NY. Retrieved February 24, 2023 (https://urbanomnibus.net/2010/08/studio-report-reimagining-towers-in-the-park/).

Stuart, Forrest. 2016. "Becoming 'Copwise': Policing, Culture, and the Collateral Consequences of Street-Level Criminalization." *Law & Society Review* 50(2):279–313. https://doi.org/10.1111/lasr.12201.

Stueve, C. Ann, and Kathleen Gerson. 1977. "Personal Relations across the Life-Cycle." Pp. 79–98 in *Networks and Places: Social Relations in the Urban Setting*, by Claude S. Fischer, Robert Max Jackson, C. Ann Stueve, Kathleen Gerson, Lynne McCallister Jones, with Mark Baldassare. New York: Free Press.

"Stuy Town Slum Clearance, 1946." 2019. *NYC URBANISM.* Retrieved March 1, 2023 (https://www.nycurbanism.com/blog/2019/8/7/stuy-town-slum-clearance-1946).

"Stuyvesant Town–Peter Cooper Village." 2023. Wikipedia. Retrieved March 1, 2023 (https://en.wikipedia.org/wiki/Stuyvesant_Town%E2%80%93Peter_Cooper_Village).

Suanet, Bianca, Theo G. van Tilburg, and Marjolein I. Broese van Groenou. 2013. "Nonkin in Older Adults' Personal networks: More Important among Later Cohorts?" *Journals of Gerontology, Series B: Psychological Sciences and Social Sciences* 68(4):633–643. doi:10.1093/geronb/gbt043.

Suls, Jerry M. 1977. "Gossip as Social Comparison." *Journal of Communication* 27(1):164–178. doi:10.1111/j.1460–2466.1977.tb01812.x.

Sun, Ken Chih-Yan. 2021. *Time and Migration: How Long-term Taiwanese Migrants Negotiate Later Life.* Ithaca, NY: Cornell University Press.

Survey of Health, Ageing and Retirement in Europe. 2015. "SHARE—Survey of Health, Ageing, and Retirement in Europe." Survey of Health, Ageing and Retirement in Europe. Retrieved July 14, 2017 (http://www.share-project.org).

Suttles, Gerald D. 1968. *The Social Order of the Slum: Ethnicity and Territory in the Inner City.* Chicago: The University of Chicago Press.

Tannen, Deborah. n.d. "Do You Speak American? American Varieties: Talking New York." PBS. Retrieved February 23, 2023 (https://www.pbs.org/speak/seatosea/americanvarieties/newyorkcity/accent/).

Taylor, Paul, Rich Morin, Kim Parker, D'Vera Cohn, and Wendy Wang. 2009. "Growing Old in America: Expectations vs. Reality." Pew Research Center, June 29. Retrieved August 26, 2012 (http://pewsocialtrends.org/files/2010/10/Getting-Old-in-America.pdf).

Telephone Topics. n.d. Mather. Retrieved April 16, 2019 (https://www.matherlifeways.com/neighborhood-programs/telephone-topics).

Thoits, Peggy A. 2011. "Mechanisms Linking Social Ties and Support to Physical and Mental Health." *Journal of Health and Social Behavior* 52:145–161. doi:10.1177/0022146510395592.

Thompson, Derek. 2019. "The Future of the City Is Childless." *The Atlantic.* Retrieved February 23, 2023 (https://www.theatlantic.com/ideas/archive/2019/07/where-have-all-the-children-gone/594133/).

Tissot, Sylvie. 2011. "Of Dogs and Men: The Making of Spatial Boundaries in a Gentrifying Neighborhood. *City and Community* 10(3):265–284. https://doi.org/10.1111/j.1540–6040.2011.01377.x.

Torres-Gil, Fernando, and Brian Hofland. 2012. "Vulnerable Populations." Pp. 221–231 in *Independent for Life: Homes and Neighborhoods for an Aging America,* edited by Henry Cisneros, Margaret Dyer-Chamberlain, and Jane Hickie. Austin: University of Texas Press.

Torres, Stacy. 2010. "Bloomberg Shuttering Lifesaving Senior Centers." *Huffington Post,* May 14. Retrieved August 5, 2015 (http://www.huffingtonpost.com/stacy-torres/bloomberg-shuttering-life_b_576507.html).

Torres, Stacy. 2014a. "Aging Women, Living Poorer." *Contexts* 13:72–74. https://doi.org/10.1177/1536504214533505.

Torres, Stacy. 2014b. "Old McDonald's." *The New York Times,* January 22, A21. Retrieved March 7, 2023 (https://www.nytimes.com/2014/01/22/opinion/old-mcdonalds.html).

Torres, Stacy. 2016a. "Aging, Ageism, and Gender." *The Wiley-Blackwell Encyclopedia of Gender and Sexuality Studies.* Oxford: Blackwell Publishing.

Torres, Stacy. 2016b. "As Los Angeles Gets Younger, Skid Row Gets Older." *Next City*. Retrieved February 23, 2023 (https://nextcity.org/urbanist-news/los-angeles-skid-row-elderly-affordable-housing).

Torres, Stacy. 2017. "Snowstorm Cleanup Deplorable in Albany." *Times Union*. Retrieved March 6, 2023 (https://www.timesunion.com/opinion/article/Snowstorm-cleanup-deplorable-in-Albany-1009736.php).

Torres, Stacy. 2018. "Aging in Places." Pp. 151–163 in *Critical Gerontology Comes of Age: Advances in Research and Theory for a New Century*, edited by Chris Wellin. New York: Routledge/ Taylor & Francis.

Torres, Stacy. 2019a. "Aging Alone, Gossiping Together: Older Adults' Talk as Social Glue." *The Journals of Gerontology: Series B* 74(8):1474–1482. https://doi.org/10.1093/geronb/gby154

Torres, Stacy. 2019b. "Ok, Boomer? Kids These Days? Why Generational Warfare Gets Us Nowhere." *CalMatters*. Retrieved February 23, 2023 (https://calmatters.org/commentary/2019/12/boomers/).

Torres, Stacy. 2019c. "On Elastic Ties: Distance and Intimacy in Social Relationships." *Sociological Science* 6:235–263. doi:10.15195/v6.a10. https://www.sociologicalscience.com/articles-v6–10–235/.

Torres, Stacy. 2019d. "We Must Prioritize Pedestrian Safety in Oakland and Other Bay Area Cities for the Good of Us All." *San Francisco Chronicle*. Retrieved March 9, 2023 (https://www.sfchronicle.com/opinion/article/We-must-prioritize-pedestrian-safety-in-Oakland-3600031.php).

Torres, Stacy. 2020a. "Closed Community Spaces Due to Coronavirus Will Leave the Homeless Out in the Cold—It's a Disgrace." *CalMatters*. Retrieved February 23, 2023 (https://calmatters.org/commentary/my-turn/2020/03/as-community-spaces-close-due-to-the-coronavirus-the-homeless-have-almost-nowhere-to-go/).

Torres, Stacy. 2020b. "'For a Younger Crowd': Place, Belonging, and Exclusion among Older Adults Facing Neighborhood Change." *Qualitative Sociology* 43:1–20. https://link.springer.com/article/10.1007/s11133–019–09441-z.

Torres, Stacy. 2021a. "For Years, I Cared for Ailing Parents. Respite Shouldn't Have Come Only With Their Deaths." *The Washington Post*, July 9. Retrieved January 3, 2024 (https://www.washingtonpost.com/opinions/2021/07/09/family-caregivers-women-minorities-relief/).

Torres, Stacy. 2021b. "Why is American Health Care So Inaccessible? It Only Got Easy When My Dad Was Dying." *USA Today*. Retrieved February 23, 2023 (https://news.yahoo.com/why-american-health-care-inaccessible-080028742 .html).

Torres, Stacy, and Griffin Lacy. 2021. "Life Course Transitions, Personal Networks, and Social Support for LGBTQ+ Elders: Implications for Physical and Mental Health." Pp. 157–179 in *Sexual and Gender Minority Health* (*Advances in Medical Sociology*, vol. 21), edited by Allen J. Le Blanc and Brea L. Perry. Boston, MA: Emerald Publishing Limited. https://doi.org/10.1108 /S1057–629020210000021012.

Torres, Stacy. 2022. "The World Might Be Done with Covid, But I'm Keeping My Distance." *The Washington Post*, August 21. Retrieved March 19, 2023 (https://www.washingtonpost.com/opinions/2022/08/21/covid-pandemic-ended-still-masking/).

Torres, Stacy, and Xuemei Cao. 2019. "Improving Care for Elders Who Prefer Informal Spaces to Age-Separated, Institutions and Healthcare Settings." *Innovation in Aging* 3(3):1–10. https://doi.org/10.1093/geroni/igz019.

Torres, Stacy, and Brittney Pond. 2023. "Researching through Loss." *Everyday Sociology Blog*, May 1. Retrieved January 2, 2024 (https://www.everydaysociology blog.com/2023/05/researching-through-loss.html).

Townsend, Peter. 1957. *The Family Life of Old People*. London: Routledge.

Trucil, Daniel E., Nancy E. Lundebjerg, and Daniel S. Busso. 2021. "When It Comes to Older Adults, Language Matters and Is Changing: American Geriatrics Society Update on Reframing Aging Style Changes." *Journal of the American Geriatrics Society* 69:265–267. https://doi.org/10.1111/jgs .16848

Tsai, Michael. 2011. "Needles Click, Yarn Unspools and All is Right at McDonald's." *Honolulu Star-Advertiser*, May 23. Retrieved March 19, 2023 (https:// www.staradvertiser.com/2011/05/23/hawaii-news/incidental-lives/needles-click-yarn-unspools-and-all-is-right-at-mcdonalds/).

Tuan, Yi-Fu. 1977. *Space and Place: The Perspective of Experience*. Minneapolis: University of Minnesota Press.

UC Berkeley Social Networks Study. 2020. "Personal Networks Over Time: Survey Instrument–Waves 1, 2 and 3." Retrieved January 3, 2024 (https://

ucnets.berkeley.edu/wp-content/uploads/2020/03/UCNets_MainSurvey_Waves-1-2-3_Questionnaire_25March2020–1.pdf).

Uchino, Bert N., John T. Cacioppo, and Janice K. Kiecolt-Glaser. 1996. "The Relationship between Social Support and Physiological Processes: A Review with Emphasis on Underlying Mechanisms and Implications for Health." *Psychological Bulletin* 119:488–531. doi:10.1037/0033–2909.119.3.488.

United Nations. 2020. "Policy Brief: The Impact of Covid-19 on Older Persons." Retrieved February 23, 2023 (https://www.un.org/other/afics/sites/www.un.org.other.afics/files/unsg-pdf-20200501-sg_policy_brief_on_covid_older_persons.pdf_).

U.S. Census Bureau. 2015. Summary File, 2011–2015, American Community Survey: 5-year Estimates. Generated by the author using American FactFinder (https://factfinder. census.gov/faces/nav/jsf/pages/index.xhtml).

U.S. Census Bureau. 2022. "Census Bureau Releases New Report on Aging in Asia." Press Release Number CB22-TPS.56. June 21, 2022. Retrieved March 6, 2023 (https://www.census.gov/newsroom/press-releases/2022/aging-in-asia.html).

U.S. Department of Health and Human Services; Centers for Disease Control and Prevention; National Center for Health Statistics. 2016. Summary Health Statistics Tables for U.S. Adults: National Health Interview Survey, 2016, Table A-10. Retrieved July 7, 2018 (https://ftp.cdc.gov/pub/Health_Statistics/NCHS/NHIS/SHS/2016_SHS_ Table_A-10.pdf).

U.S. Department of Labor. 2023. "Issue Brief: Living on Less." Retrieved January 1, 2024 (https://www.dol.gov/sites/dolgov/files/WB/oww/WB_issuebrief-living-on-less.pdf).

Utrata, Jennifer. 2011. "Youth Privilege: Doing Age and Gender in Russia's Single-Mother Families." *Gender and Society* 25(5):616–641. doi:10.1177/0891243211421781.

Vallese, Giulia. 2022. "Older People Are the Fastest Growing Age Group in Europe. It's Time We Recognize This as an Opportunity." UNFPA Eastern Europe and Central Asia. Retrieved December 31, 2023 (https://eeca.unfpa.org/en/news/older-people-are-fastest-growing-age-group-europe-its-time-we-recognize-opportunity).

Van Gogh, Vincent. 1888. "Café Terrace at Night." *Wikipedia*. Retrieved March 13, 2023 (https://en.wikipedia.org/wiki/Caf%C3%A9_Terrace_at_Night).

Van Vleck, Morgan. 2022. "Age-Inclusive Language: Are You Using It in Your Writing and Everyday Speech?" Harvey A. Friedman Center for Aging. Washington University in St. Louis Institute for Public Health. Retrieved February 23, 2023 (https://publichealth.wustl.edu/age-inclusive-language-are-you-using-it-in-your-writing-and-everyday-speech/).

"Veil of Ignorance." 2023. *Ethics Unwrapped*. McCombs School of Business—The University of Texas at Austin. Retrieved March 11, 2023 (https://ethicsunwrapped.utexas.edu/glossary/veil-of-ignorance).

Versey, H. Shellae. 2018. "A Tale of Two Harlems: Gentrification, Social Capital, and Implications for Aging in Place." *Social Science & Medicine* 214:1–11. https://doi.org/10.1016/j.socscimed.2018.07.024.

Vespa, Jonathan, and Emily Schondelmyer. 2015. "A Gray Revolution in Living Arrangements." U.S. Census Bureau. Retrieved July 6, 2018 (https://www.census.gov/newsroom/blogs/random-samplings/2015/07/a-gray-revolution-in-living-arrangements.html).

Victor, Christina, Sasha Scambler, and John Bond. 2009. *The Social World of Older People*. New York: Open University Press.

Victor, Ronald G., Kathleen Lynch, Ning Li, Ciantel Blyler, Eric Muhammad, Joel Handler, Jeffrey Brettler, Mohamad Rashid, Brent Hsu, Davontae Foxx-Drew, Norma Moy, Anthony E. Reid, and Robert M. Elashoff. 2018. "A Cluster-Randomized Trial of Blood-Pressure Reduction in Black Barbershops." *The New England Journal of Medicine* 378: 1291–1301. doi:10.1056/NEJMoa1717250

Vierck, Elizabeth, and Kris Hodges. 2003. *Aging: Demographics, Health, and Health Services*. Santa Barbara, CA: Greenwood Press.

Villa, Valentine. 2019. "Caregiving Across Generations and Cultures." *Innovation in Aging* 3, issue supplement 1: S573. https://doi.org/10.1093/geroni/igz038.2124

Wacker, Robbyn R., and Karen A. Roberto. 2013. *Community Resources for Older Adults: Programs and Services in an Era of Change*, 4th ed. Thousand Oaks, CA: SAGE Publications.

Walker, Jan, Carol Bisbee, Russel Porter, and Joanne Flanders. 2004. "Increasing Practitioners' Knowledge of Participation among Elderly Adults in Senior Center Activities." *Educational Gerontology* 30(5):353–366. doi:10.1080/03601270490433549.

Wallace, Steven P., and Susan E. Smith. 2009. "Half a Million Older Californians Living Alone Unable to Make Ends Meet." Los Angeles, CA: UCLA Center for Health Policy Research. Retrieved March 11, 2023 (https://healthpolicy.ucla.edu/publications/Documents/PDF/Half%20a%20Million%20Older%20Californians%20Living%20Alone%20Unable%20to%20Make%20Ends%20Meet.pdf).

Wallhagen, Margaret I. 2010. "The Stigma of Hearing Loss." *The Gerontologist* 50(1):66–75. https://doi.org/10.1093/geront/gnp107.

Walsh, Victor A. 2012. "Robinson Jeffers: The Poet and Stone Mason of Tor House." *Literary Traveler*. Retrieved March 7, 2023 (https://www.literarytraveler.com/articles/robinson-jeffers-the-poet-and-stone-mason-of-tor-house/).

Watson, David C. 2012. "Gender Differences in Gossip and Friendship." *Sex Roles* 67:494–502. doi:10.1007/s11199–012–0160–4.

Weil, Joyce. 2014. *The New Neighborhood Senior Center: Redefining Social and Service Roles for the Baby Boom Generation.* New Brunswick, NJ: Rutgers University Press.

Wellin, Christopher. 2010. "Growing Pains in the Sociology of Aging and the Life Course: A Review Essay on Recent Textbooks." *Teaching Sociology* 38 (4): 373–382. https://doi.org/10.1177/0092055X10380673

Wellman, Barry. 1979. "The Community Question: The Intimate Networks of East Yorkers." *American Journal of Sociology* 84(5):1201–1231. https://doi.org/10.1007/978–3–663–08443–3.

Wellman, Barry, and Milena Gulia. 1999. "The Network Basis of Social Support: A Network is More Than the Sum of Its Ties." Pp. 83–118 in *Networks in the Global Village*, edited by Barry Wellman. Boulder, CO: Westview.

Wellman, Barry, and Barry Leighton. 1979. "Networks, Neighborhoods, and Communities: Approaches to the Study of the Community Question." *Urban Affairs Quarterly* 14(3):363–390. https://doi.org/10.1177/107808747901400305

Wellman, Barry, and Scot Wortley. 1990. "Different Strokes from Different Folks: Community Ties and Social Support." *American Journal of Sociology* 96(3):558–588. https://doi.org/10.1086/229572.

Wenar, Leif. 2021. "John Rawls." *Stanford Encyclopedia of Philosophy*. Retrieved March 11, 2023 (https://plato.stanford.edu/entries/rawls/).

West, Candace, and Don H. Zimmerman. 1987. "Doing Gender." *Gender & Society* 1(2):125–151. https://doi.org/10.1177/0891243287001002200.

Wexler, Mark N., and Judy Oberlander. 2017. "The Shifting Discourse on Third Places: Ideological Implications." *Journal of Ideology* 38(4). https://scholarcommons.sc.edu/ji/vol38/iss1/4.

Whalen, Andrew. 2020. "What Is 'Boomer Remover' and Why Is It Making People so Angry?" *Newsweek*. Retrieved February 23, 2023 (https://www.newsweek.com/boomer-remover-meme-trends-virus-coronavirus-social-media-covid-19-baby-boomers-1492190).

"What Older New Yorkers Deserve: NYC Blueprint for Action 2.0." 2024. AARP New York City. Retrieved February 29, 2024 (https://local.aarp.org/news/what-new-yorkers-50-deserve-lays-out-fresh-blueprint-for-nyc-lawmakers-ny-2024-02-02.html).

White, Rob, Julie-Anne Toohey, and Nicole Asquith. 2015. "Seniors in Shopping Centres." *Journal of Sociology* 51(3):582–595. doi:10.1177/1440783313507494.

Whitman, Walt. [1855] 2023. "I Sing the Body Electric." Poetry Foundation. Retrieved March 6, 2023 (https://www.poetryfoundation.org/poems/45472/i-sing-the-body-electric).

Whyte, William H. [1980] 2001. *The Social Life of Small Urban Spaces*. New York: Project for Public Spaces.

Wireman, Peggy. 1984. *Urban Neighborhoods, Networks, and Families*. Lexington, Massachusetts: Lexington Books.

World Health Organization. 2007. "Checklist of Essential Features of Age-Friendly Cities." Retrieved March 11, 2023 (https://extranet.who.int/agefriendlyworld/wp-content/uploads/2018/04/Age-Friendly-Checklist-WHOedit.pdf).

World Health Organization. 2022. "Ageing and Health." Retrieved February 23, 2023 (https://www.who.int/news-room/fact-sheets/detail/ageing-and-health).

Yakas, Ben. 2023. "Ray's Candy Store Owner Still Loves the East Village despite Brutal Attack." *Gothamist*. Retrieved March 9, 2023 (https://gothamist.com/news/rays-candy-store-owner-still-loves-the-east-village-despite-brutal-attack).

Yeh, Jarmin. 2022. "Age-Friendly for Whom? An Aperture to the Lived Experiences of Older San Franciscans." *The Gerontologist* 62(1):100–109. https://doi.org/10.1093/geront/gnab119.

York Cornwell, Erin, and Linda J. Waite. 2009. "Social Disconnectedness, Perceived Isolation, and Health Among Older Adults." *Journal of Health and Social Behavior* 50:31–48. https://doi.org/10.1177/002214650905000103.

Young, Iris Marion. 1994. "Gender as Seriality: Thinking about Women as a Social Collective." *Signs: Journal of Women in Culture and Society* 19(3):713–738. https://doi.org/10.1086/494918.

Zaslow, Jeffrey. 2003. "Don't Trust Anyone Over 30: Boomers Struggle as Mentors." Retrieved January 27, 2019 (https://www.wsj.com/articles/SB105475169430440200).

Zerubavel, Eviatar. 1991. *The Fine Line: Making Distinctions in Everyday Life*. New York: Free Press.

Zola, Irving Kenneth. 1991. "Bringing Our Bodies and Ourselves Back In: Reflections on a Past, Present, and Future 'Medical Sociology.'" *Journal of Health and Social Behavior* 32(1):1–16. https://doi.org/10.2307/2136796.

Zunzunegui, María-Victoria, Beatriz E. Alvarado, Teodoro Del Ser, and Angel Otero. 2003. "Social Networks, Social Integration, and Social Engagement Determine Cognitive Decline in Community-Dwelling Spanish Older Adults." *The Journals of Gerontology, Series B: Psychological Sciences and Social Sciences* 58:S93–S100. doi:10.1093/geronb/58.2.S93.

Index

Aaron (Pete's Delicatessen customer), 217

activities of daily living (ADL), 4–5, 185. *See also* health issues; mobility

adolescents. *See* younger people

affinity groups, 118

Affordable Care Act (Obamacare), 106–7

age cohorts. *See* age-related identity of elders; younger people

ageism: age and career advancement, 174; aging seen as problem by society, 13–21, 93–94; awareness of, by elders, 93–94, 111–13, 132–33; "Boomer Remover," 14, 120; "Boomers Got the Vax" *(Saturday Night Live)*, 119–20; in health care system, 186–89, 205–7; internalized by elders, 105–7; loitering complaints by businesses, 251–52; "Ok, Boomer," 14; stigma of old age, 133, 145; stigma of old age and downplaying ties, 166–69; terminology for older adults, 12–13

age-related identity of elders, 89–121, 208–37; ageism internalized by elders, 105–7; Bakery Club's regrouping despite challenges, 208–15; and group identity, 92, 107–9, 225–31; loss of familiar places, 98–101, 103–5; loss of people, 101–3; and mutual support, 215–19; physical design and effect on, 219–24; safety concerns, 109–11; as series, 91,

Village Movement, 264–65; West End residential relocation in, 141

boundaries. *See* gossip

Brandeis University, 256, 257

bridgers, 192

Brissett, Dennis, 29

caregivers and family members: adult children, caretaking by/for, 34–35, 45, 49, 125, 164–65, 197; among Latinos, 17; and care crisis, 17, 18; elastic ties of acquaintances vs. reliance of, 159–60, 162, 165; obligation and responsibility complications, 21; social connections needed by, 32–33. *See also* nursing homes and institutional settings

Carl (Bakery Club member), 68

Carmen (Bakery Club member): and bakery's closing, 2; commercial gentrification and effect on, 134; elastic ties of, 154, 158–64, 166; generally, 94, 110, 210–15, 222, 231–32; and gossip, 68, 80; social integration and reciprocity, 55

Carr, Deborah, 256

Carstensen, Laura, 57

Census Bureau, 256

Center for an Urban Future, 258

Centers for Disease Control, 252

Centner, Ryan, 143

Cheang, Michael, 60

closeness. *See* elastic ties; intimacy

collegiality, 176

Columbia University College of Dental Medicine, 263–64

communication: high-involvement, 10; negative messages about aging, 15

Connie (Phyllis's friend/neighbor), 104, 232

co-op buildings. *See* housing

Coser, Lewis A., 20, 249–50

Coser, Rose Laub, 20, 249–50

cost of living. *See* financial issues; housing

COVID pandemic: and ageism, 14, 119–21; public safety of elders, 254–55

Creating Age-Friendly Health Systems Initiative, 261

crosswalk dividers, 127–28

Cruikshank, Margaret, 118

Dani (La Marjolaine Patisserie employee), 50, 98, 137

Davidson, Mark, 142–44

Degnen, Cathrine, 86, 88

dementia: caregiving for, 32–33; "dementia club," 133, 145, 158; support and housing changes needed for, 32–33, 232–33

demographic change: and future of aging, 18–19, 24–27, 241–42; and policy implications, 255–65; and solo living by elders, 16–18

depression. *See* isolation and loneliness; mental health

design of businesses. *See* physical design

Desmond, Matthew, 122, 151, 172

Diane (Bakery Club member): elastic ties of, 157; generally, 93, 94, 210–11, 213, 222–24, 233; profile of, 42–43

Didion, Joan, 1, 3

disengagement theory, 290n25

displacement: aging in displacement, 101; direct vs. indirect, 142; exclusionary displacement, 142; indirect

fast-food restaurants, 60. *See also* McDonald's (as Bakery Club gathering place)

Faulkner, William, 266

feminist theory: on gender as social construction, 114–15; and socioeconomic status, 281n29

Ferraro, Kenneth F., 25

financial issues: affordable gathering places for elders, 43–44, 89–91, 104–5; businesses attracting people asking for money, 138; elite consumption practices, 143; financial vulnerability of older white men, 233–36; gentrification and affordability of business patronage, 129–33; of health issues of elders, 106; hierarchical distinctions of older people, 105; housing eviction threat, 27; low-cost opportunities for socializing, 87; middle-class experience and intimacy, 172–74; policy considerations of, 255–65; socioeconomic status and age, 15; socioeconomic status and feminist theory, 281n29; socioeconomic status and neighborhood relationships, 58; tasks of independent living, 215, 253–54. *See also* housing

Fischer, Claude, 58, 285n18

Flora (Bakery Club member), 69, 80, 81

4 Ms (Creating Age-Friendly Health Systems Initiative), 261

Fran/Shirley (Bakery Club member), 152

Fried, Marc, 141

friendship, demands of. *See* intimacy

Galaxy Diner, 124, 125, 199, 239

gender and aging: age and status, 15; "doing gender," 115; feminist theory on gender, 114–15, 281n29; gender division in social settings, 136; LGBTQ+ elders, identity disclosed by, 118; men and suicide, 233–36; and policy issues, 256; study of, 14; wives' responsibility for health of their husbands, 197–98; women, approaches to grouping, 282n38; women, marriage and independence, 192–93; women and age-related identity, 91; women as a series, 116; women as mental health care clients, 206; women of rural vs. urban areas, 284–85n8; women without family, 18, 236–37. *See also* marriage; race and ethnicity

General Social Science Survey (GSS), 150, 169, 284n3, 285n18

Generation X, aging future of, 18–19

gentrification, 122–46; benefits of, 144; and business affordability, 129–33; defined, 140, 141–42; and health issues, 202–5; and housing affordability, 122–23; and indirect displacement of patrons, 7, 23, 100–101, 122–23, 142–46; loss of familiar places, 91, 98–101, 103–5, 140–44, 238–40, 250–55; mobility of business patrons, 123–29; physical design of businesses, 133–38; as social eviction, 250–55; surveillance/ monitoring by business staff, 122, 123, 138–40. *See also* mobility

George (Bakery Club member): generally, 93, 94, 211, 213, 223–24, 233; profile of, 42–43; social integration and relationships of, 42

Gershwin, George, 248

Gerstel, Naomi, 250

Gieryn, Thomas F., 58

Gladys (Bakery Club member): commercial gentrification and effect on, 134; elastic ties of, 154–55, 159–63; generally, 211–14, 222

Glass, Ruth, 141–42

Gluckman, Max, 86

Goffman, Erving, 114, 280n4, 283n4

gossip, 62–88; defined, 63; distancing with, 157–58; and emotional intensity in relationships, 42; and emotional ties with "difficult" network members, 88; as entertainment, 77–82; group hierarchy and solidarity established by, 64–71; health issues monitored by, 82–85, 244; isolation avoided through, overview, 22, 62–64, 86–88; and pruning of social networks, 73–77, 79; study of, 85–86, 278–79n2

Granovetter, Mark, 29, 42, 173

Gratton, Brian, 284n8

Gray Panthers, 116, 121

Greer, Scott, 174

grief. See loss and grief

group identity: affinity groups, 118; as "club" members, 92, 107–9; group in fusion, 117; and old age as a series, 91, 115–21, 244–45

Guillaume (La Marjolaine Patisserie owner), 43–44, 92, 95–99

Haber, Carol, 284n8

Hansberry, Griffin, 240

harmonious aging, 280n14

Harry (Bakery Club member), 69

health issues of elders: ageism in health care system, 186–89, 205–7; financial issues of, 106; food security, 236, 258, 260; and friends' obligations to help, 158–65; gentrification as problem of, 252–55; gossip as help for, 82–85; health care compliance/resistance, 195–200; and health-related discussions, 225–26; housing and effect on, 202–5; and management of physical/social self, 23–24, 179–80; Medicaid, 17, 257–58; Medicare, 14, 17, 90, 106–7, 116, 245, 257–58, 274n44; nutrition, 107, 225–26, 261–62; old age and health decline, 180–84; pandemic concerns, 53; routines and independence, 184–86; social integration and relationship support, 37–38, 46–56, 244, 245; successful aging, 104; third places for informal advice, 189–94, 197, 200–201. See also mobility

Helen (Bakery Club member), 66–67, 69, 193

Herd, Pamela, 241

high-involvement communication, 10

Hochschild, Arlie, 13, 25, 58, 221–22

housing: affordability of, 122–23; and age-related identity, 223; cost of, 8, 17–18, 257, 258; eviction threat, 27; gossip and advice about, 71–73, 84–85; harassment by landlords, 48–49; health issues and effect of, 202–5; help needed for tasks of, 215, 253–54; home as "first place," 29; home territories, 146, 249; policy considerations for, 255–59; social support for problems of, 37–38, 48–56; unhoused people, 244; and "urban renewal," 4. See also gentrification

Huth, Vince, 248

Hyra, Derek, 143–44

identity. *See* age-related identity of elders

immigration and immigrants, 97–98, 258

"important matters," discussing, 150, 156, 167, 169–70, 285n18, 286n27

independence and routines, 184–86

indirect displacement of patrons, 7, 23, 122–23, 142–46. *See also* gentrification

"inevitable place," 21–22. *See also* place

Institute on Assets and Social Policy, Brandeis University, 256, 257

intimacy: demands of acknowledged friendships, 155–56, 158–65; distancing tactics, 152–58; and "friend" as label, 157, 170; and friendship, 158–65; and middle-class experience, 172–74; strong ties, defined, 150; weak ties, defined, 149–50. *See also* elastic ties

"I Sing the Body Electric" (Whitman), 179

isolation and loneliness: gossip as remedy for, 62–64, 86–88; network approaches to social connectedness, 169–71; and social network loss, 56–61

Israel, elders and socializing in parks of, 60

Jacobs, Jane, 178, 267

Jasmine (La Marjolaine Patisserie employee), 111

Jeannette (Bakery Club member): commercial gentrification and effect on, 126; generally, 110, 211–15, 222; and gossip, 65–71; social integration and relationships of, 51

Jeffers, Robinson, 1, 21–22, 247–48

Jeffers, Una, 247

Jewish Association Serving the Aging (JASA), 258

Joan (Pete's Delicatessen customer), 105, 155, 195–97

Johnny's bodega, 68, 128, 181, 231, 239

Judy (Bakery Club member): commercial gentrification and effect on, 126; elastic ties of, 165; generally, 214; social integration and relationships of, 47, 52

Kihara, Barbie, 60

Kim, Ron, 252

Klinenberg, Eric, 16, 19

La Marjolaine Patisserie: business and location of, 3–4; closing of, 1–3, 11–12, 98; communal atmosphere of, 147; and loss of familiar places, 98–101, 103–5; as public living room, 6–10, 28–30, 60–61, 245–47; social life studied at, 4–6, 10–11; upscale replacement for, 103–4, 113, 123, 131–32, 137. *See also* research study; *individual names of Bakery Club members*

language, considerations about, 12–13

Laz, Cheryl, 115

Lees, Loretta, 144

LGBTQ+ elders, identity disclosed by, 118

Liang, Jiayin, 280n14

Liebow, Elliot, 172

The Life and Death of American Cities (Jacobs), 267

life expectancy (United States), 19

Linda (Dottie's daughter), 125, 164–65, 197

Loaf (business), 103–4, 113, 123, 131–32, 137

Lofland, Lyn, 146, 174, 246

London, gentrification in, 141–42

Longitudinal Aging Study Amsterdam (LASA), 26, 286nn24–25

Senior Financial Stability Index (SFSI), 256

series, old age as, 91, 115–21, 244–45. *See also* age-related identity of elders

shopping centers, for socializing, 60

Silent Generation, defined, 11

Simmel, Georg, 56, 171–72, 178

Siordia-Ortiz, Maria Guadalupe, 120

Small, Mario, 173, 174

social eviction, 16, 145

social integration, 28–61; and confiding, 45–47; and emotional ties, 42–54; public living rooms for, 6–10, 28–30, 60–61, 245–47; and reciprocity, 54–56; and relationship strength, 29–30; routines needed for, 36–42, 45; and social network loss, 56–61; third places as access to, 30–36, 38–40. *See also* gossip

social networks: bridgers, 192; "difficult" network members, 88; group hierarchy and solidarity, 64–71; loss of, 56–61; network theory, 169–73; pruning of, 71–77, 79; University of California Berkeley Social Networks Study (UCNets), 170. *See also* elastic ties

social service screening, recommendations for, 263

"social wall," 41

socioeconomic status. *See* financial issues

socioemotional selectivity theory, 57

solo living: demographic trends in (increase of, among elders), 16–18; and nursing home admission of partners, 32–33; in urban environments, 57

Spiro (Bakery Club member), 94–95, 212–13, 229

spoiled identity, 114

Stanford Center on Longevity, 264

status. *See* age-related identity of elders; power and status

stranger, insider-outsider position of, 171–72

strong ties, defined, 150. *See also* elastic ties

Stuart, Forrest, 177

stuck in place, 17, 18, 87, 175, 210, 215

Stuyvesant Town–Peter Cooper Village (New York City), 100–101

successful aging, 104

Supplemental Nutrition Assistance Program (SNAP), 236, 258, 260

Supplemental Poverty Measure (SPM, Census Bureau), 256

support between elders, 215–19. *See also* age-related identity of elders

surveillance by business staff, 122, 138–40

Survey of Health, Ageing and Retirement in Europe (SHARE), 26, 285–86n24

Susan (Bakery Club member), 63

Sylvia (Bakery Club member): and bakery's closing, 2; commercial gentrification and effect on, 124–26, 130–32, 136–37, 139–40; elastic ties of, 148–50, 156, 159, 163, 167–68, 173–75; generally, 92–94, 96, 98, 99, 101, 105, 109–12, 208–9, 213, 216–19, 225–31, 234; and gossip, 62–63, 78–80, 83; and health issues, 181, 184–88, 190–93, 195–96, 198–205; on living with emotional/physical pain, 175, 267, 269; profile of, 6–9; social integration and relationships of, 38, 45–49, 55–56; on solitariness, 251

Tannen, Deborah, 10

taxis and mobility, 38, 83, 123, 126–27

technology: assistance needed for, 216–19; isolation and loneliness issues of, 56; social connection through, 19, 20

teenagers. *See* younger people

Theresa (Bakery Club member): commercial gentrification and effect on, 134–35; death of, 239; generally, 94, 102–3, 210–15, 222–33; and gossip, 63, 67, 68, 72, 77–82; social integration and relationships of, 44, 54

third places, 28–61; accessibility to, 30–36, 38–40; bakery as public living room, 6–10, 28–30, 60–61, 245–47; defined, 16, 29; as home away from home, 59–61; informal advice exchanged in, 189–94, 197, 200–201; mobility and access to, 30–36, 38–40, 122–29; relationships and emotional ties to, 42–54; relationships and reciprocity in, 54–56; relationships and routines of, 36–42, 45; social integration and *aging in places*, 22, 56–61; "social wall" for organization of, 41; time and proximity of, 28–30, 60–61. *See also* gentrification

Tissot, Sylvie, 143, 283n4

Tom (Bakery Club member): death of, 239; generally, 90, 95, 100; social integration and relationships of, 31–33

transportation, cars as necessary, 17

Trump, Donald, age/power of, 15

Tsai, Michael, 60

UCLA Center for Health Policy Research, 256

The Unexpected Community (Hochschild), 25, 221–22

United States Census Bureau, 256

University of California Berkeley Social Networks Study (UCNets), 170

veil of ignorance thought experiment, 265

Venice Beach (California), gentrification in, 238

Village Movement, 264–65

virtual relationships, 19

Vivian (Bakery Club member), 73, 106

vulnerability of elders, 231–37. *See also* health issues; isolation and loneliness; mobility

Waite, Linda J., 286n27

Walker, Jan, 262

Walter (Bakery Club member), 69

weak ties, defined, 149–50. *See also* elastic ties

Wellman, Barry, 175

West, Candace, 115

West Side Diner, 125, 139, 204

Whitman, Walt, 179

Whyte, William H., 141

Winehouse, Amy, 266

Wireman, Peggy, 174

work, retirement from. *See* retirement from work

work as "second" place, 29

Yim, Kun Pae, 251

York Cornwell, Erin, 286n27

Yoruba proverb, 25

Young, Iris Marion, 91, 116, 282n38, 282n41

younger people: adolescent girls and loneliness, 56; birth cohorts, diversity of experience of, 15; future of aging by, 18–19; loneliness among, 19; spatial competition in public places, 221–24; teens as other marginalized age groups, 134, 139, 145; third places needed by, 254

Zerubavel, Eviatar, 41

Zimmerman, Don, 115

Zola, Irving Kenneth, 14

Founded in 1893,
UNIVERSITY OF CALIFORNIA PRESS
publishes bold, progressive books and journals
on topics in the arts, humanities, social sciences,
and natural sciences—with a focus on social
justice issues—that inspire thought and action
among readers worldwide.

The UC PRESS FOUNDATION
raises funds to uphold the press's vital role
as an independent, nonprofit publisher, and
receives philanthropic support from a wide
range of individuals and institutions—and from
committed readers like you. To learn more, visit
ucpress.edu/supportus.

www.ingramcontent.com/pod-product-compliance
Lightning Source LLC
Chambersburg PA
CBHW020821270326
41928CB00006B/396